Social
Gerontology

Social Gerontology

AN INTRODUCTION TO
THE DYNAMICS OF AGING

David L. Decker
California State College, San Bernardino

LITTLE, BROWN AND COMPANY
Boston   Toronto

To Carmen Maldonado Decker
for her more than fifty percent contribution to
our cooperative adventure of life.

Preface

Social Gerontology: An Introduction to the Dynamics of Aging is intended to provide a framework for viewing the process of aging from a variety of perspectives. C. Wright Mills (1959) wrote about the distinction between the "personal troubles of milieux" and "public issues," a distinction that must always be applied when studying aging. On the one hand individuals experience a very personal and individual aging process. In this sense the focus of attention is upon their "personal troubles," and this is an essential component of gerontology that I have tried to include in this book. On the other hand, individuals do not age by themselves; time does not stand still for everyone else while a particular individual grows older. We are a part of an age group and a sequence of generations. In this sense our individual aging occurs within the context of a structured or patterned setting, and I have tried throughout this book to indicate the lines of these social patterns. It is also important to look at the impact of aging on whole societies, even to the extent of trying to discern the historical dynamics of age changes upon world societies. I have also included this macrosocial view as an essential component of the study of gerontology.

Social gerontology is a new area of study, especially when compared with the established social sciences, but the research progress in social gerontology over the last two decades has been remarkable. This research production has allowed me to include detailed sections on such topics as the demography of aging and the political economy of aging. Much of this information is recent and has not been available previously. There have been many changes in the Social Security Law in the last three years and I have attempted to include detailed information on these changes from the most recent sources.

I have provided a chapter on aging individuals and social problems, both to indicate the degree of active involvement of older people in such social problems as crime, alcoholism, drug abuse, and suicide, and to evaluate the extent to which older people are the victims of the acts of others. While much research on social problems and the older population remains to be done, there is now enough information to provide a general outline of the relationship between deviant behavior and aging.

Every social gerontologist knows that the study of aging will be woefully inadequate until we have developed a rigorous cross-cultural perspective, and it is encouraging to read many of the newer comparative gerontological researches. I have tried to use comparative information to the greatest extent possible, in order to indicate to students the necessity of developing a worldwide gerontology that is suitable for analyzing the aging process in the broadest possible terms.

Several features have been included in the text to facilitate student learning. A brief outline appears at the beginning of each chapter, followed by a chapter overview that highlights important issues and topics to be addressed. Each chapter concludes with a summary to help students review, and with a bibliography to provide references for additional research. A complimentary Test Bank is available from the publisher to instructors requesting it on school letterhead.

It is impossible to acknowledge adequately all of the people who have aided me while I was writing this book. I would never have discovered the field of social gerontology were it not for the associates, fellows, and faculty of the Midwest Council for Social Research on Aging, especially Warren A. Peterson, Eugene A. Friedmann, Helena Z. Lopata, Charles Horn, and Harold Orbach. In recent years I have been supported, in a variety of ways, by my colleagues at California State College, San Bernardino, and especially by the Committee on Faculty Affairs and the library staff. A special note of thanks must go to Jane Rowland, who has devoted an immense amount of time to this book, and whose standard of excellence in her work I shall always remember and appreciate. I would also like to thank Little, Brown and Company, and the sociology editor, Katie Carlone, for being alternately patient, helpful, and encouraging, as well as thoroughly professional. And finally, to Carmen Maldonado Decker, Monica Decker, and Ricardo Decker, whose influence has been the most enduring and enjoyable.

David L. Decker

Contents

I

Introduction to the Field of Social Gerontology

Aging and the Individual

The Social Structure of Aging

Introduction to the Field of Social Gerontology

The study of aging is a recently developed discipline that views both the individual and the society as entities that are changed by the passage of time. A society changes over time, not only in response to specific events but also in terms of population structure. The individual also changes, not only biologically but also personally and socially. And the interaction between individual and society is what gives the world its distinctive character at any particular point in time.

Social gerontology organizes knowledge about aging, a task that is made difficult by the complexity of the aging process. It requires an understanding of the biological factors that operate to produce the aging of the human body. It also requires an understanding of how the aging of the individual affects and is affected by the demographic structure of the society. And it requires an appreciation of similarities and differences between the attitudes toward aging in different societies. Obviously, the study of aging crosses many of the traditional lines separating the disciplines of the natural and social sciences. But the interdisciplinary perspective of gerontology also provides an opportunity to integrate knowledge gleaned from those various disciplines. It is the integrative perspective of gerontology that provides challenge and stimulation for the student of aging.

CHAPTER **1**

The Development of Social Gerontology

Overview. The scientific study of aging is very new. In the past, people gained insight into the aging process only through personal observation or discussion, or by relying on folk knowledge or myths about aging. Most research in this field has been done only in the last two decades, and the knowledge base is currently expanding rapidly. The growing interest in gerontology has necessitated the development of research methods capable of measuring the processes of aging.

Governmental programs that deal with some of the problems of aging are also quite recent. The United States has been particularly slow to establish such programs, especially compared with European nations. As in the case of gerontological research, however, the number of programs designed to meet the needs of the older population has increased rapidly in the last two decades.

The Myths of Aging

Growing old is nothing new. From the beginnings of human existence some people have survived into old age; consequently, aging has long been a subject of myth. Only very recently, however, has aging also been a subject of scientific inquiry.

Gruman (1966) says that myths of aging and death usually express one of three themes: the antediluvian theme, the hyperborean theme, and the rejuvenation theme. The antediluvian theme is based on the belief that long ago people lived very long lives. The best-known source of support for the antediluvian myth is the Bible, especially the Book of Genesis, in which some ancient Hebrews are reported to have lived for several hundred years. As Stahmer (1978: 29) has pointed out,

> Among the ancient Jews, the great longevity of one's ancestors was an indication that they were among God's chosen; longevity was a reward for their steadfastness. This is implied in Deuteronomy (11:21) in Moses' charge to his people that if they obey God's commandments, "Then you will live long, you and your children, in the land which the Lord swore to your forefathers to give them, for as long as the heavens are above the earth."

In the hyperborean theme a distant culture is thought to produce long-lived peoples. This theme is still very much alive today, although there has been some effort to move from myth to scientific inquiry by investigating the vital statistics of long-lived peoples. (See Chapter 3 for more details on the Abkhasians and other groups that fit the hyperborean theme.)

The third theme, rejuvenation, was the motive behind the search for the fountain of eternal youth. Ponce de León is well known in American history because of his search for the fountain of youth in what is now Florida. It is ironic that many older people retire to Florida, though few profess a belief in the fountain of youth. The rejuvenation theme is still very much alive, however, in the form of either myth or science, and is expressed in such fads as vitamin E or jogging.

Another theme running through much of human history is that of gerontophobia, or a general dislike or fear of old age that is related to agism. Studies (Freedman, 1978; Tamke, 1978) have found gerontophobia to be a persistent theme in English literature. Tamke (1978: 71) notes that English Victorian literature portrayed a socially withdrawn and passive role for older people:

Most popular adult Victorian literature about aging reflects the same values and attitudes and behavioral imperatives that we find in children's literature: that old age was a time for reflection about death and a withdrawal from the world; that the aged should take a passive rather than an active role, except as teachers of the young; and that if the aged showed secular passions or desires more appropriate to the young or otherwise behaved inappropriately, they deserved punishment.

The scientific study of aging will not immediately exorcise all myths about aging from the population, but at least it will counter the harmful ones with evidence. Palmore (1977) has developed a short quiz composed of twenty-five true/false questions that attacks some of the commonly held myths about aging. He notes that the following statements, which are widely accepted as true, have been found to be false:

1. Most old people have no interest in, or capacity for, sexual behavior.
2. Most old people are set in their ways and unable to change.
3. The majority of old people are socially isolated and lonely.
4. The majority of older people have incomes below the poverty level.

While many such myths have been shown to be untrue, others remain. It will surely be some time before many of them are eradicated, and it is possible that some of the current thinking about aging will eventually be contradicted by new evidence. In any case, gerontology has firmly established itself as the scientific study of the aging process.

The Emergence of Gerontology

As mentioned earlier, aging has been exposed to systematic scientific inquiry only recently. Even the word *geriatrics* was not used until the year 1909, when Ignatz L. Nascher, a Viennese physician, coined it. It was much later, in 1939, that the first organization devoted to gerontology was formed. This organization, the Club for Research in Ageing, was established by a group of British scientists. This group was also responsible for the establishment of the American Research Club on Ageing in the United States, also in 1939 (Philibert, 1964).

Although before 1939 there had not been an organized group of gerontologists in the United States, there had been some books published in the field. In 1922 G. Stanley Hall, a psychologist with a background in childhood and adolescent psychology, published the book *Senescence, the Second Half of Life.* Hall was concerned that people in the second half of life be regarded as more than merely "over the hill" and on a downward course to destruction. In 1939 an influential book by E. V. Cowdry, *Problems of Ageing,* appeared. In 1945

Leo Simmons published the first major survey of anthropological gerontology, *The Role of the Aged in Primitive Society.* Until after World War II these books constituted the only body of literature on aging that existed in the United States, and little more was available in the rest of the world.

Prior to the establishment of the Research Club in the United States, the Macy Foundation had been instrumental in encouraging research on aging. Beginning in 1937, it sponsored an annual conference on the problems of aging. The Macy Foundation was also responsible for the establishment of the first federal government bureau concerned primarily with the problems of aging. This occurred in 1940, when the foundation gave the United States Public Health Service the seed money to establish a unit of gerontology (Philibert, 1964).

Most of the founding members of the American Club for Research on Ageing were biologists, and it was not until the mid-1940s that a distinct group of social gerontologists emerged. The early history of gerontology in the United States was dominated by biological and clinical scientists, and the social gerontologists were somewhat peripheral (Streib and Orbach, 1967). In the mid-1940s, however, social scientists began to turn their attention to the social aspects of aging. In 1943 Ernest W. Burgess, chairman of the Social Science Research Council's Research Committee on Social Adjustment, began what has been described as "the first organized attempt to delineate the socio-logical aspects of aging" (Donahue, 1964: 9).

Burgess, a major figure in the history of American sociology, is best known for his writings on urban sociology and the sociology of the family. He developed an interest in social gerontology rather late in his professional career, but nonetheless made important contributions to the field. The first major publication in American social gerontology was produced by a committee headed by Burgess and was entitled *Social Adjustment in Old Age.* This work was originally produced in 1946 and was reorganized and rewritten before being published in 1948. Burgess also stimulated many graduate students at the University of Chicago to conduct research on aging, and it is largely through his efforts that much early research in social gerontology was centered at the University of Chicago. In 1952 Burgess became the first social scientist to be elected president of the Gerontological Society.

In 1945 the American Club for Research on Ageing decided to incorporate the club and to change its name to the Gerontological Society. In 1952 a membership section "Psychology and Social Sciences" was organized within the society. Although the society has changed its internal structure over the years, it remains the dominant professional society in the field. It publishes the *Journal of Gerontology,* a bimonthly journal that contains original articles on the problems of aging from the fields of biology, medicine, psychology, and the social sciences, and *The Gerontologist,* a publication devoted to issues of applied research, the general well-being of the older population, and discussions of public policy issues that are relevant to the gerontologist.

While some significant contributions to the field of gerontology were published before 1945, most gerontological research has been published since that year. In the period since 1945 the production of gerontological research has accelerated, and each succeeding decade has seen a large increase in the number of articles and books on the subject. In short, as an organized effort, and as a recognized area of academic study, gerontology is a post-World War II development.

The Development of Government Programs

In the government sector of the United States, the three major developments affecting older people are the Social Security Act of 1935, the Older Americans Act of 1965, and the establishment of the National Institute on Aging in 1974. From the standpoint of health and economic well-being, the Social Security Administration is still the most important of the three. The idea of a social security system was nothing new in 1935, since many European nations already had social security programs by that time; however, the particular program developed in the United States as the inspiration of Franklin D. Roosevelt was something new. Roosevelt wanted a contributory pension scheme in which working people could save money toward their old age while they were still able to work. He felt strongly that older people did not want to be on the dole but wanted to draw benefits from an insurance system supported by the contributions of workers: "Our American aged do not want charity, but rather old age comforts to which they are rightfully entitled by their own thrift and foresight in the form of insurance" (Roosevelt, 1938, vol. 1: 103). He wanted a social security system that would include practically every worker and would be simple enough for everyone to understand and accept. To keep it simple, he originally wanted to run it through the post office:

> The rural free delivery carriers ought to bring papers to the door and pick them up after they are filled out. The rural free delivery carrier ought to give each child his social insurance number and his policy or whatever takes the place of a policy. The rural free delivery carrier ought to be the one who picks up the claim of the man who is unemployed, or of the old lady who wants old-age insurance benefits. (quoted in Perkins, 1946: 283)

Although the social security system was not all that Roosevelt had envisioned and does not operate in the simple style that he preferred, it remains the basis of financial support and health insurance for older people in the United States. The Social Security Act and the Older Americans Act, which have developed many programs at the state and local level, are discussed in greater detail in Chapter 9.

In 1974 the National Institute on Aging was established by Congress to conduct and support gerontological research. The Institute was intended to provide for the support of biomedical, social, and behavioral research and to assist in developing programs that would train personnel for the betterment of later life.

Gerontology in Higher Education

In recent years gerontology has emerged as an area of study in American colleges and universities. The long-term direction of gerontological education is the primary concern of the Association for Gerontology in Higher Education (AGHE), a group that was founded in 1972 and adopted its present name in 1973 (Hickey, 1978). The goals and structure of gerontological education are topics of ongoing discussion, although it seems to be agreed that gerontology is an interdisciplinary field that must draw upon both the natural sciences and the social sciences (Peterson, 1978).

An area of disagreement in regard to gerontological education is whether gerontology should be an autonomous professional field or whether it is more appropriately a subfield of more established academic disciplines. Sociologists, psychologists, and biologists have developed courses in gerontology as a specialized area within the broader discipline of which they are a part. This means that most academic gerontologists are sociologists, psychologists, and so on first and specialists in gerontology second. However, at least partly because of government support for various social service programs, a corps of service providers who work with the older people has emerged. The result has been that some colleges and universities have attempted to meet the educational needs of this service corps by developing programs that portray gerontology as an autonomous field. The eventual definition of gerontological education, and even of the field itself, remains unclear, however.

Today at least five distinct structural arrangements govern the gerontology curricula of colleges and universities (Peterson, 1978):

1. Intradepartmental structure—in which gerontology courses are taught as part of the offerings of a traditional academic area. The gerontology program might be an area of specialization within a department of sociology or psychology.
2. Interdepartmental committee—in which gerontology courses are taught by faculty from a number of different disciplines; the gerontology student might be required to take a course of study that included all of these disciplines. A student might be required to take gerontology courses offered by the departments of sociology, psychology, and biology.

3. Gerontology center. This may appear to be more like the departmental structure of the traditional academic disciplines, but the faculty who make up the center are usually members of traditional departments, and the resulting program may be very much like that offered by the interdepartmental committee.
4. Department of gerontology—in which gerontology has been granted the status of a department equal to the traditional academic disciplines. In this setting gerontology courses are offered by the department, usually by its own faculty. Whereas in the first three structures a course in the sociology of aging would be taught by a sociologist as part of the sociology curriculum, in this structure a member of the department of gerontology would offer a course in the sociology of aging as part of the gerontology curriculum. Also, with a department of gerontology a school would usually offer a degree in gerontology.
5. School of gerontology—such a school might have a number of different departments (e.g., Department of Social Gerontology, Department of Psychological Gerontology, etc.) and might offer degrees in gerontology at various levels (e.g., B.A. or B.S., M.A. or M.S.).

All of these structures may be found in American colleges and universities. It is now possible for students to take a course in gerontology or complete a certificate, a bachelor's degree, or an advanced degree. Gerontological education is expanding and will probably continue to do so in the foreseeable future, although at a reduced pace.

Major Concepts in Social Gerontology

It is often useful to try to reduce human existence to its most essential elements, for example, to describe life as resulting from the interaction of time, space, objects, and people. As individuals, or as humans in a collective sense, we can be described in terms of our relationship to time, space, objects, and people. In this context the study of aging, or social gerontology, is the study of time. Social gerontologists are dealing with the historical period in which people live, the passage of time and its effects on people, the social meanings of the passage of time, and the perception of time within particular cultural settings. In addition, gerontologists relate time to space, to objects, and to people. Unlike most other social scientists, however, gerontologists are using time as the axis on which life moves. Some researchers have described older people as "immigrants in time," meaning that older people have moved through time, have experienced the meaning of time, and have come to know the pleasures and the ravages of time.

If social gerontology is the study of time, it is not really the study of "old folks," a common misconception of the field. To the extent that social gerontology studies "old folks," it is attempting to see the effects of time, and since we are all vitally affected by the passage of time, we are, of course, interested in the findings. Ultimately, we are personally interested in how the passage of time affects us, and in a personal sense the study of social gerontology is really the study of ourselves. Students of aging soon learn that we study older people not as a strange cult or a foreign culture but as future versions of ourselves as we move through time. The inevitable conclusion that we reach is that older people are not "them" but "us."

It is ironic that in many societies time is seen as a barrier that separates various age groups. It is ironic because the longer view shows us that we are fellow passengers through time, and the panorama of time itself is observable because of the different age groups that are always present in a society.

Generation, Maturation, and Social Age

Since social gerontology is the study of time, it is important to know the different ways of analyzing time. This involves some of the concepts that are most basic to gerontology: generation, maturation, and social age.

A generation is a very simple measurement of time that places each person in a lineal order: a man is behind his father and ahead of his son; a woman comes after her mother and before her daughter. Generation can also be used in a collective sense, namely, that we are members of a particular historical cohort. In recent American history there have been frequent references to the "beat generation" and the "generation of the sixties," and we will probably be hearing about the "seventies generation" before long. In this sense a generation is the group of people who reached adulthood within a certain period. This idea of a generation is more than a convenient referent; it is often used to indicate that individuals are formed in some degree by membership in a particular generation. As Mannheim says (1952: 291), members of a generation have a "collective mentality":

> The fact of belonging to the same class, and that of belonging to the same generation or age group, have this in common, that both endow the individuals sharing in them with a common location in the social and historical process, and thereby limit them to a specific range of potential experience, predisposing them for a certain characteristic mode of thought and experience, and a characteristic type of historically relevant action.

The essence of Mannheim's statement is that we are products of our times, captives of time and space, and that there really is no escaping such restraints. Each generation will exhibit certain unique characteristics, and future generations will always differ from past ones.

Most people, when they think about aging, probably have in mind the effects of maturation. All organisms undergo certain changes during the life cycle, and humans are no exception. Much of social gerontology is oriented toward observing maturational effects as they are manifested in social behavior. As we grow older, do we react to objects, events, people, and even ourselves differently than at earlier ages? If we do, are our reactions to maturational processes organic in nature, or are they essentially social? These are the kinds of questions that confront the social gerontologist, and the answers are almost never simple. Certainly, we know that a lot of changes occur as part of the aging process, from readily observable changes, such as the wrinkling of the skin, to unobservable metabolic changes. But what does wrinkled skin have to do with the way people behave? Moreover, if there are behavior changes, are they a result of organic changes or of other people's reactions to organic changes, our own reactions to such changes, our own fear of the reactions of others to such changes, or all of the above? At present gerontologists have more questions than answers on the subject of maturation.

A third basic concept of social gerontology is that of social age (Neugarten and Datan, 1973). No matter what our generation or our stage of maturation, there are social definitions of time that give meaning to our age. In some societies a person of 50 may be considered old, while in another society a person of 70 may not be regarded as old. Conversely, a person of 15 may be regarded as a child or as an adult, depending on the definition of social age. Social age is also closely related to a person's movement through social institutions, for example, through the various stages of the family life cycle or an occupational career. A mentally retarded person may be socially defined as a child, despite his or her chronological age, because of failure to move through the usual stages of the major social institutions.

These three concepts—generation, maturation, and social age—are basic to much research in social gerontology, and it is crucial to be able to distinguish among them. Throughout this book the importance of these concepts will become apparent, and especially in Chapter 7, where the development of specific theories of aging will be treated in detail. It will also be important to know how these concepts are accounted for in the research process. These concepts are essential for an understanding of the social gerontological perspective and the relationship of social gerontology to the traditional social sciences.

Gerontology and the Social Sciences

Whether gerontology ever emerges as a distinct academic discipline, or whether it even should, will remain a debatable question for years to come. Whatever happens, however, it is almost certain that social gerontology will have a significant impact on the theoretical perspectives of the traditional social sciences. Social gerontology has already encouraged researchers to consider social processes and social change as an essential part of societal and individual behavior. Consider an example from the field of criminology: How can we explain criminal behavior? In trying to explain behavior at the individual level, the social scientist might try to show that criminals are mentally and personally different from noncriminals. A social perspective might find that criminals are disproportionately drawn from the poverty areas of cities; perhaps they come from particular kinds of families, or maybe they have learned criminal behavior by associating with other delinquents. A sociohistorical approach would consider the effect of particular economic and political circumstances on the crime rate, and a demographer would point to the effect of birthrates and migration patterns to explain the volume of crime. What social gerontology asks, however, in addition to the insights provided by these other perspectives, is the effect of life cycle changes on criminal behavior. It causes the social scientist to look at the effects of generation, maturation, and social age on criminals, their victims, and the types of crimes they commit.

The advent of the social gerontological perspective does not mean that criminologists have never before looked at crime from such a perspective. Neither does it invalidate the contributions of other perspectives. The new perspective provides a systematic approach that allows researchers in all the social sciences to ask new questions and rethink some old problems in the quest to explain human behavior. It encourages them to view social life and behavior as an ongoing, dynamic process.

Research Methods in Social Gerontology

The development of the social gerontological perspective has necessitated the development of some new approaches in research methodology. A large number of research strategies and techniques are employed by contemporary social gerontologists, including ethnographic field studies; historical research; content analysis of literature, film, newspapers, and television; thematic apperception tests; semantic differentials, and standard surveys. But contemporary research strategies are not equipped to handle the basic subject matter of gerontology, the phenomenon of time. To use the imagery of film, most social research produces a photograph of the subject matter under investigation, but the aging process is a full-length feature film. The photo image is especially true of survey research, but it is also true of most other research. Even ethnographic field work, which is very concerned with seeing social life in action, is usually completed in a few months or years. The dilemma faced by the social gerontologist is how to capture the effects of time using atemporal research strategies and techniques.

Aside from content analysis and historical research, which are better able to take account of time, most research strategies use one of three possible research designs: cross-sectional, longitudinal, or cohort analysis.

Table 1.1 THE IMPORTANCE OF RELIGION IN
YOUR LIFE

Age	Percentage reporting "very important"
18–24	34
25–39	45
40–54	58
55–64	65
65–69	69
70–79	71
80+	73

Source: Adapted from National Council on the Aging, *The Myth and Reality of Aging in America* (Washington, D.C., 1975).

Cross-sectional Research

The cross-sectional research design is most frequently used in social gerontology. It involves testing individuals of various ages and comparing the responses of people in different age categories. In most cases the group being studied is selected by random sampling. The sample could represent a wide variety of different universes—a neighborhood, an institution, an entire community, or even an entire nation. The group could be tested on an infinite number of topics, but typically the testing situation includes basic demographic information, some self-reports on activities in which the group has been involved, and perhaps some questions regarding the group's attitudes toward certain topics or issues. The respondents can then be aligned into age groups, and comparisons can be made of the responses of members of those groups to the items being studied. Table 1.1 is a simple example of a cross-sectional research design. It is derived from a study that asked respondents how important religion was in their lives. The table shows the number of people from the different age groups who replied that religion was "very important." It indicates a direct relationship between aging and the importance of religion. At this stage of the analysis there is no problem, because the information indicates that in the United States in 1975 older people were much more likely than younger people to report that religion was very important to them.

It is tempting to conclude from Table 1.1 that people become more concerned with religion as they grow older; however, no such conclusion is warranted. To infer the dynamics of the aging process from this information would be a serious logical error involving the acceptance of a large number of unsubstantiated assumptions. It could be that people become more concerned with religion as they age, but it could also be that the table reflects a long-term historical change in public attitudes toward religion, or that those who are concerned about religion live longer and therefore outnumber the nonreligious members of their cohort by the time they reach advanced ages. The point is that the cross-sectional research design does not allow the researcher to infer the aging process as the cause of differences in concern with religion between people of different ages.

Longitudinal Research

The longitudinal research design is much better, though not perfect, as a means of studying the aging process because it attempts to measure changes in individuals over time. An example of a longitudinal research design is the multidisciplinary Duke Longitudinal Study of Aging (Palmore, 1970). This study was designed to allow for repeated observations of the same group of people over time, to observe the aging process in a selected group of men and women from the beginning of the study until the time of their death. Since the goal of the study was to report on normal aging, the panel selected for the study consisted of noninstitutionalized people residing in a community, and the focus was on the normal and typical features of those people. "The reports deal with common medical problems, common mental health problems, normal patterns of intellectual functioning, patterns of family and sexual behavior, the normal association of activities with life satisfaction, and typical attitudes toward aging, health, and death" (Palmore, 1970: vii). The advantages of the longitudinal approach are that each panel member serves as his or her own control so that the process of aging can be observed; observations at a number of points in time allow the researchers to distinguish between long-term trends and temporary fluctuations; problems associated with asking subjects to recall information from the past are eliminated; possible early warnings of disease or death can be studied; cohort differences (discussed later) can be isolated from the aging process; and the effects of one change on other changes can be studied (e.g., the effect of declining health on family relations) (Palmore, 1970: viii).

Since the Duke study involved a rigorous set of tests that lasted for two days and required the subjects' presence at the Duke Medical Center, and since the subjects had to agree to be retested over the remaining years of their life, the researchers opted to use volunteers rather than to enlist the aid of a random sample of respondents. They therefore tried to create a panel of volunteers who were 60 years of age or older and reflected the age, sex, and ethnic and socioeconomic characteristics of the city of Durham, North Carolina. It took four years for the research team to assemble and test the original panel of 256 respondents.

One of the major drawbacks of the longitudinal design of the Duke study is that, since the panel of subjects is not randomly drawn, it is not possible to generalize from this group to a larger group of older people. The findings from this panel can stimulate research to confirm the existence of some pattern in the general population, but the Duke study itself cannot make such generalizations.

Since the Duke study relies on volunteers for research subjects, it is not possible to know the kinds of systematic biases that might be included in the study. Do research volunteers tend to be different from people who will not volunteer? At least with regard to their willingness to volunteer, they are different, but other ways in which they may be different are not known. Although cross-sectional research may rely on a random sample of respondents, it faces a similar problem in that a certain proportion of people will refuse to participate.

One of the most significant problems of any longitudinal study is panel attrition—especially when the panel is composed solely of older people, since death is a major cause of panel attrition. In the Duke study 71 percent of the original panel was available for the second round of testing, which occurred about three years after the initial testing. Most of those who were not tested on the second round either had died or were ill. Because of panel attrition, the ones remaining for the second and subsequent rounds of testing tended to be physically, mentally, and socially a highly active group. The problem of attrition further limits the researchers' confidence in the information they collect.

Cohort Analysis

Both cross-sectional and longitudinal studies have their strengths and weaknesses, although for measuring the effect of time the longitudinal design is preferable because it can capture the effects of aging with the fewest uncontrollable effects. There is a method, known as cohort analysis, that combines some of the features of both research designs and eliminates some of their drawbacks. Basically, cohort analysis involves the use of a number of discrete random-sample surveys that collect similar information at different points in time. If we wanted to know whether people's concern with religion increased with age, we could use a cohort analysis design. We know from Table 1.1 that using cross-sectional research it was found that older people reported greater concern with religion than younger people, but we were unable to decide whether the differences between the age groups was a result of the aging process, a generational phenomenon, or a demographic shift. Using a cohort analysis design, it would be possible to isolate the effect of aging from generational and demographic factors without the problems of maintaining a panel. This can be accomplished by comparing the responses of people of various ages regarding their concern for religion at different points in time. Sometimes a cohort analysis can be reconstructed retrospectively when adequate information on an age cohort has been collected at various times over a number of years. Some polling services have asked national samples the same questions over a long period (Glenn and Zody, 1970). By dividing the respondents into cohorts—say five- or ten-year cohorts—it is possible to see how a particular cohort responded to a question at different times: once in 1950, another time in 1960, a third time in 1970. If one cohort was between the ages of 40 and 45 in the year 1950, then it would be between the ages of 50 and 55 in the year

1960 and between the ages of 60 and 65 in the year 1970. By comparing responses to the question about concern with religion, it is possible to draw some conclusions as to the changes, if any, that have occurred within the cohort. Let us assume that the cohort has shown increasing concern with religion from 1950 to 1970; then we can conclude that the change is not purely a generational phenomenon because we are dealing with only one generation yet we have observed some change *within* this generation. The change could be a result of a demographic shift, since men between the ages of 40 and 65 experience a higher mortality rate than women in the same age group. Even if the cohort as a whole shows increasing concern with religion over time, it may be that the women of the cohort have always had greater concern with religion than the men of the cohort and that, owing to the greater mortality of the men, the cohort has actually changed in its demographic composition. For this reason it is always necessary in cohort analysis to treat males and females separately—that is, to control for sex—when analyzing the data (Glenn and Zody, 1970).

If, after controlling for sex and any other variable that seems appropriate, there still seems to be increasing concern with religion as people grow older, then it is necessary to compare our cohort with other cohorts over the same period. Have younger and older cohorts experienced the same increase in concern with religion from 1950 to 1970? If so, it may well be that a general change has occurred in the society; perhaps recent events have caused people of all ages to turn their attention toward matters of religion. On the other hand, if it is believed that people begin to show increased concern with religion at a particular age, it may be possible to observe changes in other cohorts at the same age but in different years. It might be possible to observe an older cohort as it passed from age 40 to age 65 during the years from 1940 to 1965. If the same pattern appears for different cohorts but at different times, then there is substantial evidence for arguing that the effect is a result of the aging process.

The cohort analysis design has an advantage over the longitudinal design in terms of efficiency. Some retrospective analyses are possible, and the problems of panel attrition and voluntary subjects are avoided. It has an advantage over the cross-sectional study in that it can study changes over time by comparing a series of randomly selected cohorts. However, cohort analysis requires properly selected samples of respondents; sample error can produce potentially misleading results; and when carrying out retrospective researches based on data collected previously, the researcher is limited to the topics covered in the surveys and repeated at several intervals.

What's in a Name?

People are justifiably sensitive about the names applied to them, not so much because of the name itself but because of the implied meanings of the name. It is bad enough to be called Charlie when your name is Henry, but it is even worse to be called Dumbo when your name is Henry. The same thing applies to the names given to groups of people. I attended a college in which our mascot was the raven, the intelligent, elegant bird immortalized in Edgar Allen Poe's lines, "Quoth the raven, Nevermore!" But some of our athletic opponents insisted on referring to us as the crows, as in "to eat crow." As ravens we were dignified, proud, and aggressive, but as crows we were dispirited and ordinary. Some might argue that indeed the raven is classified as a member of the crow family, but to us the difference between the two was immense. A name is not just a name; contained in a name is an image of ourselves and of how others view us. We want others to refer to us by a desirable name because we hope the name reflects their positive image of us.

When dealing with age groups, names can be a problem even when there are no bad intentions. What names do older people as an age group like and dislike? According to a national sample survey (National Council on the Aging, 1975), there is no overwhelming consensus regarding a preferred name, and about one-third of those interviewed who were over 65 years of age said that they were indifferent as to which names are used. Of those who did care, about 50 percent liked the phrases "a mature American," "a retired person," and "a senior citizen," and less than 15 percent said that they did not like these phrases. At least half of this sample said that they did not like the phrases "an aged person" and "an old man/woman." The following phrases were liked and disliked in about equal proportions: "an elderly person," "a middle-aged person," "an older American," "a golden ager," and "an old-timer."

It is easy to understand why people over 65 would dislike the expressions "an aged person" and "an old man/woman"; they seem so absolute. Everyone is aged to some extent, but the phrase "an aged person" suggests that the aging is complete and a state of total agedness has been reached. If we want a name to apply to people over 65, why not use the ones that are most popular in a sample of people over 65? "A mature American" might be used in some circumstances, but it presents some problems in that it seems to imply that people under 65 are immature. "A retired person" is appropriate for those who are retired, but it is too specific to permit general usage. "Senior citizen" is more acceptable for general use, although it has been criticized as euphemistic. Perhaps an entirely new name could be used: the stage of adolescence is peopled by adolescents, so maybe the state of senescence could be peopled by senescents; or, taking a clue from gerontology, the noun *gerontes* could be adapted to modern usage, even though the original gerontes were the supreme magistrates of the Spartan senate and were all over 60 years of age. Reasonable as these alternatives might be, they would not be useful until they had gained some popular acceptance.

The problem of a name is not an easy one, but the most reasonable solution until a widely accepted name emerges is to use straightforward descriptive terms. For comparing age groups, the most descriptive terms are *younger, middle-aged,* and *older.* In this context *older* does not imply any absolute qualities. When referring to senior citizens, therefore, I will use the term *older,* as in "older Americans," "older people," "older men," "older women," "older voters," and so on. In some instances the younger–older dichotomy will be used. In the long run, as we learn more about aging, *older* and *old* should become respectable terms that can be used without apology and without any suspicion that a negative meaning is intended.

Summary

Aging has long been a subject of myths, but only recently has it been a subject of scientific inquiry. Many myths of aging have been found by modern research to be false; indeed one of the tasks of gerontologists has been to counter those that are most harmful.

Social gerontology emerged as a recognized area of academic study and research after World War II. The last couple of decades have seen a very rapid expansion of interest and research in gerontology. Government programs for older people are also relatively new, especially in the United States, but a large number of programs have been developed in recent years.

Gerontology has become an established area of study on many campuses in the United States. It is now possible to receive an academic degree in gerontology, but several different types of programs have been developed, and the eventual place of gerontology in higher education is still a topic of debate.

The development of social gerontology has also produced a new theoretical perspective as well as new research techniques, both of which have influenced, and will continue to influence, the traditional disciplines of the social sciences.

In the next chapter we will see some of the reasons why social gerontology has emerged as an area of study and interest. The age structure and composition of many societies has changed and is continuing to change. The emergence and rapid expansion of gerontology is largely a result of these changes.

SELECTED REFERENCES

Vern L. Bengtson and Neal E. Cutler, "Generations and Intergenerational Relations: Perspectives on Age Groups and Social Change," in *Handbook of Aging and the Social Sciences,* eds. Robert H. Binstock and Ethel Shanas (New York: Van Nostrand Reinhold, 1976), pp. 130–159.

James E. Birren and Vivian Clayton, "History of Gerontology," in Aging: *Scientific Perspectives and Social Issues,* eds. Diane S. Woodruff and James E. Birren (New York: D. Van Nostrand, 1975), pp. 15–17.

Wilma Donahue, "Aging: a Historical Perspective," in *Research Utilization in Aging* (Bethesda, Md.: Public Health Service Publication no. 1211, 1964), pp. 7–15.

Richard Freedman, "Sufficiently Decayed: Gerontophobia in English Literature," in *Aging and the Elderly,* eds. Stuart R. Spicker, Kathleen M. Woodward, and

David D. Van Tassel (Atlantic Highlands, N.J.: Humanities Press, 1978), pp. 46–61.

Norval D. Glenn and Richard E. Zody, "Cohort Analysis with National Survey Data," *Gerontologist* 10 (1970): 233–240.

G. J. Gruman, *A History of Ideas About the Prolongation of Life: the Evolution of Prolongevity Hypothesis to 1800* (Philadelphia: American Philosophical Society, 1966).

Tom Hickey, "Association for Gerontology in Higher Education—a Brief History," in *Gerontology in Higher Education: Perspectives and Issues,* eds. Mildred M. Seltzer, Harvey Sterns, and Tom Hickey (Belmont, Calif.: Wadsworth, 1978), pp. 2–11.

George L. Maddox, "Selected Methodological Issues," in *Normal Aging: Reports from the Duke Longitudinal Study,* 1955–1969, ed. Erdman Palmore (Durham, N.C.: Duke University Press, 1970),. pp. 18–27.

Karl Mannheim, *Essays on the Sociology of Knowledge* (New York: Oxford University Press, 1952).

National Council on the Aging, *The Myth and Reality of Aging in America* (Washington, D.C., 1975).

Bernice L. Neugarten and Nancy Datan, "Sociological Perspectives on the Life Cycle," in *Life-Span Developmental Psychology: Personality and Socialization,* eds. Paul B. Baltes and K. Warner Schaie (New York: Academic Press, 1973), pp. 53–69.

Erdman Palmore, ed., *Normal Aging: Reports from the Duke Longitudinal Study, 1955–1969* (Durham, N.C.: Duke University Press, 1970).

Frances Perkins, *The Roosevelt I Knew* (New York: Viking Press, 1946).

David Peterson, "An Overview of Gerontology Education," in *Gerontology in Higher Education: Perspectives and Issues,* eds. Mildred M. Seltzer, Harvey Sterns, and Tom Hickey (Belmont, Calif.: Wadsworth, 1978), pp. 14–26.

Michel A. Philibert, *"An Essay on the Development of Social Gerontology,"* mimeographed (Ann Arbor: University of Michigan, Division of Gerontology, 1964).
———, "The Emergence of Social Gerontology," *Journal of Social Issues,* 2 (1965): 4–12.

Franklin D. Roosevelt, *The Public Papers and Addresses of Franklin D. Roosevelt,* vols. 1–5, ed. Samuel I. Rosenmen (New York: Random House, 1938).

Harold M. Stahmer, "The Aged in Two Ancient Oral Cultures: the Ancient Hebrews and Homeric Greece," in *Aging and the Elderly,* eds. Stuart F. Spicker, Kathleen M. Woodward, and David D. Van Tassel (Atlantic Highlands, N.J.: Humanities Press, 1978).

Gordon F. Streib and Harold L. Orbach, "The Development of Social Gerontology and the Sociology of Aging," in *The Uses of Sociology,* eds. Paul F. Lazarsfeld, William H. Sewell, and Harold Wilensky (New York: Basic Books, 1967), pp. 612–640.

Susan S. Tamke, "Human Values and Aging: The Perspective of the Victorian Nursery," in *Aging and the Elderly,* eds. Stuart F. Spicker, Kathleen M. Woodward, and David D. Van Tassel (Atlantic Highlands, N.J.: Humanities Press, 1978), pp. 63–81.

CHAPTER **2**

The Demography of Aging

Overview. As we saw in Chapter 1, the study of aging is a recent development, and at least part of the reason is that many societies have experienced a significant increase in their older populations. This change in age structure is a new phenomenon: The world has never before experienced the kinds of changes that are currently taking place. There are a number of ways of expressing the demographic changes that are occurring, but a simple example will indicate their significance. In 1820 over half the population of the United States was under 17 years of age, but by 2030 over half will be over 38 years of age. In a little over two centuries the United States will have been transformed from a very young society to a mature society. Another way of looking at this demographic shift is to note that the number of people in the United States age 65 and over will have doubled between the years 1950 and 1980 and will have doubled again by the year 2030. The change in the demographic structure of the United States is very important, and it will have occurred in a relatively short period. Other societies are further advanced in this demographic transformation than the United States, and many others are sure to follow the pattern established by these societies.

Although many people are not familiar with the field of demography, most people have heard of various demographic concepts, especially birth and death rates. Most people are also familiar with the ideas of life expectancy and geographical mobility, both of which are elements of the demographic study of a population. The population under study is usually a single society, but it may also be the entire world, or it may be a part of a society, such as a state or a particular age group. Whatever its focus, demographic analysis is always concerned with the vital processes of a group, that is, how it maintains itself through the events of birth, death, and migration. By observing the vital processes of a society or group over a long period, it is possible to ascertain the population composition at a particular point in time and to note how that composition has changed over time. By making certain assumptions about how birth, death, and migration rates will change in the future, it is possible to make projections about the probable composition of the population at some future date.

Human demography is, in some respects, similar to the demographic and ecological study of animals. Population biologists examine the size of an animal population, make estimates as to the vital rates of the population, and study its migratory patterns and its ways of adapting to its habitat. These studies sometimes conclude that a particular species is in danger of extinction if there is no change in its vital rates, or that a species is growing at a rate that could pose problems for other animal or human populations. The migration patterns of some animals, such as the return of the swallows to San Juan Capistrano each March, are memorialized in song.

Humans are different from animals in many ways, and this makes the demographic study of humans quite complex and not entirely predictable. Humans have the ability to think, to make decisions on the basis of their thought processes, and to base their actions on those decisions. Whereas many animal species are highly predictable in their behavior, humans are continuously changing, at times even showing rapid changes in their vital rates. This is not to say that there may not be some relationships between the demographic processes of humans and animals. Emmel (1976), for example, states that there is well-documented evidence of a pattern of sex ratio changes with age in both mammals (including humans) and birds. A sex ratio refers to the sex composition of a population—the number of males per 100 females. The general rule is that among older cohorts of birds there are more males than females, whereas among older cohorts of mammals there are more females that males. The general pattern for mammals is usually found among humans—females usually have a longer life expectancy—with the result that the older age groups usually contain more females than males. An implication of such evidence, since it extends to an entire class of animals, is that the phenomenon is biologically determined. Whether there are biologically determined processes that affect human demography is still unknown, although it seems likely that there are some.

Many of the changes in human societies are very gradual and may seem incredibly slow to the casual observer; but long-term trends are often observable, and the consequences of these gradual changes can be immense. Students often dismiss demographic information as "dry statistics," but with a little imagination these pieces of information form an image of American society and how it is changing, especially with regard to age structure. Remember that tables of numbers and graphic presentations are intended to serve as anchors. To gain the most from a table or graph, you have to search for the consequences and implications of the information presented.

Determining the Age Structure of a Population

Most of those who are interested in the aging process study it at the individual and interpersonal level. It is, however, very important to understand the aging of a society, to look at aging from a total-society point of view. We will find that, like individuals, some societies are very young while others are comparatively old. Whether a society is young or old in a demographic sense has very little to do with how old it is in a historical sense. The United States, for example, is a young nation in world history, but in demographic terms it is an aging society.

Unlike individuals, an aging society is probably no more likely to die than a young society, because a society is young or old only in a descriptive sense. We might describe a society as old or young in the same way that we might describe it as a Catholic country or an oil-rich nation. It is possible for an old society to become a young one, just as a young society may become an aging society. Also, all young societies have some old members, and all old societies have some very young members, just as a poor society probably has some rich members and rich societies have some poor members. So when the concept of age is applied to a society, it is intended to describe a dominant characteristic of the society and to indicate how the age structure of the society is changing.

Median Age

There are a number of ways in which the age structure of a society can be indicated. One of the simplest indicators of age structure is median age. The median age of a society is the age at which the population is divided into two equal parts, one half older than the median age and the other half younger. The median age of the United States shows that this country has been aging for at least 150 years. In 1820 (the earliest year for which there is information on the median age), the median age of the United States was 16.7 years; in 1870, it was 20.2 years; in 1920, it was 25.3 years; in 1970, it was 28.1 years. In the last 150 years the median age has increased by over eleven years, and while the aging process is very slow, the long-range change is quite significant.

Although the median age is a fairly simple indicator of the complex workings of a society, it gives a useful illustration of the value of demographic analysis. Actually, a simple indicator like median age is quite valuable because we can use it to demonstrate how the population structure has changed as well as to estimate or project future changes and to compare one society with another. In addition, a single indicator can be used to show the relationship between the major groups within a society; for example, the median age can be used to compare males and females or blacks and whites or other groups within the society.

Population information can be used in a number of ways. Perhaps the most important use of such information is as an aid in the development of government policies and programs. In the United States changes in the social security system, the establishment of programs under the Older Americans Act, and the establishment of the National Institute on Aging have all been influenced by demographic studies that show American society to be aging. In addition, private groups, such as Planned Parenthood and the Gray Panthers, and various businesses rely on population information and projections in planning their activities.

Population Pyramids

The median age of a society is a useful but simple measure of its age structure. Other methods go into more detail. Among them is the population pyramid, a graph that shows each age category, divided between males and females, as a percentage of the total population at some particular time. Figure 2.1 presents population pyramids for the United States for the years 1900, 1940,

1970, and 2030. In each pyramid the population is divided into five-year age categories (although other age categories, such as one-year or ten-year age groupings, could be used). The male portion of each age category is on the left-hand side of the pyramid and the female portion on the right-hand side. The youngest age group (the "under 5 years of age" group) is at the base of the pyramid, with older five-year age groups above it. The population pyramids shown in Figure 2.1 have the category "65 and over" at the top, although it is more common to further divide the older segment of the population into five-year age groups (e.g., 65–69, 70–74, 75 and older). The "65 and over" grouping is used here because most of the other information that will be presented uses this age category.

The population pyramid for the year 1900 shows best why the graph is called a pyramid: Using the five-year age groups, each older age group is slightly smaller than the next-younger age group. Since males are placed on the left side of the pyramid and females on the right side, and since the numbers of each are nearly equal, the pyramid is symmetrical. The median age of the United States population depicted in the population pyramid for the year 1900 is 22.9.

By 1940 the population pyramid of the United States no longer looked exactly like a pyramid. The proportion of the population over the age of 65 had increased, but the base of the pyramid had contracted, leaving the 15–19 year old age group as the largest. The contracting of the base is a result of a decline in the birthrate that began during the years when the 10–14 year olds were born and continued to decline for those under 9 years old. This indicates a declining number of births for the years 1925–1940. The decline in the birthrate during this period was a response to the social and economic conditions of the Great Depression. The declining birthrate between the years 1925 and 1940 has caused the population to age, so that the median age of the population is now 29.0 years.

The population pyramid for 1970 does not even resemble a pyramid, but it does indicate a number of important features of the American population. One of the most outstanding of these is the large proportion of the population over age 65, especially the large number of females over age 65. The small number of births between the years 1925 and 1940 gives the 1970 pyramid a constricted middle; that is, the number of people between the ages of 30 and 45 in 1970 is unusually small. This pyramid is also constricted at the bottom as a result of the decline in the birthrate in the decade from 1960 to 1970. The median age of the 1970 population was only 28.1 years, however, or slightly younger than that of the 1940 population.

The population pyramid for the year 2030, which is based on population projections for that year, is now T-shaped. The pyramid shows the dramatic increase in population over age 45 and especially the increase in population

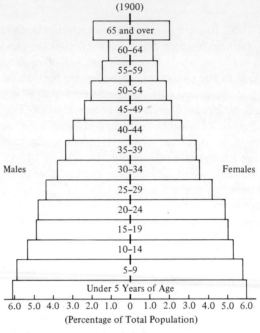

(1900)

65 and over	
60–64	
55–59	
50–54	
45–49	
40–44	
35–39	
30–34	
25–29	
20–24	
15–19	
10–14	
5–9	
Under 5 Years of Age	

Males   Females

6.0 5.0 4.0 3.0 2.0 1.0   0   1.0 2.0 3.0 4.0 5.0 6.0

(Percentage of Total Population)

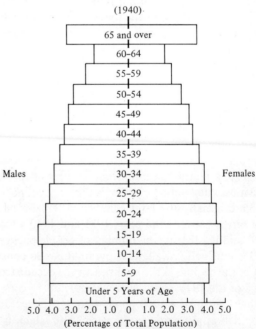

(1940)

Males   Females

5.0 4.0 3.0 2.0 1.0   0   1.0 2.0 3.0 4.0 5.0

(Percentage of Total Population)

Figure 2.1 *Population Pyramids for the United States for the Years 1900, 1940, 1970, and 2030*

24

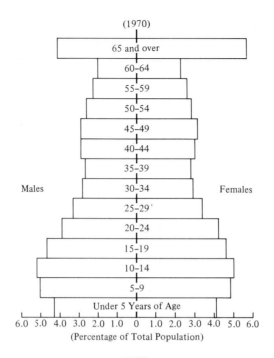

(1970)

65 and over
60–64
55–59
50–54
45–49
40–44
35–39

Males   30–34   Females

25–29'
20–24
15–19
10–14
5–9
Under 5 Years of Age

6.0 5.0 4.0 3.0 2.0 1.0 0 1.0 2.0 3.0 4.0 5.0 6.0

(Percentage of Total Population)

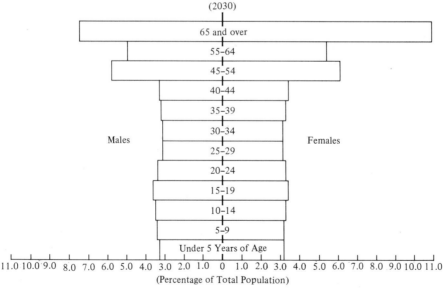

(2030)

65 and over
55–64
45–54
40–44
35–39
30–34

Males   Females

25–29
20–24
15–19
10–14
5–9
Under 5 Years of Age

11.0 10.0 9.0 8.0 7.0 6.0 5.0 4.0 3.0 2.0 1.0 0 1.0 2.0 3.0 4.0 5.0 6.0 7.0 8.0 9.0 10.0 11.0

(Percentage of Total Population)

Source: Constructed from data in U.S. Bureau of the Census, *Historical Statistics of the United States, Colonial Times to 1970,* bicentennial edition (Washington, D.C.: U.S. Government Printing Office, 1975), and the U.S. Bureau of the Census, "Projections of the Population of the United States: 1977 to 2050," *Current Population Reports,* Series P-25, no. 704 (Washington, D.C., U.S. Government Printing Office, 1977).

over age 65. It also shows the type of age structure that results from a society that has a constant birthrate over a large number of years. The younger five-year cohorts are very similar in size, which is in sharp contrast with the age structure of the United States in 1900 when a rapidly expanding population produced ever larger new cohorts at the bottom of the age scale.

Vital Rates

As mentioned earlier, the basic elements that determine the composition of a population are the birthrate, the death rate, and migration. Any of these elements can be the most important at a particular time. The death rate can heavily influence a society if a disease or disaster strikes; immigration has always played a significant role in the population composition of the United States, especially during the period of heavy migration (1870–1910) but also today; in periods of normal death rates (and with the exception of societies that are heavily influenced by migration), the most important determinant of the age structure of a society is usually the birthrate. Some researchers have stated that even heavy migration to the United States has not had a great impact on the age structure, the only result being a very slight reduction in the median age (Spengler, 1975).

For most of the 100,000 years of human existence, societies have experienced both high birthrates and high death rates. People have reproduced themselves at a fairly slow pace, with some periods of no growth and even some declines in total population. Most of the increase in the human population has occurred in the last 300 years. Prior to the seventeenth century the typical lifespan was probably no longer than 35 or 40 years. A high birthrate was necessary just to maintain the human population.

The problem of a population explosion is quite recent in the context of the much longer period in which humans were faced with the problem of sustaining their numbers. When the human population began to grow at a fairly fast pace, however, it was not really because of an increased birthrate but instead because of a decrease in the death rate. Societies begin to grow, and to age, when there is a decrease in the number of people who die each year. The first stage of the modern population explosion is usually thought to have begun about the year 1650 in some of the industrializing European societies. The reasons for the decline in the death rate at about this time are unclear, although three causes have been suggested: (1) an increase in resistance to some fatal diseases, such as scarlet fever; (2) the development of techniques for preventing some diseases, such as inoculation against smallpox; and (3) some improvement in sanitary and health conditions, such as better nutrition and separation of sewage from drinking water (Peterson, 1975). Whatever the reasons, the world population increased greatly as a result of continued high birthrates (perhaps increased by a tendency toward earlier marriage) combined with lowered mortality. Whenever this combination of high birthrates and lowered mortality occurs in a society, the predictable result is a population explosion.

The Theory of Demographic Transition

The interaction between birth and death rates and its consequences for the population structure of a society are summarized in the theory of demographic transition. The theory states that it is possible to divide societies into three broad categories:

> High birthrate, high death rate = preindustrial society.
> High birthrate, low death rate = society in transition.
> Low birthrate, low death rate = modern society.

The theory sees societies as moving from the more or less primitive condition of high birth and death rates into the transitional stage, in which the society has reduced the death rate but has not yet altered the birthrate, and emerging as a modern society when the birth and death rates have been stabilized at a low level. Because of the interaction between the birth and death rates of each of the modal societies in the theory, the age composition of each type will be quite different. The preindustrial society will be a young society, with many babies born each year but with low life expectancy. The transitional society is beginning to age, especially since the decline in the death rate will increase the number of older people; but because the birthrate remains high, the older people may not greatly increase as a proportion of the entire society. The modern society is an aging society, for while the reduced death rate allows the number of older people to increase, the decline in the birthrate allows the older people to become an increasingly larger proportion of the total society.

The United States is a society that is aging, and it is possible to show the aging process by looking at the changes in its birth and death rates over the last century. The relevant figures are given in Table 2.1. The table shows that since 1840 the birthrate in the United States has declined markedly and that,

Table 2.1 TOTAL POPULATION, MEDIAN AGE, PERCENTAGE OVER AGE 65, BIRTH RATE, AND DEATH RATE FOR THE UNITED STATES, 1840–1976

Year	Total population	Median age	Percentage over age 65	Birth rate (per 1,000)	Death rate (per 1,000)
1840	17,069,000	17.8	—	51.8	—
1870	39,818,000	20.2	3.0	—	—
1900	76,094,000	22.9	4.1	32.3	17.2
1940	132,594,000	29.0	6.8	19.4	10.8
1960	180,671,000	29.5	9.2	23.7	9.5
1976 (est.)	215,118,000	29.0	10.7	14.7	9.0

Sources: U.S. Bureau of the Census, *Historical Statistics of the United States, Colonial Times to 1970,* bicentennial edition (Washington, D.C., 1975), and "Projections of the Population of the United States: 1977–2050," in *Current Population Reports,* Series P–25, no. 74 (Washington, D.C., 1977).

Table 2.2 APPROXIMATE POPULATION, BIRTH RATES,
PERCENTAGE OVER AGE 65, AND MEDIAN AGE OF UNITED STATES,
WORLD, MORE DEVELOPED REGIONS, AND LESS DEVELOPED REGIONS,
1970

	Total population	Median age	Percentage over age 65	Birth rate	Death rate
World	3,988,000,000	26	5.5	31.8	12.8
United States	204,879,000	28	9.8	18.2	9.4
More developed regions	1,133,000,000	33	9.6	17.2	9.2
Less developed regions	2,855,000,000	23	3.8	37.8	14.4

Source: United Nations, *Concise Report on the World Population Situation in 1970–1975 and Its Long-Range Implications,* Population Studies no. 56 (New York, 1974).

at least since 1900, the death rate has declined. The result has been an aging of the society, as is shown by the generally increasing median age but especially by the increasing percentage of Americans over 65. In 1870, only 3.0 percent of the United States population was over 65; but in 1976, however, 10.7 percent was in this age group.

The demographic transition theory can also be illustrated by comparing some of the vital rates of economically developed societies with the rates of less developed societies, as has been done by the United Nations (1974). This information is presented in Table 2.2. Societies are classified as either more developed or less developed. Two-thirds of the world's population is found in the less developed regions. The median age is only 23 years, which is ten years younger than that of the population of more developed regions. Slightly less than 4 percent of the people in the less developed regions are over age 65, but nearly 10 percent of those in the more developed regions are over age 65. The relative youth of the less developed regions and the relative maturity of the more developed regions is a reflection of the high birth and death rates of the less developed societies as compared to the relatively low birth and death rates of the more developed societies.

The Dependency Ratio

The age structure of a society is more than a matter of passing curiosity because a number of consequences flow from it. One of the most important ways in which a society is affected by its age structure has to do with the economy and the system of retirement. If a society is going to retire some of its members from the labor force, it is essential to know how many workers there are compared to the number of nonworkers. One of the simplest ways of calculating the relationship between the number of workers and the number of nonworkers is to use the dependency ratio. The dependency ratio uses the formula

$$\frac{\text{0–17 years of age} + \text{65} + \text{years of age}}{\text{18–64 years of age}}$$

This formula tells us the proportion of dependent persons in a society (here defined as everyone under 18 years of age plus everyone over 65) compared to the working population (defined as everyone between the ages of 18 and 64). The dependency ratio for the United States in 1976 was .69, which means that the dependent population was 69 percent as large as the working population. The completed formula for 1976 was as follows:

$$\frac{\text{65,191,000 age 0–17} + \text{22,934,000 age 65} +}{\text{126,933,000 age 18–64}}$$

In 1950, the dependency ratio for the United States was slightly lower, .64. In 1960, however, it was .82; in 1970, .78. The relatively high dependency ratios of 1960 and 1970 resulted from the large number of babies born after World War II, which produced a large population under age 18.

A variant of the dependency ratio is the old-age dependency ratio, which summarizes the relationship between the number of older people and the working population. The old-age dependency ratio is calculated by comparing the number of people over age 65 to the number between 18 and 64 years of age, or

$$\frac{\text{65} + \text{years}}{\text{18–64 years}}$$

In 1976, the old-age dependency ratio in the United States was .18, which means that there were slightly less than two people over age 65 for every ten people between the ages of 18 and 64. In 1950, the old-age dependency ratio was .13; in 1960, it had risen to .17, and it was still .17 in 1970. The old-age dependency ratio is particularly important in estimating the need for social security taxes as well as the need for government services for the older population.

When we compare the dependency ratio of the United States with the old-age dependency ratio, we see that since 1960 the dependency ratio has decreased whereas the old-age dependency ratio has increased. This indicates that an increasing proportion of the dependent population is old and a smaller proportion is young. It also indicates that some of the increased demand for government services for older people can be shifted from the decreased demand for services for the young population. As a practical matter the shift of government services from the young population to the old population may not be accomplished easily. A particular community, for example, may experience a decrease in the need for some of its elementary schools, especially schools located in neighborhoods populated largely by older adults with few school-age children. It might be possible to transform the neighborhood school into a senior center, a place for activities and services devoted to the older population. It will not be as easy, however, to replace elementary school teachers with workers qualified to work with older citizens. Nevertheless, this is the type of social transformation that is implied by the changing age structure of a community as indicated by changes in the dependency ratio and the old-age dependency ratio.

Population Projections

Perhaps the most valuable aspect of the demographic study of human populations is that past trends can be used to make projections about the future. Using birth, death, and immigration rates it is possible to make projections about a population at some future date. Projections are by their nature subject to error, especially if one of the actual rates deviates markedly from recent patterns. The demographic rates of the preceding years, for example, would not have led anyone to predict the 1947–1957 baby boom in the United States, because the birthrate in this period was much higher than any of the previous rates. In the last decade population projections for the United States have tended to overestimate the total population, mainly because the birthrate has declined more than was expected. Even if the projected rates are reliable in the long run, they may prove inaccurate in the short run. A population projection may correctly project an average of two children per family, but if a large number of couples delay having children until relatively late in the childbearing period, it affects the projections, especially in the early years. Population projections are not likely, therefore, to predict the future population composition of a society exactly, but they are capable of producing reasonably accurate forecasts, especially if the population dynamics are stable.

Unfortunately for population forecasters, population dynamics are seldom stable over a long period. The population of any society is likely to be affected by social and economic events that are unpredictable, such as wars, depressions, and technological advances. Peterson (1975), for example, includes the following technical innovations that are likely to affect population trends before the end of the twentieth century:

wider use of lasers in surgery
reductions in birth defects
increased use of artificial aids (such as heart pacers) and organ transplants
effective dietary control
ocean farming
ability to choose the sex of unborn children
some weather control
increased water availability in arid lands, such as through desalination or the
    use of icebergs
greater availability of nuclear power, including mass means of destruction

There will undoubtedly also be other technical advances by the end of this century that have not even been imagined yet. One such innovation could have a tremendous impact on the future population of the United States and the world. A nuclear war could decimate the human, animal, and vegetable population, or the effective application of cryogenics might retard the aging process to a significant degree. Since it is impossible, however, to estimate the potential impact of any such events or innovations on the population structure, demographers do not attempt to include them in their population projections.

The U.S. Bureau of the Census issues periodic population projections for the United States based on assumptions about future birthrates, death rates, and net immigration (U.S. Bureau of the Census, 1977). Three sets of projections are given—high, medium, and low. Each set assumes that the death rate and the rate of net immigration will remain relatively constant. Current projections show that the United States will have a population of between 246 million (the low projection) and 283 million (the high projection) in the year 2000. The most likely population is the medium projection, which shows a population of 260 million people for the year 2000. The discussion that follows is based on the medium projection (called the Series II projections).

Table 2.3 shows the population projections for the United States at ten-year intervals to the year 2050. It is interesting to note that the population of the United States is expected to increase at every ten-year interval, despite the assumption that each family will have 2.1 children. If this 2.1 replacement rate were to continue beyond the year 2050, the population size would be stabilized; but because of the large number of people of childbearing age there will be continued population growth through the year 2050. Although the population will continue to grow, the median age of the population will rise, going from about 30 years in 1980 to 38 years in 2030. From 2030 to 2050 the median age of the population will decrease slightly. The biggest jump in the median age will occur between 1980 and the end of the twentieth century. One of the reasons for this jump is that during those years the large baby boom cohort will be middle-aged and will therefore push up the median age.

Table 2.3 POPULATION PROJECTIONS FOR THE UNITED STATES, 1980–2050

	Total population	Median age	Number 65+	Percentage 65+	Old-age dependency ratio
1980	222,159,000	30.2	24,927,000	11.2	.17
1990	243,513,000	32.8	29,824,000	12.2	.20
2000	260,378,000	35.5	31,822,000	12.2	.20
2010	275,335,000	36.6	34,837,000	12.7	.20
2020	290,115,000	37.0	45,102,000	15.5	.26
2030	300,349,000	38.0	55,024,000	18.3	.32
2040	308,400,000	37.8	54,925,000	17.8	.31
2050	315,622,000	37.8	55,494,000	17.5	.30

Source: U.S. Bureau of the Census, "Projections of the Population of the United States: 1977–2050," in *Current Population Reports*, Series P-25, no. 704 (Washington, D.C., 1977).

One of the most impressive figures given in Table 2.3 is the projected number of Americans over age 65. There will be a doubling of the number of people over age 65 between the years 1980 and 2030. Although these figures are projections, they should be very reliable because everyone who will be over age 65 by 2030 is already born. In other words, we already know how many older people there will be if the cohort follows a normal life expectancy pattern. If the mortality rate for this group is lower than expected because of medical advances or other causes, this group will be even larger. After the year 2030 the number of older Americans will stabilize, even dipping slightly in the year 2040.

There is no doubt that the number of people over age 65 is going to increase for the remainder of this century and into the first half of the twenty-first century, but it is not clear what proportion of the total population will be in this age category. The projections show this group increasing from about 11 percent in 1980 to over 18 percent in 2030. This increase is likely to occur unless there is an unexpected increase in the birthrate during this period, which would have the effect of lowering the proportion of older people in the population.

Table 2.3 also presents the old-age dependency ratio. This ratio shows that the proportion of people over age 65 is going to increase in relation to the working population. The increase will be modest from 1980 to 2010, but by 2020 the ratio will be .26 and in 2030 it will be .32. This means that in 2010 there will be about one person over age 65 for every five persons between the ages of 18 and 64, but that by the year 2030 there will be one person 65 + years of age for every three people between the ages of 18 and 64. For the American system of social security, which has traditionally been a pay-as-you-go system of income security for the retired, the old-age dependency ratio foretells a significant increase in social security taxes. (See Chapter 9.)

The population projections for the United States for the next 70 years indicate that the population is going to grow older—that even though the population of the entire society is going to increase, the proportion of the society over age 65 is going to increase at an even faster pace. Figure 2.2 shows the growth and projected growth of the entire United States population and the proportion of the population over age 65 from 1950 to 2050. As the figure makes clear, the population of the United States is going to increase at a fairly steady rate, but the older population is going to increase gradually through the year 2010 and then markedly between 2010 and 2020 and from 2020 to 2030. From 2030 to 2050 the older population will not increase at all but instead will stabilize at about 55 million people. The large increase in the number of people over age 65 between the years 2010 and 2030 is, again, a result of the post-World War II baby boom; the people who will turn 65 in 2010 were born in 1945, and those who will turn 65 in 2030 were born in 1965.

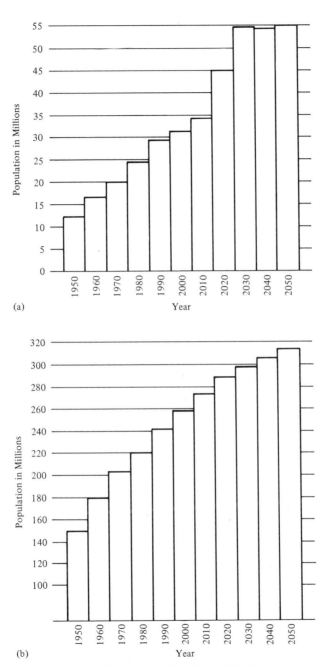

Figure 2.2 *Population and Population Projections, 1950–2050: (A) Number of People Age 65 and Over (B) Total Population of the United States*

Life Expectancy

In general, life expectancy has increased throughout human existence, although the pattern is probably not as consistent as might be imagined. Laslett (1976) reports that life expectancy in one English village was probably about 45 years at birth in the period 1538–1599, but between the years 1650–1699 it had dropped to 34 years at birth. In eighteenth-century Massachusetts and New Hampshire, life expectancy at birth was 28.15 years, while in seventeenth-century Plymouth Colony life expectancy was as high as 50 years. The large variations in life expectancy figures result from varying conditions in different places at different times; a plague epidemic could produce a decrease in life expectancy at a particular time, just as the elimination of a disease could increase life expectancy at another time.

Life expectancy is derived from a life table, which is the life history of a hypothetical group of people, such as those born in a particular year. The people in this cohort are assumed to die at a fixed rate until there is no one left in the cohort. Life expectancy refers to the total number of years lived by all the members of the cohort divided by the number of people in the cohort. In other words, life expectancy is the average number of years lived by the members of a cohort. This life expectancy figure can be computed for the members of a cohort at any age, but usually it refers to life expectancy at birth. The life expectancy at birth for all people in the United States born in 1970 was 70.9 years. This means that all the people born in the United States in 1970 will, on the average, live 70.9 years. Of course, some of the people in this cohort will die in the first year of life, which decreases the life expectancy of the entire cohort. The life table then gives a life expectancy at the age of 1 for the survivors, which in 1970 in the United States was 71.3 years. This means that everyone who was born in 1970 and survived for one year has a remaining life expectancy of 71.3; thus, on the average, those who lived through the first year will live to be 72.3 years of age—1 year lived + 71.3 years remaining life expectancy. The life table gives the life expectancy at every age for this cohort. Each year that the members of a cohort survive increases the number of years they are expected to live. By age 70 the surviving members of this cohort will still have a remaining life expectancy of 12.2 years.

Table 2.4 shows the life expectancy at birth for people born in selected years between 1900 and 1976, and the projected life expectancy for those who will be born in the year 2050. The differences in life expectancy between males and females is usually quite significant, so separate life expectancies are computed for each sex. As the table indicates, the life expectancy of females is always higher than that of males, and since 1900 sex differences in life expectancy have been increasing.

Life expectancy gives the mean number of years of expected life for a cohort, but it is also possible to compute the median expectation of life, which is a

Table 2.4 Life Expectancy at Birth in the United States, 1900–2050, in Years

	Male	*Female*	*Both sexes*
1900	46.3	48.3	47.3
1910	48.4	51.8	50.0
1920	53.6	54.6	54.1
1930	58.1	61.6	59.7
1940	60.8	65.2	62.9
1950	65.6	71.1	68.2
1960	66.6	73.1	69.7
1970	67.1	74.8	70.9
1976	69.1	77.0	
2050	71.8	81.0	

Sources: U.S. Bureau of the Census, *Historical Statistics of the United States, Colonial Times to 1970*, bicentennial edition (Washington, D.C., 1975), and "Projections of the Population of the United States: 1977 to 2050," in *Current Population Reports*, Series P–25, no. 704 (Washington, D.C., 1977).

better indicator of the average probable lifespan of a member of a cohort. The median expectation of life tells us the age to which 50 percent of the cohort will survive, a figure that is higher than the life expectancy at birth. In 1970 the median expectation of life was close to 75 years, compared to the life expectancy at birth of 70.9 years. This means that 50 percent of those born in 1970 can expect to reach age 75; a person born in 1970 has a 50:50 chance of living to age 75.

Life expectancy still varies considerably from one area of the world to another and from one nation to another. Table 2.5 shows estimated life expectancies for the major world areas and for some nations in 1970. Whereas Northern America, Europe, and the USSR have life expectancies at birth of over 70 years, South Asia and Africa have life expectancies of less than 50 years. Among individual nations, Sweden records the highest life expectancies, 71.7 for men and 76.5 for women. The life expectancies of much of Europe and North America are quite similar.

While an increase in life expectancy at birth reflects a decrease in the mortality rate, it does not really tell us at what age the improvement has occurred. We know that life expectancy at birth in the United States has increased from 47.3 years in 1900 to 70.9 years in 1970, an increase of 23.6 years. Almost all of the increase occurred between 1900 and 1950; since 1950 the life expectancy has increased only slightly. If we compare the life expectancy at birth with the life expectancy at age 65 for the United States for the period between 1900 and 1970, we find that life expectancy at age 65 has increased only by a little more than three years for all Americans. This means that most of the increase in life expectancy in the United States has been at ages under 65; in other words, for those who live to age 65, life expectancy has increased by only about three years. If, however, we look at the life expectancy at age 65 for white males and white females and for all other males and all other females, we can observe some significant differences. The figures are given in Table 2.6. Whereas white males have increased their life expectancy at age 65 by only about one and a half years since 1900, white females have increased their life expectancy by more than four and a half years. Likewise, all other males have increased their life expectancy at age 65 by about two and a half years, while all other females have increased their life expectancy by more than four years. Although Americans as a whole have not added many years to their life expectancy at age 65 since 1900, females have added more than males have.

Table 2.5 ESTIMATED LIFE EXPECTANCIES FOR MAJOR WORLD AREAS AND SELECTED NATIONS, ABOUT 1970

	Life expectancy at birth		
World area	*Male*	*Both sexes*	*Female*
Northern America		71.4	
Europe		71.3	
USSR		70.4	
Oceania		68.3	
East Asia		62.9	
Latin America		61.9	
South Asia		49.5	
Africa		45.2	
Nation			
Sweden	71.7		76.5
Netherlands	71.0		76.4
Iceland	70.8		76.2
France	68.6		76.1
Norway	71.0		76.0
Denmark	70.8		75.7
Canada	68.8		75.2
Puerto Rico	69.0		75.1
England and Wales	68.7		74.9
Australia	67.9		74.2
United States	66.6		74.0
Mexico	61.0		63.7
Philippines	48.8		53.4
Nicaragua		49.9	
Pakistan	53.7		48.8
Haiti		44.5	
Zambia		43.5	
Niger		41.0	
India	41.9		40.6
Mali		37.2	

Sources: United Nations, *Concise Report on the World Population Situation in 1970–1975 and Its Long-Range Implications*, Population Studies no. 56 (New York, 1974), and *Demographic Yearbook* (New York, 1972).

Table 2.6 Life Expectancy at Age 65, by Sex, in the United States, 1900–1970

	1900	1910	1920	1930	1940	1950	1960	1970
White males	11.5	11.3	12.2	11.8	12.1	12.8	13.0	13.2
White females	12.2	12.0	12.8	12.8	13.6	15.0	15.9	16.8
All other males	10.4	9.7	12.1	10.9	12.2	12.8	12.8	13.0
All other females	11.4	10.8	12.4	12.2	14.0	14.5	15.1	15.8

Source: National Center for Health Statistics, *Vital Statistics of the United States, 1973,* vol. II (Rockville, Md., 1975), Section 5.

Characteristics of the American Older Population

Residential Distribution

Older people are not randomly distributed throughout the United States. More are found in some areas than in others. The U.S. Bureau of the Census divides the nation into four regions, which contained the following numbers and percentages of people over age 65 in 1975:

Northeast	5,545,000	11.2%
North Central	6,119,000	10.6%
South	7,145,000	10.5%
West	3,592,000	9.5%

Although the Northeast has a somewhat larger proportion of older people, both the North Central region and the South have larger numbers of older people. The West has both the lowest proportion and the fewest number of people over age 65.

The states with the largest numbers of older people are also the most heavily populated states. Table 2.7 shows that seven states had older populations that exceeded 1 million in 1975. California and New York each had over 2 million people over 65. Over half of all Americans age 65 or over reside in one of the nine states with the largest numbers of older people.

The states with the largest numbers of older people are generally not those with the highest proportion of the population over age 65. Florida is the only exception, because Florida has both large numbers and a high percentage of older people. The states with high proportions of older people are not generally among the most heavily populated states, and most of them are midwestern farm states. Florida has a high percentage of older people because residents of other states have migrated to Florida upon retirement to enjoy its favorable climate. Most of the other states with high proportions of older people have also been affected by migration: out-migration by young people. The loss of the younger population has caused these states to age. Within some of these

Table 2.7 States with Largest Numbers and Largest and Smallest Percentages of Residents Over Age 65, in 1975 (Numbers in Thousands)

States with largest number of people over age 65

	State	Number
1.	California	2,056
2.	New York	2,030
3.	Pennsylvania	1,377
4.	Florida	1,347
5.	Texas	1,158
6.	Illinois	1,153
7.	Ohio	1,066
8.	Michigan	815
9.	New Jersey	767
10.	Massachusetts	672

States with largest percentage of people over age 65

State	Number	Percentage of residents
Florida	1,347	16.1
Arkansas	271	12.8
Iowa	364	12.7
Missouri	601	12.6
Kansas	285	12.6
Nebraska	194	12.6
South Dakota	85	12.5
Oklahoma	334	12.3
Rhode Island	113	12.2
Maine	125	11.5

States with smallest percentage of people over age 65

State	Number	Percentage of residents
Alaska	9	2.4
Hawaii	57	6.6
Nevada	44	7.5
Utah	91	7.5
New Mexico	90	7.9
S. Carolina	229	8.1
Colorado	210	8.3
Maryland	340	8.3
Virginia	424	8.5
Georgia	430	8.7
Delaware	50	8.7

states, such as Kansas, about 20 percent of the counties in the state have more than 20 percent of the population over age 65.

The states with the smallest percentages of older people (see Table 2.7) are in the West and South. Some of these states have experienced a heavy in-migration of young people, and others have high fertility rates. The effect of both of these processes is to keep the proportion of older people relatively low.

There are some differences in the life expectancies of various states. (See Table 2.8.) Hawaii has the highest overall life expectancy, and many of the midwestern and western states have life expectancies above the national average. Washington, D.C., has the lowest life expectancy at birth, although most of the states with low life expectancies are in the South. Hawaii also has the longest life expectancy at age 65, followed closely by Florida and then by some of the midwestern agricultural states: Nebraska, South Dakota, and Kansas. The states with low life expectancies at age 65 are scattered around the country, from Pennsylvania and Delaware to Nevada and Louisiana.

Although everyone is aware of the large numbers of retired people who have migrated from cold-weather states to warm-weather states, in comparison with younger age groups older Americans do not have a high migration rate. The general rule is that there is an inverse relationship between age and geographical mobility, and there is no large increase in mobility among older people, not even around the typical retirement age of 65 years. There are, however, very definite patterns of movement among older people, and most of the migration is out of the Northeast and North Central states and into the South and West. Table 2.9 summarizes the migration patterns of the population over 65 for the period between 1960 and 1970. The states that experienced the

Table 2.8 HIGH AND LOW LIFE EXPECTANCIES AT BIRTH AND AT AGE 65 FOR THE FIFTY STATES AND THE DISTRICT OF COLUMBIA

Life expectancy at birth (in years)

High states		Low states	
1. Hawaii	73.6	1. Washington, D.C.	65.7
2. Minnesota	73.0	2. Alabama	66.1
3. Utah	72.9	3. South Carolina	68.0
4. North Dakota	72.8	4. Mississippi	68.1
5. Nebraska	72.6	5. Georgia	68.5

Life expectancy at age 65 (in years)

1. Hawaii	16.2	1. Pennsylvania	14.4
2. Florida	16.1	2. Delaware	14.4
3. Nebraska	15.9	3. Nevada	14.4
4. South Dakota	15.8	4. Louisiana	14.4
5. Kansas	15.8	5. West Virginia	14.5

Source: Adapted from Herman B. Brotman, "Life Expectancy: Comparison of National Levels in 1900 and 1974 and Variations in State Levels, 1969–1971," *Gerontologist*, 17 (1977):12–22.

greatest loss of people over 65 through migration were the Northeast and North Central states with the largest older populations: New York, Illinois, Pennsylvania, Ohio, and Michigan. The states that gained the most older people through migration were the warm-weather states of the South and West: Florida, California, Texas, Arizona, and Arkansas.

Today the United States is an urban society, so it is not surprising that most people over 65 live in urban areas. About 73 percent of all older people live in urban areas. (See Table 2.10.) Within urban areas, the largest proportion of older people is found in central cities (34 percent), and only 21 percent live in the suburbs. This is a reversal of the pattern for the general population, in which more people live in the suburbs than in the central cities of urban areas. Slightly less than 9 percent of older people live in small cities; another 9 percent live in towns. About 27 percent live in rural areas, most on farms or in communities of less than 1,000 population. The rural towns and small urban towns have the highest concentrations of older people, who account for 13.6 percent of the population of rural towns and 12.2 percent of the population of urban towns. In contrast, older people make up only 7.8 percent of the population of suburbs. Kennedy and DeJong (1977) studied the residential patterns of ten cities in the United States to determine whether the central-city areas were segregated by age. They found that there is some segregation by age, although the degree of segregation is moderate and much lower than the

Table 2.9 ESTIMATED MIGRATION OF PEOPLE OVER AGE 65, BY REGION AND STATE, 1960–1970

	Net migration	Rate of migration (%)
A. Regions		
Northeast	−333,605	− 3.8
North Central	−219,903	− 2.3
South	+444,196	+ 5.0
West	+232,960	+ 5.0
B. States with large numbers of out-migrants		
1. New York	−202,942	− 5.9
2. Illinois	−105,145	− 5.5
3. Pennsylvania	− 88,470	− 4.0
4. Ohio	− 58,753	− 3.4
5. Michigan	− 50,146	− 3.9
C. States with large numbers of in-migrants		
1. Florida	+366,122	+36.0
2. California	+142,886	+ 5.3
3. Texas	+ 52,762	+ 3.5
4. Arizona	+ 46,176	+25.2
5. Arkansas	+ 17,750	+ 4.9

Source: Jacob S. Siegel, "Some Demographic Aspects of Aging in the United States," in *Epidemiology of Aging*, eds. Adrian M. Ostfeld and Don C. Gibson (Washington, D.C.: U.S. Government Printing Office, 1975), pp. 40–42.

Table 2.10 URBAN–RURAL RESIDENCE OF PEOPLE 65 YEARS OF AGE AND OLDER IN THE UNITED STATES, 1970

	Number	Percentage of people over 65	Percentage of area population
Urban Areas (73.0%)			
Central cities	6,842,000	34.1	10.7
Suburbs	4,264,000	21.3	7.8
Small cities (over 10,000 population)	1,788,000	8.9	10.8
Towns (2,500 to 10,000 population)	1,737,000	8.7	12.2
Rural Areas (27.1%)			
Rural towns (1,000 to 2,500 population)	903,000	4.5	13.6
Other rural	4,532,000	22.6	9.6
Total	20,065,000	100.0	

Source: U.S. Bureau of the Census, *1970 General Population Characteristics*, Final Report (Washington, D.C.: 1973), United States Summary.

amount of racial segregation in most United States cities. They also concluded that there had been no increase in the amount of age segregation in the cities during the period 1960–1970.

Sex and Race Composition

Since the life expectancy of American females is significantly greater than that of American males, it is not surprising that the older population is largely female. There are usually more males born than females, and there are usually slightly more males than females until a cohort reaches adulthood. Because of the higher death rates of males, females usually outnumber males at the higher ages. Table 2.11 shows the sex composition of the United States for age cohorts in the year 1970. As mentioned previously, the sex ratio compares the number of males to the number of females. For children under 5 years of age in 1970 the sex ratio was 104, which means that there were 104 boys for every 100 girls between the ages of 0 and 4 years. A sex ratio above 100 indicates that there are more males than females, while a ratio below 100 indicates that there are more females than males. We can see that for the United States in 1970 all cohorts under 25 years of age were composed of more males than females, but all cohorts over 25 years of age were composed of more females than males. The predominance of females increases with the age of the cohort. For the last cohort, those over 75 years of age, the sex ratio is 64; in other words, in 1970 there were only 64 males over age 75 for every 100 females.

The United States has not always had more females than males in the older cohorts. Table 2.11 also shows the sex ratios for those over 65 from 1870 to 1970, as well as the projections for this cohort for the years 2000 to 2050. From

1870 to 1930 the sex ratio indicates that there were more older males than older females; but beginning in 1940 there were more females than males, and females continued to become a larger proportion of the older cohort until 1970. By 1970 the sex ratio of all people over age 65 was 72. Population projections for the future anticipate that there will continue to be more females than males in the over-65 cohort, with sex ratios ranging between 66 and 69.

Although aging among minority groups is treated in greater detail in Chapter 4, it is important to note that the demography of aging is significantly different among both American blacks and Americans of Spanish origin than among American whites. Primarily because of higher birthrates, a smaller proportion of the minority population is over age 65. In 1975, 11.0 percent of the white population was 65 or over, whereas only 7.4 percent of blacks and 3.6 percent of persons of Spanish origin were over age 65.

Educational Levels

Because each new generation in American society has aspired to more education, and because the opportunities to secure an education have expanded over time, the over-65 segment of the American population is less well educated than younger generations. Table 2.12 shows that the educational level of Americans over age 65 has improved from 1952 to 1975 and that the educational level will continue to increase. Whereas the median educational level of the older population in 1975 was 9.0 years, by 1990 it will have increased to 11.9 years. This means that the median educational level of the older population is going to increase by nearly three years within a fifteen-year time span. This increase in median educational level will bring the older population very close to the median educational level of the entire adult population; more important, the rising educational level of the older population means that in the future the older population is going to be more sophisticated in pursuing its political and economic interests. Although the difference between the educational levels of older males and females is not large, females have had slightly higher educational levels in the past, and this advantage is expected to continue at least to 1990.

Table 2.12 MEDIAN YEARS OF EDUCATION FOR PEOPLE OVER AGE 25 AND OVER AGE 65 IN THE UNITED STATES, 1952–1990, BY SEX

	1952	1965	1975	1990 (Projection)
Over age 25, both sexes	10.1	11.8	12.3	12.6
Over age 65, both sexes	8.2	8.5	9.0	11.9
Females over age 65	8.3	8.6	9.4	12.0
Males over age 65	8.0	8.3	8.9	11.8

Source: U.S. Bureau of the Census, "Demographic Aspects of Aging and the Older Population in the United States," in Current Population Reports, Special Studies, Series P–23, no. 59 (Washington, D.C., 1976).

Table 2.11 AGE AND SEX COMPOSITION OF THE UNITED STATES POPULATION, 1970, AND SEX COMPOSITION OF THE POPULATION 65 + YEARS OF AGE, 1870–2050

Age	Males Number	Males Percentage	Females Number	Females Percentage	Sex ratio
Under 5	8,752,000	50.9	8,415,000	49.1	104
5–9	10,134,000	51.0	9,754,000	49.0	104
10–14	10,595,000	50.9	10,205,000	49.1	104
15–19	9,802,000	50.8	9,499,000	49.2	103
20–24	8,649,000	50.3	8,543,000	49.7	101
25–29	6,796,000	49.7	6,891,000	50.3	99
30–34	5,708,000	49.3	5,862,000	50.7	97
35–39	5,484,000	49.1	5,690,000	50.9	96
40–44	5,838,000	48.7	6,143,000	51.3	95
45–54	11,236,000	48.3	12,051,000	51.7	93
55–64	8,817,000	47.3	9,834,000	52.7	90
65–74	5,454,000	43.7	7,028,000	56.3	78
75+	2,996,000	38.9	4,699,000	61.1	64

Year	Males Number	Males Percentage	Females Number	Females Percentage	Sex ratio
1870	578,230	50.1	575,419	49.9	100
1880	867,564	50.3	855,895	49.7	101
1890	1,233,719	51.0	1,183,569	49.0	104
1900	1,555,418	50.5	1,525,080	49.5	102
1910	1,985,976	50.3	1,963,548	49.7	101
1920	2,483,071	50.3	2,450,144	49.7	101
1930	3,325,211	50.1	3,308,594	49.9	101
1940	4,406,120	48.9	4,613,194	51.1	96
1950	5,796,974	47.2	6,472,563	52.8	90
1960	7,503,097	45.3	9,056,483	54.7	83
1970	8,415,708	41.9	11,649,794	58.1	72
Projections					
2000	12,717,000	40.0	19,105,000	60.0	67
2010	13,978,000	40.1	20,858,000	59.9	67
2020	18,468,000	40.9	26,634,000	59.1	69
2030	22,399,000	40.7	32,624,000	59.3	69
2040	21,816,000	39.7	33,108,000	60.3	66
2050	22,055,000	39.7	33,439,000	60.3	66

Sources: U.S. Bureau of the Census, *Statistical Abstract of the United States* (Washington, D.C., 1973), *Historical Statistics of the United States, Colonial Times to 1970,* bicentennial edition (Washington, D.C., 1975), and "Projections of the Population of the United States: 1977–2050," in *Current Population Reports,* Series P-25, no. 704 (Washington, D.C., 1977).

Summary

The United States has been experiencing a major change in the age composition of its population, becoming a much more mature society than it was only a few decades ago. The median age of the society has increased from about 17 years in the year 1820 to 28 years in 1970 and is expected to increase to about 38 years by 2030.

The major indicators of demographic change are the birthrate, the death rate, and the migration rate, but the birthrate is particularly important in the age shift in European and North American societies. Most industrialized societies have experienced reduced death rates when compared with earlier periods of human history, and most have also experienced a population explosion when the decrease in the death rate was not accompanied by a decrease in the birthrate. Once a society brings the birthrate more or less in line with the death rate, the society begins to age—the average age of the society increases and the proportion of older people in the society increases.

The transformation that is under way in the age composition of the United States population is not expected to be complete until about the year 2030. By the year 2030 the number of people age 65 and over in the United States will have grown from about 20 million in 1970 to about 55 million. While life expectancy at birth has increased by more than 20 years from 1900 to 1970, it is not expected to increase by more than about five years in the next century.

Older people do not move as often as younger people, but most of those who do, move from the "snowbelt" areas of the country to the "sunbelt" areas, especially Florida and California.

SELECTED REFERENCES

William Peterson, *Population,* 3rd ed. (New York: Macmillan, 1975).

Joseph J. Spengler, *Population and America's Future* (San Francisco: W. H. Freeman, 1975).

U.S. Bureau of the Census, "Historical Statistics of the United States, Colonial Times to 1970," bicentennial edition (Washington, D.C., 1975).

——— "Demographic Aspects of Aging and the Older Population in the United States," in *Current Population Reports,* Special Studies, Series P–23, no. 59 (Washington, D.C., May 1976).

——— "Projections of the Population of the United States: 1977 to 2050," in *Current Population Reports,* Series P-25, no. 704 (Washington, D.C., 1977).

CHAPTER 3

The Biology and Epidemiology of Aging

Overview. Although some impressive studies of the biology of aging have been reported, much work remains to be done. Much future research will be guided by one of the major theories of aging that have already been expounded. However, until there is some agreement on the validity of those theories, the question of what constitutes biological aging will remain unanswered.

Although there is no widely accepted theory of why biological aging occurs, some research has been done on the effects of aging. Everyone is aware that certain kinds of changes occur throughout the life cycle, and we even have ways of alleviating some of the deleterious effects of this process.

While few advances have occurred in altering the basic biological components of aging, the aging process has been affected by medical advances. Most important, the elimination of infectious diseases as major causes of death has allowed many more people to live longer. But while infectious diseases pose a declining threat, older people are faced with the problems brought on by chronic noninfectious diseases.

There are no simple ways of overcoming the changes that occur in the human body with advancing age, but the two elements that contribute to good health at all ages—a balanced diet and proper exercise—are especially important for older people.

It is well known that certain physical changes occur with aging, especially superficial changes such as graying of the hair and wrinkling of the skin. But the most significant physical changes that occur with age are not visible to the naked eye, and even biological gerontologists are not always certain of the precise dynamics of many age-related changes.

All organisms undergo continuous change, and the cumulative effect of this process is thought of as biological aging. Measuring the effects of aging on the human body presents many of the same methodological problems that are faced in measuring the social and mental aspects of aging. In the first place, the length of human life presents research problems that are not associated with the study of shorter-lived animals such as rats. Because rats exhibit some of the same biological processes as humans, but have a life expectancy of only a couple of years, they are often used as subjects for research with the hope that the results will provide some insight into the processes of human aging. Rats are not humans, however, and it is not legitimate to imply that the aging process of rats is identical to that of humans. When humans are used in aging research, it is possible to use a cross-sectional approach to compare the measurements of some vital functions for different age groups. It is possible, for example, to measure diastolic blood pressure or maximum breathing capacity in a sample of people of different ages. But the cross-sectional research design contains many of the same problems in biological research as it does in sociological or psychological research. Differences between the blood pressure levels of people of various ages could be a result of aging, but they could also be caused by factors affecting different age cohorts, such as different environments; different diets; different means for preserving, storing, and preparing foods. To some unknown degree, these or other factors could alter the process of biological aging. Longitudinal or cohort analyses of the physical changes that occur with age are preferred.

Another research problem faced by biological gerontologists is the difference between *in vivo* and *in vitro* research, a distinction that is especially important in cellular research. Cells that are a part of a living organism are said to be *in vivo,* that is, in their natural environment. It is possible, however —and usually advantageous—to isolate cells from their natural setting by placing them in a culture in which they can survive while being observed. The problem is that cells *in vitro* may not act and react exactly the same way they would if they were a part of a living organism.

Another research problem faced by biological—and other—gerontologists is that of defining and isolating the aging process. Two types of changes are associated with advancing age: normal processes and pathological processes. Aging is usually identified as a set of normal processes, that is, the kinds of changes that are experienced by all the members of an age cohort. They may involve declines in certain performance capacities, but they are not debilitating. Pathological changes involve the presence of an abnormal condition, usually thought of as a disease, and are usually accompanied by deleterious effects. Although it might seem easy to distinguish between normal and pathological aging, the two are so closely related at times that it is almost impossible to separate them. An example is atherosclerosis (to be discussed later in this chapter), a chronic condition that is so widespread among older Americans that some experts believe it is a normal feature of aging while others believe it is a disease that has reached epidemic proportions among older people. The distinction between normal and pathological aging is important. If the strategy is to explore the normal course of biological aging, seeking the answer to the question of why we grow old, then the approach would be to follow a course of basic biological research, concentrating on the elements of human maturation and development. If, on the other hand, the strategy is to concentrate on the pathological conditions that affect older people, the approach would be to develop an applied program of research that would attempt to ameliorate those conditions.

Which approach should be taken? What are the benefits to be derived from each? If the strategy of eliminating the pathological conditions of aging is chosen, then there are estimates of the effect this approach could have if

Table 3.1 GAIN IN YEARS OF LIFE EXPECTANCY AT AGE 65 FROM ELIMINATION OF LEADING CAUSES OF DEATH

| | Males | | Females | | |
| | White | Nonwhite | White | Nonwhite | Total |
Causes of death					
Major cardiovascular–renal	9.6	9.3	10.2	10.8	10.0
Malignant neoplasms	1.3	1.3	1.1	1.0	1.2
All accidents (except motor vehicle)	0.1	0.1	0.2	0.1	0.1
Motor vehicle accidents	0.1	0.1	—	—	0.1
Influenza and pneumonia	0.2	0.4	0.2	0.3	0.2
Infective and parasitic	0.1	0.2	—	0.1	0.1
Diabetes mellitus	0.1	0.1	0.2	0.2	0.2
Tuberculosis	0.1	0.1	—	—	—
Total	11.6	11.6	11.9	12.5	11.9

Source: Jacob S. Siegel, "Some Demographic Aspects of Aging in the United States," in *Epidemiology of Aging*, eds. Adrian M. Ostfeld and Don C. Gibson (Washington, D.C.: U.S. Government Printing Office, 1972), p. 61.

successful. Table 3.1 shows the increases in life expectancy at age 65 that would result from the elimination of the current major causes of death. The table shows that a significant increase in life expectancy—an average gain of ten years—would result from the elimination of cardiovascular–renal diseases. This category of diseases includes a wide variety of heart diseases as well as kidney dysfunctions, and it would require a series of significant medical discoveries to eliminate the entire category. Eliminating just the diseases of the heart as a cause of death would add 4.9 years to life expectancy at age 65. Elimination of the second category, malignant neoplasms, which includes a variety of cancer diseases, would add 1.2 years to life expectancy at age 65. Elimination of all eight major causes of death in the United States would add 11.9 years to life expectancy at age 65. The successful application of a strategy to eliminate the major causes of death would yield approximate life expectancies of 89.8 years for white males who survived to age 65, 89.6 years for nonwhite males, 93.7 years for white females, and 93.3 years for nonwhite females.

In contrast, there are no good estimates of the increases in life expectancy that might result from a research program on normal aging—that is, from studying the most basic processes of aging—although the upper limits of any estimates that could be developed would probably exceed the life expectancy figures just noted. A basic program of research might reduce some of the chronic conditions associated with aging, also, allowing people to lead fully active lives for a longer time.

At present the relationship between normal and pathological processes of aging are so closely related that they affect each other in a dialectical fashion.

The normal processes of aging alter the human body to the extent that it is increasingly vulnerable to acute attacks of disease. While it may be that nobody ever died of old age, the normal processes of aging can render a person nearly defenseless against disease processes that would not seriously threaten a younger person.

Biological Theories of Aging

There are currently five recognized theories of biological aging, plus one discovery that has achieved the status of an axiom, which guide most research on the biology of aging. The axiom is the "aging clock" idea developed by Leonard Hayflick, and the five theories are as follows:

1. The error theory
2. The free radical theory
3. The cross-linkage theory
4. The autoimmune theory
5. The pituitary theory

There are a number of potential relationships among these theories, and it is very possible that a theory of biological aging might incorporate portions of several or all of them; but each is currently being pursued as an independent theory that may hold the key to understanding the biology of aging.

Hayflick's Aging Clock

All animal species have a more or less predictable lifespan, and humans are no exception. The concepts of human life expectancy and a life table are discussed in detail in Chapter 2, but calculations of human life expectancy do not tell us what the maximum potential lifespan is. How long could a human live? Are there, indeed, finite limits to the human lifespan, limits beyond which it would be impossible (under current conditions) to continue living? Although the subject is not closed, there is general agreement that at the human cellular level there is a definite limit that is built—some say programed—into the human lifespan. Leonard Hayflick (Hayflick, 1965, 1974, 1977; Hayflick and Moorhead, 1961) and his associates have been able to demonstrate that normal human cells will survive and reproduce in a culture for a certain period, but will eventually enter a state of degeneration and then die. Hayflick has calculated that human cells will reproduce themselves about fifty times (plus or minus ten times) before they die. On the basis of normal rates of metabolism, he has estimated that the full potential human lifespan is no longer than 110–120 years. If Hayflick is correct, even if all the pathological causes of death were eliminated, a human would eventually die as a result of the expiration of the programed lifespan of the cells. Since human cells have this aging clock, the extension of the human lifespan beyond the 110–120 year age limit would require some change in the normal rate of cellular activity. However, very few people today even approach the full potential lifespan because they die of some disease process at an earlier age.

The cellular aging clock has been validated in research studies using human cells in cultures; it is possible that cells in living bodies would react differently. Further research, however, has found that cells taken from very young humans and placed in a culture will reproduce more times than cells taken from older people, which implies that the cells taken from older people have already undergone a certain number of cell divisions and therefore have fewer reproductions left than the cells taken from embryos. This further supports the idea of the aging clock and provides some evidence that the phenomenon is not just an artifact of the research laboratory but also occurs within the human body.

The discovery of the cellular aging clock will not immediately extend the human lifespan, although it does inform us that even the elimination of diseases will not confer immortality upon us; the discovery also tells us that any long-term answers to the extension of human life will have to be based on a better understanding of the structural components of the human organism than currently exists.

The Error Theory

The human cell is a very complex structure. Ultimately, the entire body is dependent on the metabolic activity of cells. Cellular activity involves the interaction of a number of components, including deoxyribonucleic acid (DNA), the command center located in the nucleus of the cell, and ribonucleic acid (RNA), which is involved in the production of proteins. DNA directs RNA to manufacture proteins, and RNA does so, using amino acids and enzymes. This protein synthesis is accomplished by means of a genetic code that is contained in both DNA and RNA. However, cells can and do make mistakes in the production of DNA, RNA, and the proteins; at the very least, over a lifetime some cells will make some random errors. The more time passes, the greater the accumulation of cellular errors. If an error occurs in DNA, a permanent change in the chemical structure of the cell—a mutation—may occur. An error in DNA can lead to the production of an altered RNA, which in turn can lead to an altered protein synthesis. A random error in cellular activity thus can reverberate throughout the cellular system. The error theory of aging argues that aging is basically a result of a lifetime accumulation of cellular errors. Eventually, some cells may contain so many faulty molecules that the cell will not be able to sustain normal functions (Orgel, 1963, 1970). Since the human body is dependent on cellular activity, any change in this activity can mean that some normal and perhaps critical functions will not be performed or will be performed inadequately.

The Free-radical Theory

A second theory, which focuses on the dysfunctions of normal cellular activity with aging and on how these dysfunctions can produce deleterious effects, is the free-radical theory. The damage to the cells according to this theory is caused by the presence of free radicals. Free radicals are unstable atoms of the cell, usually pieces of molecules, that have broken off and established independence. They do not remain independent very long, but attach themselves to other molecules. In doing so, they can cause a certain amount of damage, or, even worse, the impact of the attachment may cause atoms from the host molecule to break off and become free radicals themselves. The end result of the movement of free radicals is cellular damage, perhaps even causing damage to DNA or to proteins. All cells will normally produce a certain number of free radicals, but exposure to radiation can greatly increase their number and, therefore, the amount of cellular damage. According to the free-radical theory, human aging is a result of the accumulation of damage caused by the presence of free radicals (Harman, 1960, 1968).

It is believed that the damage caused by free radicals can be reduced through the use of antioxidants (Harman, 1961; Tappel, 1968). Of the several antioxidants currently available, two of the most familiar are BHT (butylated hydroxytoluene) and vitamin E. The current interest in vitamin E as an antiaging element has derived from the free-radical theory of aging and from research on some animals, which has found that supplementing the diet with vitamin E increases the lifespan.

The Cross-linkage Theory

A theory of aging that is very closely related to the free-radical theory is the theory of cross-linkage. This theory holds that human aging is a result of the formation of bridges (cross-linkages) between the protein molecules that form the intercellular material in the body. Once these cross-linkages have been formed, they are apparently immune to the efforts of the body's repair enzymes to break them apart. Cross-linking is a phenomenon that usually occurs in collagen, a protein found throughout the human body. Collagen surrounds cells and blood vessels and is part of the substance that surrounds muscles.

The cross-linkage theory of aging hypothesizes that humans experience less muscular flexibility, less efficient cardiac contraction, and reduced tissue oxygenation because of the formation of cross-linkages. The problems caused by cross-linkages lead to other problems, such as increased hypertension and greater difficulty in the passage of vital materials throughout the body, and may even contribute to the development of neoplasia (Bjorksten, 1968; Kohn, 1977; Weg, 1978). Although it would not be possible to avoid the formation of cross-linkages, it is thought that their number could be reduced by lowering the caloric intake of the daily diet, and especially by avoiding overeating.

The Autoimmune Theory

Most of the theories of biological aging concentrate on basic molecular and cellular processes, but the autoimmune theory has developed out of clinical observations of older medical patients (Makinodon, 1977). It is known that the human immune system becomes less efficient with age. In the human immune system immunocompetent cells (either B cells or T cells) respond to foreign matter in the body by treating it as a threat to the body. The immune system protects the body by causing it to produce antibodies that will attack the foreign matter. With age, however, the normal immune functions decline, and as a result older people are more susceptible to infections from bacteria and viruses. In addition, it is thought that the increased susceptibility of older people to cancer is a result of the decline in the immune system—an efficient immune system would destroy cancer cells as they appeared.

The autoimmune theory postulates that the breakdown of the body's immune system may cause the body to produce antibodies that attack and destroy normal, healthy cells as if they were foreign matter. It is this process that gives the theory the name *autoimmunity;* in essence, the immune system turns against the host organism that it is supposed to defend (Walford, 1969; Makinodan, 1977).

There is a possibility that the efficiency of the immune system and the suppression of the autoimmune reaction could be extended by dietary means (especially by reducing intake and by reducing fat) or by reducing the body temperature. There is also a possibility that greater control could be achieved through the use of chemicals or perhaps through surgical removal of the spleen. The idea of removing the spleen is based on some research with mice in which it was discovered that the spleen contained both autoimmune cells and cancer cells and that removing the spleen increased the lifespan of the mice. Another possible procedure for dealing with the autoimmune reaction is the infusion of young, healthy immune cells in older people. The cells for the infusion could come from a compatible young donor, or perhaps in the future people will be able to preserve (at very cold temperatures) their own immune cells for infusion in later life.

The Pituitary Theory

Some researchers believe that the secret of aging may be found in the pituitary; it is known that the pituitary gland is essential for life because it controls the thyroid, the adrenal cortex, the ovary, and the testis, and regulates human growth, reproduction, and metabolism. Basically, this theory states that aging is a result of a lack of pituitary hormones. It is known, for example, that when young people suffer from a pituitary destroyed by disease, they exhibit many of the physical characteristics associated with old age. Unlike the aging of older people, however, this psuedoaging can usually be reversed by replacement of the missing hormone.

The pituitary gland secretes several hormones that are essential for the maintenance of normal bodily functions, but some researchers believe that it secretes a specific life-maintaining hormone known as ACTH (adrenocorticotropic hormone). It appears from clinical cases of individuals who exhibit premature senescence that aging could result from either a lack or an excess of hormones (Herman, 1976). If an excess of ACTH can cause premature aging, perhaps because of overstimulation and overuse of the body's organs, then in a normal state the pituitary could contribute to aging by overstimulating a body that can tolerate only so much wear and tear. By producing hormones that stimulate the organs, it causes the organs to expend their useful life in a shorter period than would be the case if they operated at a basal level without stimulation (Everitt, 1976).

Very closely related to the pituitary theory is the work of Denkla (1974, 1975, 1976), who has found a hormone called DECO (decreasing O_2 consumption) that appears to veto the functioning of thyroxine as people grow older. If this is the case, then many of the changes associated with aging could result from the action of DECO, now sometimes referred to as the death hormone (Rosenfeld, 1976). This would mean that the body contains within itself the means of its own ultimate destruction—a death hormone that could make the body susceptible to other, more obvious disease processes.

Physical Changes with Age

Most people undergo noticeable physical changes as they age, although these changes occur at different ages in different people. The biological age of a particular person may be quite different from that of other people who are of the same chronological age. This variation in aging is very much like the different rates of maturation in children—it is well known that some children mature at a faster rate than others.

One way of measuring the changes that occur with age is to compare the functional performance levels of some of the basic physiological processes. Figure 3.1 presents a comparison between an average 30-year-old and an average 80-year-old on six processes that represent some of the major organ systems of the body. The performance level of the average 30-year-old is taken as the 100 percent level of functioning. The figure shows that the average 80-year-old experiences a decline in each of these physiological processes. The basic metabolic rate of the 80-year-old is about 85 percent of that of the 30-year-old, whereas the cardiac output is only 65 percent, the maximum breathing capacity only 40 percent, the renal plasma flow 45 percent, the

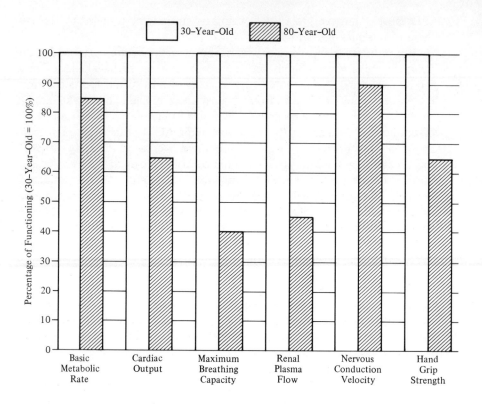

Figure 3.1 *Comparison Between an Average 30-Year-Old Person and an Average 80-Year-Old Person on Six Basic Physiological Processes*

Source: Adapted from Seymour Bakerman, *Aging Life Processes* (Springfield, Ill.: Charles C Thomas, 1969).

nervous conduction velocity 90 percent, and the hand grip strength 65 percent. Although all of the physiological processes show a decline, some declines are very modest while others are quite large. The usual cautions about using cross-sectional comparisons of age groups, as well as the factor of individual variations, must be remembered. It is quite possible that a particular 80-year-old might exceed the performance level of the average 30-year-old in some ways.

It is not known exactly why humans experience these declines in performance level other than "because of age," although it is suspected that some of the decline is a result of changes in body composition. Table 3.2 is a comparison of body composition between a 25 year old male and a 70 year old male. It is known that most people become shorter after middle age, and that after gaining weight in middle age, most people lose weight in their later years

Table 3.2 COMPARISON OF BODY COMPOSITION OF MALE AGED 25 AND
MALE AGED 70

25-year-old male		70-year-old male
14%	Fat	30%
61%	Water	53%
19%	Cell solids	12%
6%	Bone mineral	5%
1.068	Specific gravity	1.035

Source: Isadore Rossman, "Anatomic and Body Composition Changes with Aging," in *Handbook of the Biology of Aging*, eds. Caleb E. Finch and Leonard Hayflick (New York: Van Nostrand Reinhold, 1977), pp. 189–221.

(Rossman, 1976). Nevertheless, the comparison between a 25 year old male and a 70 year old male shows that the older male has more than doubled the proportion of fat in his body. The increase in body fat accounts for some of the decrease in water but is also a result of a decline in the lean body mass, and possibly some tissue shrinkage. The decrease in cell solids is due to a loss of protein and potassium and is also related to the decrease in muscle. The general result of aging is a decrease in muscle, which is replaced by fat, and this change is related to many of the declines in the functional performance levels of the body's organs. The loss in bone mineral is not as significant as other changes in body composition, although changes in the skeletal system are usually more significant for females than for males. The decline in specific gravity from age 25 to age 70 is also related to the increase in fat in the body. Since fat is the only body tissue that is lighter than water, when the proportion of body fat increases, the specific gravity decreases. A specific gravity value of 1.10 would indicate a fat-free human body. Thus, the change in specific gravity from 1.068 at age 25 to 1.035 at age 70 reflects the increase in body fat (Rossman, 1977).

The Skeletomuscular and Dental Systems

Growing old is commonly associated with the onset of arthritis and rheumatism. While not everyone suffers from these conditions, aging is associated with a decrease in bone mass, loss of movement in some joints, and degeneration in joint cartilage (Weg, 1975). The loss of bone mass can lead to osteoporosis, a condition that can lead to increased risk of bone fractures as well as loss of height and a curved back. More women than men suffer from the effects of osteoporosis, and this sex difference is reflected in the large number of bone fractures sustained by women. Women experience a bone loss of about 40 percent between the ages of 40 and 80, while in men bone loss typically begins between the ages of 55 and 65. The causes of osteoporosis are not known, although it may be related to poor diet (especially low calcium intake), lack of exercise, and diminished levels of estrogen, among other things (Kart, Metress, and Metress, 1978; Tonna, 1977).

Osteoarthritis, one form of arthritis, is a degeneration of bone joints that usually occurs with aging. Osteoarthritis is basically a wearing away of the joint cartilage, and it can lead to joint stiffness and pain. The condition develops very gradually and to some extent will affect anyone who lives long enough. The other major form of arthritis is rheumatoid arthritis, an inflammatory condition that is not necessarily a disease of old age; by no means will most older people experience its painful, disfiguring, or crippling effects.

The muscles of the body usually decrease in size with age, and after maximum strength has been reached (between the ages of 20 and 30) there is some decline, although the loss is quite modest. There is no other deleterious effect on functioning that inevitably comes with the aging of the muscular system (Kart, Metress, and Metress, 1978; Gutmann, 1977).

Human teeth are somewhat different from most other living tissue in that the teeth replace themselves only once and then stop growing. Other mammals have continuously growing teeth, and most nonmammalian vertebrates have continual replacement of lost teeth. Even without replacement teeth, however, it is estimated that human teeth could last up to 200 years (Tonna, 1977). Caries and periodontal disease do not appear to be age related, although large numbers of people of all ages experience dental problems. Loss of teeth can be problematic in older people because they are likely to have already lost some teeth. Thus, the older person is more likely to become edentulous, or to have the total number of teeth reduced to the level where chewing some foods may be difficult and digestion may be hindered.

The Skin

No part of the human body is more closely associated with age than the skin. For many people, the undeniable sign of advancing age is the appearance of wrinkles; for some, wrinkles are a matter of utmost concern. Yet wrinkles are one of the best examples of normal aging. From a purely physical standpoint they pose no threat to good health, nor do they produce any deleterious effects. This, of course, does not mean that wrinkles may not cause social, psychological, and/or existential problems for some people.

Wrinkling of the face, neck, and hands is a result of many years of exposure to the elements, as well as loss of skin elasticity and subcutaneous fat. Especially because of the loss of subcutaneous fat, some bones may become more prominent with age, and because the fat tissues serve as a body heat insulator many older people feel cooler than younger people (Selmanowitz, Rizer, and Orentreich, 1977; Kart, Metress, and Metress, 1978).

The Cardiopulmonary and Cerebrovascular Systems

Diseases of the heart are the number one cause of death of older Americans, and cerebrovascular diseases are number three. Prolongation of human life could be most immediately and significantly achieved by eliminating these diseases. Some researchers have concluded that "the cardiovascular system was not designed for a very long life" (Kohn, 1977:311). The heart tends to be less efficient as it ages, and the arterial system places ever-greater pressure on the heart because of its own loss of elasticity and progressive thickening.

Central to much of the discussion of the cardiovascular system are two processes: arteriosclerosis and atherosclerosis. Arteriosclerosis, usually thought of as hardening of the arteries, is the loss of elasticity that occurs in the aging arterial system. It can be considered a normal process because it occurs in everyone to some extent, and it is strongly age related. The result of progressive arteriosclerosis is to restrict the rate of blood flow to some parts of the body.

Atherosclerosis, while widespread in the older population of the United States, may not be an inevitable feature of aging. There are differences in the amount of atherosclerosis found in different societies and even within the same society. Atherosclerosis is the narrowing of the walls of the arteries that result from the accumulation of fat, cholesterol, and other materials. In a severe case an artery may be completely closed off, either by the accumulated material itself or by a blood clot that cannot pass through. It is believed that atherosclerosis may be a result of a diet that is rich in animal fat, cholesterol, and refined sugar, and that it can be complicated by obesity, stress, inactivity, and cigarette smoking.

Arteriosclerosis and atherosclerosis are usually implicated as contributing factors in the major diseases of the cardiovascular and cerebrovascular systems, including hypertension, congestive heart failure, and strokes, which means that older individuals are at greater risk of suffering from these diseases than younger people (Kohn, 1977).

The respiratory system also tends to lose some of its elasticity with age, and the maximum breathing capacity is reduced. Osteroporosis can further restrict the action of the lungs by compressing them tighter when the rib structure weakens. The lessened effectiveness of the immune system can also make it more difficult for an older person to battle respiratory infections (Kart, Metress, and Metress, 1978).

The Gastrointestinal/Excretory Systems

The human stomach does not change a great deal with age, although there is an increase in the prevalence of atrophic gastritis with advancing age. This condition is a result of the thinning of the gastric mucosa and the muscular wall and can lead to diminished absorption of iron and vitamin B_{12}. Although the colon is not thought to change much with age, older people are more likely to be bothered by constipation and are prone to laxative abuse (Bhanthumnavin and Schuster, 1977).

The liver is usually able to function well throughout a normal lifespan, even though cirrhosis of the liver is one of the leading causes of death in the United

States. Cirrhosis is very closely related to heavy use of alcohol, and long-term use of alcohol does affect a proportion of the older population; but liver dysfunction is not a normal feature of aging. More common than liver ailments are gallstones. One estimate places the incidence of gallstones at between 15 and 33 percent among people over age 70 (Kart, Metress, and Metress, 1978).

Older people often experience some change in bladder function. It is known that their bladder capacity is less than half of that of a young adult, and that in older people the desire to urinate often does not occur until the bladder is full. In addition, many older men have problems related to the prostate gland, which can produce a variety of effects, including urine retention and the need to urinate several times during the sleeping hours (Kart, Metress, and Metress, 1978).

The Endocrine, Brain, and Nervous System

Some of the changes in the endocrine system were discussed earlier in this chapter in the context of theories of aging. One disease of this system, diabetes, has not yet been discussed and is of particular importance. The incidence of diabetes usually increases with age, although there are enough undetected cases to make an exact count impossible. Perhaps the most important reason for the relatively large numbers of older diabetics is that modern control of the disease allows diabetics to live long lives. As with many other health conditions, management of diabetes can be achieved through a program that begins with a properly balanced diet.

The human brain shows definite signs of age throughout the lifespan; after a person reaches adulthood a slight but consistent loss of neurons occurs. For most people, the decline in neurons is of no great consequence, and they are able to function mentally very well throughout their lives (Vogel, 1977).

All age groups contain a certain number of people who experience neurological problems, and the older age group is no exception. One estimate of the total number of psychiatric disorders requiring psychiatric hospitalization found that in the United States people over 65 had a rate of hospitalization more than three times higher than the rate for those under 65.

Psychiatric disorders are classified as either functional or organic in origin. Functional disorders are those for which there is no apparent physical cause (i.e., the cause is emotional in nature), while an organic disorder is a result of an identifiable physical cause. While most psychiatric disorders of people under 65 are diagnosed as functional, the majority of people over 65 are diagnosed as having organic disorders (Wang, 1977; Hendricks and Hendricks, 1977). The distinction between functional and organic disorders may not be nearly as reliable as has been assumed, however, especially when diagnosing older patients. Some psychiatrists suspect that some—perhaps many— older people who have functional psychiatric problems are mistakenly diagnosed as suffering from organic disorders simply because it is assumed that an organic disorder is a reasonable diagnosis in view of the possibility of neurological degeneration in an older patient (Butler and Lewis, 1977).

Senility, which is usually called senile dementia or organic brain syndrome, is characterized by impairment of cognitive functions, including disorientation and memory loss. In some cases the condition is acute and may be temporary and reversible, while in others it is chronic and irreversible. The syndrome is often associated with cerebral arteriosclerosis, a condition that is widespread in the older population, but there are also cases of the disease in which no arteriosclerosis is present (Shelanski, 1975). There is still much to be learned about organic brain syndrome; for one thing, it probably has several causes and can take several different forms. In some cases heredity appears to be a factor, while in others diet, smoking, and strokes are implicated. The underlying causes of the syndrome can sometimes lead to death, but some people experience improvement and/or adequate adjustment to the condition. Butler and Lewis (1977: 77) refer to the adjustment to memory loss made by an 83 year old woman who "made lists of things to remember; she tied letters to be mailed to the doorknob so she would see them when she went out; she attached her wallet and keys onto her belt or slip strap. She asked friends to call and remind her of appointments . . ." In another example, a Harvard professor with an IQ of 170 was found to have an IQ of 130 after a stroke, a loss that was recognized by the patient himself but was undetected by his physician (Ostfield, 1975).

In some cases of organic brain syndrome, it would be extremely difficult or very dangerous to determine the exact cause; in other cases, such as cerebral atherosclerosis, knowing the cause does not lead to any effective program of control. Damaged brain tissue cannot be restored, so very often the goal is to prevent further cerebral impairment and avoid any aggravating factors (Wang, 1977).

The Epidemiology of Aging

In Chapter 2, "The Demography of Aging," it was pointed out that the aging of the United States population has occurred largely because of a decreasing birthrate and a decline in infant mortality. The decline in infant and early-life mortality is closely related to changes in the structure of disease and death, that is, the kinds of life-threatening processes found in a society. In a European society of a few centuries ago, a community or an entire region could be seriously affected by the large number of deaths caused by a plague. In North America, some of the indigenous tribes were almost destroyed by diseases brought to them by the early European explorers. Every society can be described by its structure of disease and death and the ways in which that structure affects its population.

In the United States and a number of other societies, the population has aged because of a reduction in infant and early-life mortality, which has allowed larger proportions of each age cohort to live to late adulthood. Much of the twentieth-century reduction in mortality can be attributed to increased control over infectious diseases. Table 3.3 shows the ten leading causes of death in the years 1900 and 1969. In 1900 the leading cause of death was pneumonia and influenza, followed by tuberculosis and then by diarrhea and enteritis, all of which are infectious diseases. In total, 57 percent of the deaths attributed to the ten leading causes were from infectious diseases. Only 37 percent of the deaths were from the chronic noninfectious diseases, that is, diseases of the heart, cerebral hemorrhage, or cancer.

Table 3.3 LEADING CAUSES OF DEATH IN THE UNITED STATES FOR ALL AGES, 1900 AND 1969

Rank	Cause of death	Rate per 100,000 population	Percentage of all deaths
	1900		
1	Pneumonia and influenza	202	11.8
2	Tuberculosis	194	11.3
3	Diarrhea and enteritis	143	8.3
4	Diseases of the heart	137	8.0
5	Cerebral hemorrhage	107	6.2
6	Kidney infections	89	5.2
7	Accidents	72	4.2
8	Cancer	64	3.7
9	Diphtheria	40	2.3
10	Meningitis	34	2.0

Percentage of deaths from infectious diseases: 57
Percentage of deaths from chronic noninfectious diseases: 37

Rank	Cause of death	Rate per 100,000 population	Percentage of all deaths
	1969		
1	Diseases of the heart	366	38.5
2	Cancer	160	16.8
3	Cerebrovascular diseases	103	10.8
4	Accidents	58	6.1
5	Influenza and pneumonia	34	3.6
6	Diabetes mellitus	19	2.0
7	Arteriosclerosis	16	1.7
8	Bronchitis, emphysema, and asthma	15	1.6
9	Cirrhosis of the liver	15	1.6
10	Suicide	11	1.2

Percentage of deaths from infectious diseases: 6
Percentage of deaths from chronic noninfectious diseases: 85

Sources: National Center for Health Statistics, "Mortality Trends for Leading Causes of Death, United States—1950–69" (Washington, D.C.: U.S. Government Printing Office, 1974); Matilda White Riley and Anne Foner, *Aging and Society*, vol. 1, *An Inventory of Research Findings* (New York: Russell Sage, 1968).

By 1969 the leading causes of death had changed considerably, shifting toward the chronic noninfectious diseases and away from the infectious diseases. Pneumonia and influenza dropped from the number one to the number five cause of death and from 202 persons per 100,000 population to 34 persons per 100,000 population. Tuberculosis, diarrhea and enteritis, kidney infections, diphtheria, and meningitis dropped out of the top ten causes of death. By 1969 only 6 percent of deaths from the ten leading causes were from infectious diseases, while 85 percent were from chronic noninfectious diseases. The leading causes of death in 1969 were diseases of the heart, cancer, and cerebrovascular diseases (usually strokes). Infectious diseases have been brought under control or at least are no longer usually life threatening.

People who do not die of an infectious disease will eventually die of something else. Although death has not been eliminated, for a lot of people it has been delayed. Some people who would have died of an infectious disease at a young age in a previous era now live a long life and die of a chronic noninfectious disease. The leading causes of death at age 65 in the United States are very much like the leading causes of death for the general population, although the mortality rates are much higher among the old, as is shown in Table 3.4. The three leading causes of death are still diseases of the heart, cancer, and cerebrovascular diseases. By age 65, diseases of the heart have a rate of 2,831 (per 100,000 population), compared to a rate of 366 for the general population. Diseases of the heart account for 46 percent of all deaths for people age 65 or older, and the top three causes account for more than 75 percent of all deaths.

There are some differences between the sexes in the causes of death, although as shown in Table 3.5, these differences are relatively minor. Cancer

Table 3.4 Leading Causes of Death in the United States for People Age 65 and Older, 1968

Rank	Cause of death	Rate per 100,000 population	Percentage of all deaths
1	Diseases of the heart	2,831	46
2	Cancer	925	15
3	Cerebrovascular diseases	904	15
4	Influenza and pneumonia	246	4
5	Arteriosclerosis	167	3
6	Accidents	149	2
7	Diabetes mellitus	137	2
8	Bronchitis, emphysema, and asthma	113	2
9	Cirrhosis of the liver	36	1
10	Kidney infections	35	1

Source: National Center for Health Statistics, *Health in the Later Years of Life* (Washington, D.C.: U.S. Government Printing Office, 1971).

Table 3.5 RANK ORDER OF CAUSES OF DEATH FOR MALES AND
FEMALES OVER AGE 65 IN THE UNITED STATES, 1968

Rank	Males	Females
1	Diseases of the heart	Diseases of the heart
2	Cancer	Cerebrovascular diseases
3	Cerebrovascular diseases	Cancer
4	Influenza and pneumonia	Influenza and pneumonia
5	Bronchitis, emphysema, and asthma	Arteriosclerosis
6	Accidents	Diabetes mellitus
7	Arteriosclerosis	Accidents
8	Diabetes mellitus	Bronchitis, emphysema, and asthma
9	Cirrhosis of the liver	Kidney infections
10	Peptic ulcer	Hypertension

Source: National Center for Health Statistics, *Health in the Later Years of Life* (Washington, D.C.: U.S. Government Printing Office, 1971).

is number two and cerebrovascular diseases number three for males, while the order is reversed for women. Cirrhosis of the liver and peptic ulcer are on the men's list but not on the women's, while kidney infections and hypertension are on the women's list but not on the men's.

The theory of demographic transition discussed in Chapter 2 is relevant for understanding the structures of disease and death in different societies. The industrialized societies usually have controlled infectious diseases, and their mortality figures reflect high rates for chronic noninfectious diseases, especially heart disease, cancer, and stroke. Societies that have not begun industrialization or are passing through the transition usually show relatively high rates of death from infectious diseases and relatively low rates from the chronic noninfectious diseases. Table 3.6 illustrates this process for a few selected countries. The table shows that developed societies such as England and Wales, the United States, and Hungary have relatively high rates of mortality for heart disease, cancer, and stroke and relatively low rates for influenza, pneumonia, and tuberculosis. Mexico and the Philippines, which have not yet completed the demographic transition, have a reversed structure of disease: relatively low rates of mortality from the chronic noninfectious diseases and relatively high rates for the infectious diseases. The developed countries have very similar patterns, although Japan has a slight variation; the number one cause of death in developed countries is heart disease, number two is cancer, and number three is stroke. Japan thus has the same three leading causes of death as other developed countries, but stroke is number one and heart disease number three. The societies in transition, Mexico and the Philippines, do not have any chronic noninfectious diseases among the top three causes of death. In both countries influenza and pneumonia are number one, while numbers two and three are infectious diseases or accidents.

Table 3.6 MORTALITY RATES FOR SELECTED COUNTRIES FOR LEADING CAUSES OF DEATH, 1966

	Canada	England/ Wales	Hungary	Italy	Japan	Mexico	Philippines	Spain	United States
Heart disease	270	379	277	263	83	35	32	131	371
Cancer	134	225	197	164	111	36	22	130	155
Stroke	78	164	157	132	174	22	14	122	105
Influenza and pneumonia	30	82	33	32	22	138	114	43	33
Tuberculosis	—	—	23	11	20	22	86	16	—
Leading causes of death									
1.	heart disease	heart disease	heart disease	heart disease	stroke	influenza and pneumonia	influenza and pneumonia	heart disease	heart disease
2.	cancer	cancer	cancer	cancer	cancer	gastritis, duodenitis, enteritis, colitis	tuberculosis	cancer	cancer
3.	stroke	stroke	stroke	stroke	heart disease	accidents	gastritis, duodenitis, enteritis, colitis	stroke	stroke

Source: United States Senate, Special Subcommittee on International Health, Education, and Labor Programs, *Leading Causes of Death in Selected Areas of the World* (Washington, D.C.: U.S. Government Printing Office, 1972).

Health Services

No age group in the United States has more contact with medical practitioners than older people. Older people in this country, "occupy 33 percent of the nation's hospital beds and 95 percent of the long-term care beds, use 70 percent of the home health services, and spend 25 percent of the American health dollar" (Kart, Metress, and Metress, 1978: 270). Yet, the speciality of geriatrics is practiced by only a few physicians, and in general the quality of geriatric education in American medical schools is inadequate. Very few physicians are trained in geriatrics, which is not surprising since only 45 of the 112 schools even offer elective courses in geriatrics. None of these schools requires any course work in gerontology or geriatrics (Sauvageot, 1978).

Like younger people, older people suffer from acute illnesses; but older people are more dependent on medical services than younger people because of chronic health problems. About 46 percent of the men and 40 percent of the women over 65 are limited in their activities because of chronic conditions (National Center for Health Statistics, 1971). The leading chronic causes of impairment are heart conditions, arthritis and rheumatism, visual impairments, hypertension, and mental and nervous conditions.

In any one year about two-thirds of those in the 65-and-over age group visit a physician at least once, although women are somewhat more likely to visit a physician than men. About one person in four over age 65 is hospitalized each year, but men are more likely to be hospitalized than women. The most common reasons for hospitalization are heart disease, cancer, stroke, fractures and pneumonia.

Older people who do not need the facilities of hospitals but are in need of medical care that they cannot provide themselves are often placed in nursing homes. The chronic conditions that most frequently result in nursing home

Table 3.7 AGE, RACE, AND SEX COMPOSITION OF NURSING AND PERSONAL CARE HOMES IN THE UNITED STATES, 1969 (RATE PER 1,000)

Age	Race	
	White	Nonwhite
Men		
65–74	9.5	10.5
75–84	39.0	18.2
85+	129.8	27.3
Women		
65–74	12.7	7.1
75–84	67.3	21.8
85+	205.8	58.2

placement are strokes, heart disease, arthritis and rheumatism, advanced senility, and hearing impairments. Table 3.7 shows the composition of the residents of nursing and personal care homes by race and sex in the United States. As would be expected, the rate of institutionalization increases with age for all groups, men and women, whites and nonwhites. White women have the highest rates of residence in nursing homes, at all age levels. Although nonwhite women have higher rates of nursing home residence than nonwhite men, in general white men have higher rates than nonwhites of either sex (National Center for Health Statistics, 1971).

Diet

If there is one factor that holds immediate promise for an increase in the healthy lifespan of the average person, it is improving the quality of the food diet. Rockstein and Sussman (1979: 128) maintain that "if all the health problems associated with obesity and its related diseases were eliminated, a 4-year increase in mean longevity could be expected." Obesity, of course, is only part of the nutritional problem. There are also problems associated with undernutrition.

A number of factors are associated with undernutrition in the older population, not the least of which is money. Individuals with relatively high incomes are much more likely to have an adequate nutrient intake, whereas low-income people are more likely to have an inadequate dietary intake (Sherwood, 1970). Perhaps more important than income is a person's educational level. Older individuals with higher educational levels have been found to have more healthful diets, although studies have found that in general older people in the United States are less informed about good nutritional practices than younger people. The relationship between knowledge about good nutritional practices and the maintenance of good dietary habits would imply that there is a need for educational programs on nutrition aimed at the older population. There is some evidence, however, that established eating patterns are difficult to change (Sherwood, 1970). The long-term answer to the problem of poor nutrition among older persons is to provide nutritional education and to establish healthy eating patterns from early childhood.

Quite apart from income levels and educational awareness, there are social factors that influence eating habits, especially in an older population. Socially isolated individuals are more likely to have a poor dietary intake than socially active people, at least partly because people who live alone have been found to choose foods that are easily available and easy to prepare (Keys, 1952).

Undernutrition has been thought to be less of a problem in the older population of the United States than overnutrition. The reason for this is that some research on laboratory animals has shown that dietary restriction (underfeeding) increases the lifespan. When mice, fish, and other animals have been fed only enough to maintain their body weight, they have lived longer than would normally have been expected. However, the exact reasons for the increased longevity are not yet known (Barrows and Roeder, 1977). Many of the reputed long-lived peoples—for example, the Abkhasians and the Hunza— have been shown to have a low daily caloric intake, perhaps about half the average daily caloric intake of Americans. Of course, there are limits to the advantages of underfeeding in humans. Seriously underfed people have a shorter, not longer, normal life expectancy.

A number of researchers have noted that a certain proportion of the American population suffers from nutritional inadequacy, but an even larger proportion suffers from being overweight. Although estimates vary, some researchers have found up to 50 percent of older women to be at least 10 percent overweight and more than 30 percent of older men to be overweight, while about 10 percent of the women and 20 percent of the men were 10 percent or more underweight (Weg, 1978). The importance of excess weight can be demonstrated by noting that an excess of 25 pounds can reduce the life expectancy of a middle-aged man by about 25 percent; also, people who are only 14 pounds overweight have a mortality rate higher than the lung cancer rate of long-term heavy smokers (Rockstein and Sussman, 1979).

Vital nutrients in appropriate amounts are essential at all ages, and the nutritional needs of older people are not far different from those of middle-aged adults. Table 3.8 presents a comparison of the minimum daily requirements of certain vitamins and minerals for people aged 20–24, 45–54, and 65 and over. These figures are for an average adult; all diets must be adapted to the individual's height, weight, and special needs. The table indicates that people over 65 have a slightly reduced minimum daily calorie requirement. The reduced need for calories poses a special nutritional problem for older people

Table 3.8 AVERAGE DAILY INTAKE OF CALORIES AND SELECTED NUTRIENTS AND PERCENT OF THE MINIMUM DAILY REQUIREMENT, FOR THREE U.S. AGE GROUPS

	20–24 Years		45–54 Years		65 + Years	
Calories	2,265	(88%)	1,901	(85%)	1,521	(75%)
Protein (gm)	86.5	(123%)	79.3	(116%)	61.1	(94%)
Calcium (mg)	888	(191%)	710	(152%)	631	(131%)
Iron (mg)	13.1	(108%)	12.5	(101%)	10.5	(105%)
Vitamin A (IU)	4,501	(128%)	5,249	(150%)	5,315	(152%)
Vitamin C (mg)	96.2	(166%)	83.1	(145%)	89.4	(157%)
Thiamine (mg)	1.42	(157%)	1.23	(160%)	1.08	(177%)
Riboflavin (mg)	2.02	(162%)	1.77	(169%)	1.55	(185%)
Niacin (mg)	18.9		18.4		14.0	

Source: Compiled from National Center for Health Statistics, *Dietary Intake Findings, United States, 1971–1974* (Washington, D.C.: U.S. Government Printing Office, 1977).

because it is increasingly important that the food consumed contain the appropriate amounts of essential vitamins and minerals.

The table also gives the average amounts of the minimum daily requirements that Americans in these age groups have been found to consume. The figures indicate that most people, including people over 65, are meeting the minimum daily requirements. The one exception is the amount of protein in the diet of people over 65, which is only 94 percent of the minimum daily requirement. The protein content of the diet could easily be adjusted through a modest increase in calories. The optimal daily calorie intake is not achieved in any of the age groups, although none is at the danger level. However, the limited caloric intake of persons 65 and over makes it extremely important that the daily diet be carefully selected to ensure that adequate nutrients are included.

Some researchers have argued that the minimum daily requirement for calories is too high, that is, that Americans consume too many calories (Leaf, 1975). The Vilcabamba, an Ecuadorian people who are reputed to have an unusually long life expectancy, were found to have an average intake of only 1,200 calories per day. Other long-lived peoples have been found to have intakes in the range of 1,700 to 2,000 calories a day. One estimate is that an intake of 1,650 to 1,825 calories would be salutary for older Americans (Kart, Metress, and Metress, 1978). In any case, while the caloric intake of the 65-and-over population in the United States may be at the low end of the desirable range, it is not alarmingly inadequate.

Exercise

In recent years larger numbers of Americans have begun to participate in a wide variety of sports and other forms of exercise and physical activity. There has been a rekindling of interest in tennis, running, and racket-ball, and in the future we may see a resurgence in such activities as bicycling, swimming, and volleyball. For too many years active participation in sports was thought to be most appropriate for young children and adolescents, and many adults simply gave up activities that they had enjoyed during their youth. The belief that "physical activity is for kids" was also reflected in, for example, the physical education requirement on many college campuses, which has traditionally been waived for "overage" students, usually meaning students over age 25.

The President's Council on Physical Fitness surveyed older adults in the United States to determine why they do not exercise. It discovered that people are generally not well informed about the need for physical activity. The council found that many people believe the need for exercise diminishes with age, although regular activity is beneficial to everyone. Many people also hold an exaggerated view of the dangers of physical activity. There have been some well-publicized instances of people dying while engaging in strenuous activity; and while it is not a good idea for someone who is overweight and has not exercised for a long time to jump into strenuous activity, there is minimal danger from physical activity for someone who undertakes a gradual program after a thorough physical exam. The survey also found that people very often overrate the benefits of the kinds of physical activity they do engage in. For example, bowling once a week or playing an occasional round of golf or mowing the lawn probably does not exercise the heart muscle sufficiently. There must be an adequate level of exertion on a regular basis. This does not mean that a person has to run 10 kilometers a day, but it does mean adequate exercise at least three times a week. The council's study also found that older adults tend to underrate their abilities and capacities, to think they cannot perform many physical activities (Wiswell, 1978). People of all ages *are* capable of participating in a regular program of exercise, and while adjustments in the amount and type of physical activity may be required, age is not a barrier to and certainly not a reason for inactivity.

Summary

Although most of us are aware of many of the superficial changes that occur in the human body with age, the basic process of aging cannot be observed and is currently the object of much research. Hayflick has calculated that human cellular activity can continue for a maximum of 110 to 120 years, give or take a few years. But since no one dies of cessation of cellular activity, Hayflick's discovery does not tell us all we need to know about the specific processes of aging. There are, however, a number of theories that are trying to explain these processes. The error theory, the free-radical theory, and the cross-linkage theory all concentrate on the cellular and molecular processes to try to determine the effects of time on the operation and functioning of the human body. The autoimmune theory and the pituitary theory are searching for the same effects by concentrating on the body's immune and hormone systems. Whether any of these theories ever gains wide acceptance will depend on a wide variety of research projects that are yet to be completed.

Doubtless the human body changes with age, both in performance capacities and in body composition. It is known that the bones change with age, so that some older people suffer from osteoporosis and osteoarthritis. Arteriosclerosis is also very common in an aging population, and diabetes becomes increasingly present as a cohort ages. Even though a person is more likely to suffer from a chronic condition with increasing age, many people are able to make adequate adjustments to such conditions for long periods. The increased incidence of chronic diseases nevertheless causes older people to make greater use of medical services and facilities than younger people.

Research in the biology of aging has not yet produced any miracle solutions to the problems of aging, and there is no guarantee that any such solutions will be found in the near future. In the meantime the best way to attain a long and healthy life is to maintain a proper diet and to keep the body in good condition through a regular program of exercise.

SELECTED REFERENCES

Seymour Bakerman, *Aging Life Processes,* Springfield, Ill.: Charles C Thomas, 1969.

Caleb E. Finch and Leonard Hayflick, eds., *Handbook of the Biology of Aging* (New York: Van Nostrand Reinhold, 1977).

Cary S. Kart, Eileen S. Metress, and James F. Metress, *Aging and Health: Biologic and Social Perspectives* (Menlo Park, Calif.: Addison-Wesley, 1978).

Joel Kurtzman and Phillip Gordon, *No More Dying: The Conquest of Aging and the Extension of Human Life* (Los Angeles: J. P. Tarcher, 1976).

Albert Rosenfeld, *Prolongevity* (New York: Knopf, 1976).

Ruth B. Weg, *Nutrition and the Later Years* (Los Angeles: University of Southern California Press, 1978).

CHAPTER **4**

Variations in the Experience of Aging

Overview. The ultimate aim of social science is to make statements about human behavior that account for differences that occur throughout the world. If this goal is to be achieved, then social scientists must do comparative research—studies must include comparisons of human behavior in one society with human behavior in other societies. Social gerontologists would like to be able to draw some conclusions about the nature of aging by studying it in a wide variety of societies. Comparative research is, however, a very difficult, time-consuming, and expensive enterprise, and thus it is not surprising that much more comparative research on aging needs to be done.

There have been some notable attempts to gather information about the cultural variations in aging and to make some preliminary statements about those variations. There is always some hope that our own society might be able to gain some useful insights into the social meaning of aging, or even that we might learn how to live fuller and more productive lives for a longer time, by observing other societies.

While there are wide variations in the experience and meaning of aging from one society to another, we do not have to look far to see such variations. Within any society there is some variation in the aging process, perhaps by social class, by religion, or by racial or ethnic group. In the United States we find all of these elements contributing to the meaning of aging. Of special importance are the differences in the aging patterns of racial and ethnic groups.

The aging process is so different in various cultures and subcultures that it appears almost to be specific to each setting. With such wide cultural variations it is difficult to devise concise generalizations about cross-cultural patterns of aging. Some sociologists and anthropologists, however, have recently begun to construct detailed statements about the similarities and dissimilarities between the patterns of aging that appear in different societies (Cowgill and Holmes, 1972). Much of the current work in comparative aging has been inspired by the classic work by Leo W. Simmons (1945), *The Role of the Aged in Primitive Society.*

The Universals of Aging

Cowgill and Holmes (1972) have been able to identify eight elements that are believed to be present in all societies. These elements, which they call the universals of aging, are as follows:

1. "The aged always constitute a minority within the total population." That the "aged" are a minority within a society does not necessarily mean that they are dominated by the majority, but it does mean that age is a key characteristic used by the members of a society to define themselves and others, even though the significant age groups could vary greatly from one society to another. The aged in one society could be defined as everyone over age 45, while in another society the aged would be everyone over age 70. It is quite

possible that the social definition of the aged in the United States could change significantly in the next 50 to 100 years as the number of people over age 65 increases substantially. Cross-cultural research shows quite clearly that age is not destiny, that the social definition of age is very changeable.

2. "In an older population, females outnumber males." Females usually outlive males, especially in industrialized societies, where the life expectancy of females continues to increase faster than that of males, with the result that the older population is disproportionately female. While there are some exceptions to the general rule, they are usually temporary and subject to change.

3. "Widows comprise a high proportion of an older population." If the older population of a society consists of more females than males, it is to be expected that there will be more widows than widowers. High proportions of widows in an older population is also a sign of the general tendency of females to marry males of approximately the same age or slightly older than themselves. Given the longer life expectancy of females, the only ways in which the older population could be composed of nonwidows would be if females never married, married males slightly younger than themselves, remarried after becoming widows (primarily to younger males), or practiced polygyny (i.e., older wives sharing a husband). While these possibilities exist, they have not yet been widely practiced.

4. "In all societies, some people are classified as old and are treated differently because they are so classified." Aging is such an intimate part of life that it is recognized in all societies, and the old are recognized as being in a position distinct from that of younger people. While this may seem a commonsense observation, it should be remembered that there are very few universal features in human societies. Not all societies, for example, recognize the relationship between sexual intercourse and pregnancy; and even though the incest taboo is usually regarded as universal, there are extremely wide variations in its application (Murdock, 1949). In this context the universal recognition of old age is of some significance; furthermore, the old are treated differently: There are specific responses that are most appropriate for the old. All societies have different folkways for interacting with those who are defined as old; at the very least, a society will have a set of role expectations that govern the interaction of one old person with another old person, an older person with a younger person, and a young person with another young person.

5. "There is a widespread tendency for people defined as old to shift to more sedentary, advisory, or supervisory roles involving less physical exertion and more concerned with group maintenance than with economic production." Industrial societies have systems of occupational retirement that allow older people to lessen their level of physical exertion; nonindustrial societies also have methods that allow older people to give up some of their more physically demanding activities: The warrior may become a head man or a priest; a

grandmother in an extended household may surrender the responsibility for cooking the meals and performing many of the household chores to the daughter-in-law and turn her attention to the supervision and training of the grandchildren. It would probably be an oversimplification to refer to this apparently universal change as retirement, since there is usually no sudden or complete cessation of activities, as often occurs in modern occupational retirement, but there is a general movement away from physically demanding tasks by those defined as old.

6. "In all societies, some old persons continue to act as political, judicial, and civic leaders." In industrialized societies, some high positions in the political and judicial systems are filled by older people, but these positions are not reserved for older people. In many nonindustrialized societies, some leadership positions are reserved for the elders. One explanation for this apparent difference between industrialized and nonindustrialized societies is the role of information control. In traditional and nonindustrial societies, older people are thought to be vital to the maintenance and survival of the society because they control much of the available information about social customs, habits, history, and ritual. Given their possession of this vital information, older people are highly esteemed, and many leadership positions may be reserved for them because they are deemed most worthy of those positions. In industrial societies, information control is no longer possible: Rapid technological and social change makes much traditional information obsolete, and information that is thought to be valuable is available through books or other impersonal information storage systems. In this system the information controlled by an older person is not highly valued, and leadership positions are not reserved for them because they are not thought to be any more worthy of a position than a younger person, and perhaps less so (Watson and Maxwell, 1977).

7. "In all societies, the mores prescribe some mutual responsibility between old people and their adult children." There is wide variation in the social demands of the adult child/parent relationship, although there is an impressive amount of evidence that there is some mutual responsibility even in societies that emphasize the conjugal relationship over consanguinity and in societies in which the extended family is secondary to the demands of the nuclear family. There are exceptions to the general rule under the most extreme conditions, but even then there is some recognition of residual responsibilities. Turnbull (1977: 187), for example, reports that the Ik, a tribe in northern Uganda, gave up essentially all filial responsibilities during a severe drought that caused widespread starvation.

"Children are not allowed to sleep in the house after they are put out, which is at about three years old, four at the latest. From then on they sleep in the open courtyard, taking what shelter they can against the stockade. They may ask for permission to sit in the doorway of their parents' house but may not lie down or sleep there." The same applies to dependent old people, but then only if their children let them stay in the compound. The drought and resulting hunger have reduced the mutual responsibilities between the generations to a minimum, but there remain signs that those responsibilities are not entirely forgotten. Turnbull (1977: 189) reports an instance in which a father tried to go to his son's house to die, in essence making a claim on his son's responsibility to bury him when he died: The father had gone to his son's home to beg him to let him into his compound because he knew he was going to die shortly. But the son said that he could not let his father stay in his home because his father was a very important man and his death would have called for an enormous and expensive funeral feast. So he refused, the son drove him out, and the father died alone. The son's unsympathetic reaction to his father's plea should not overshadow the fact that the father was making a claim on the son's sense of filial responsibility and that the son recognized the responsibility, so much so that he drove the father out of the village so that he would not be forced to fulfill the responsibility. This occurred under the most miserable of human conditions, in a society ill equipped to handle crises.

8. "All societies value life and seek to prolong it, even in old age." The fear of growing old is probably confined to young people, and most people are able to accommodate the changes that occur with advancing age. There is no age at which a general dissatisfaction with life occurs, and if some older people lose the desire to live, it is usually because of a debilitating health condition, the loss of close friends or relatives, or some other specific reason, not because of age in and of itself. Those people who seriously pursue immortality are probably a small minority, but they are like most other people in their desire to prolong a healthy and useful life as long as possible.

Variations in Aging

Even though some aspects of aging may be found in all or nearly all societies, there are more ways in which the aging process varies from one society to another. Cowgill and Holmes (1972) have identified twenty-two variations just by comparing preindustrial, or traditional societies, and industrial, or modern, societies. Among the most significant differences they noted were the following:

1. "Modernized societies have older populations, i.e., higher proportions of old people." Because of the higher birth and death rates of preindustrial societies, the proportion of older persons is lower than in industrial societies. At least, this is true if the older segment of the population is defined as being over some specific chronological age, such as 60, 65, or 70. Table 4.1 shows the estimated total and over-60 populations of the more developed and less developed regions of the world for 1970, as well as projections for these regions

Table 4.1 ESTIMATES OF TOTAL POPULATION AND OVER AGE 60
POPULATION FOR MAJOR WORLD REGIONS, 1970, AND PROJECTIONS FOR
THE YEAR 2000 (IN THOUSANDS)

Region	Total population	Population age 60+	Total percentage of population age 60+
	1970		
World	3,631,797	290,697	8.0
More developed regions	1,090,297	153,741	14.1
Less developed regions	2,541,501	137,024	5.4
	2000		
World	6,493,642	584,605	9.0
More developed regions	1,453,528	231,105	15.9
Less developed regions	5,040,114	353,917	7.0

Source: United Nations, *The Aging: Trends and Policies* (New York, 1975).

for the year 2000. It is estimated that in 1970 there were slightly more people over age 60 in the more developed regions, even though the total population of these regions is less than half that of the less developed regions. The result is that in the more developed regions the age 60 and over group constitutes over 14 percent of the population, whereas they constitute only slightly more than 5 percent of the population in the less developed regions. It is projected that by the year 2000 a larger proportion of the human population will be 60 or over—9 percent, compared to 8 percent in 1970. In the more developed regions, however, nearly 16 percent of the people will be 60 or over, while in the less developed regions the percentage will have risen to 7. It should be remembered that 60 is an arbitrary chronological age chosen for purposes of comparison. It would not be an exact indicator of the social definition of an older age group in the various societies.

2. It is thought that the status of older people is higher in preindustrial societies, in which older people constitute a low proportion of the total population and the rate of social change is slower. Some recent detailed studies have supported the conclusion that as a society modernizes, the status of older people in that society declines; but a couple of qualifications must be added to this generalization. First, the decline in the status of older people in modern societies is in relation to younger people and is not necessarily the same as an absolute decline in material well-being. Palmore and Manton (1974), for example, remark that older people in more modern countries usually have a higher standard of living than their counterparts in other societies, even though their relative status is lower. This is because people of all ages in modern societies have a generally higher standard of living. Second, the lower social status of older people does not necessarily mean that they will be treated poorly in

interpersonal relationships. In a study that analyzed the responses of more than 5,000 males in six developing nations, Bengtson and associates (1975) concluded that individuals who have been exposed to modernizing experiences do not have significantly different attitudes toward aging or older people than people who have not been exposed to such experiences.

3. The individualistic value system of Western societies reduces the economic security of older people, and responsibility for providing economic security is shifted to the state. Since extended families are not common in modern industrial societies, and because the values of individual achievement are more compatible with the needs of an industrial economy, the family as a system of economic support is not available to older people. This leaves the older person vulnerable to the vagaries of the economic system; under such circumstances the state usually steps in to provide older people with basic material necessities.

Not all gerontologists accept the explanation that human history is made up of the difference between the pre- and post-Industrial Revolution eras and the effect this is supposed to have had on aging and older people. Laslett (1976) has discovered that the position of the old in preindustrial society, at least in England but probably in other places as well, was not at all what it is usually thought to have been. It is usually assumed that modern industrial societies were once like contemporary preindustrial societies; it is just as reasonable to believe that this was not the case. It is also possible that contemporary gerontologists suffer from a prejudice that is found among most modern peoples, namely, a tendency to romanticize and idealize the position of older people in preindustrial periods. Laslett (1976: 115) maintains that there may be much more continuity in the preferred social position of older people than is usually imagined: "The conclusion might be that then, as now, a place of your own, with help in the house, with access to your children, within reach of support, was what the elderly and the aged most wanted for themselves in the preindustrial world."

Longevity in Various Cultures

One of the most persistent topics in gerontology is the question of whether some peoples are unusually long-lived. The topic will remain a lively issue for years to come because there are no records that prove beyond all doubt the ages of supposedly long-lived people. The three peoples that are most often referred to as having unusually large numbers of very old people are the Vilcabambans of Ecuador, the Abkhasians of Russia, and the Hunza of Pakistan (Leaf, 1975; Benet, 1974; Davies, 1975).

Those who doubt the reports regarding the longevity of these peoples point to the fact that long-lived people have been known to overstate their age.

Sachuk (1970), for example, notes that of a group of 160 people who registered as centenarians in Switzerland, only three were found to qualify after a check of the records. Societies that have accurate birth and death records are not among those that claim to have large numbers of very old people or even extremely long-lived individuals. *The Guinness Book of World Records* lists a Frenchman who died at age 113 as the longest-lived person with a documented and undisputed date of birth. This is far from the world record of 168 years claimed by the USSR for Muslim Shirali, who died in 1973, although the accuracy of that claim is questioned by some gerontologists (Medvedev, 1974).

When there are no accurate government documents that can provide proof of birth dates, a great deal of investigation is required to determine a person's age. At present there is no way to determine a person's age through clinical testing, not only because individual rates of aging vary significantly but also because longevity is influenced by genetic, dietary, and environmental factors. In many cases birth dates can be established even when government documents do not exist. Apparently, however, personal estimates of age are unreliable. For example, Leaf (1975) found that the age of one of the most celebrated residents of Vilcabamba, a man by the name of Miguel Carpio, was being exaggerated. Carpio was reported to be 121 when Leaf visited the region in 1970, but was said to be 132 when Leaf returned four years later. This age exaggeration was proved by later researchers (Mazess and Forman, 1979), who found that Carpio was actually 93 when he died in 1976. These researchers were able to determine the age of Carpio and other reputed nonagenarians and centenarians in the Vilcabamba region by using available birth, marriage, and death records to reconstruct genealogies. They found that in Vilcabamba people commonly began exaggerating their age at about age 70. The investigation discovered that none of the 23 centenarians had lived to age 100 and none of the 15 nonagenarians had lived to age 90. Their calculations showed that the average age of those who claimed to be centenarians was about 86, the range being from 75 to 96.

Even if the ages claimed for some individuals are exaggerated, there remains the possibility that a particular region could produce exceptionally long-lived people. In most of Europe and North America the number of centenarians is quite limited—around three per 100,000 population—and only about one person in 40 million lives as long as 110 years (Medvedev, 1974). According to the 1970 census, the Abkhasians of Soviet Georgia have 60 centenarians per 100,000 population, and other nearby areas report rates as high as 103 per 100,000 population. A census of Vilcabamba found a rate of 1,100 centenarians per 100,000 population, although this rate is based on a small population. The 1971 census of Vilcabamba nevertheless found about 11 percent of the population over 60, compared to a national average of about 6 percent. In 1974 another census also found about 11 percent over 60 (Mazess and Forman,

1979). When adjustments were made to take into account the number of younger people who had moved out of the town into the cities, as well as the number of older people who had moved into the town from the surrounding rural areas, the proportion over 60 was found to be only 7 percent, a figure only slightly higher than that for the country as a whole.

In trying to account for the unusual longevity of these peoples, most attention has been focused on their diet, genetics, amount of daily physical activity, and relatively isolated settings. The results of health studies have been paradoxical. "The function and metabolism of longevous people of 100–110 years are on the same level as is usual for people of 55–60 years. Research in other countries concerning centenarians with well-established ages does not usually give such paradoxical results" (Medvedev, 1974). Other researchers have introduced social explanations as accounting for claims of longevity (Medvedev, 1974). In Soviet Georgia, for example, there is a long cultural tradition of reverence for the very old, a tradition that may encourage people to exaggerate their age; the attention focused on people who claim extreme longevity by the Soviet and the world press may have the same effect. In some instances, also, there appear to be specific factors that have caused people to falsify personal documents, such as men who have used their fathers' documents to avoid being drafted into the army. Ultimately, however, the social explanation is no more convincing than the claims of extreme longevity because in neither case is reliable documentation supplied to support the claim.

The real importance of the longevity argument may lie in the fact that people are very interested in the possibility that long-lived peoples exist somewhere on earth. This interest may be a result of our natural curiosity about people who are significantly different from ourselves. More likely, however, interest in longevity is the product of a combination of optimism and hope. People are optimistic that it is possible for humans to live a long, healthy life, to be 110 years of age but to be in the physical shape of a 50 year old person; and they hope that by discovering and studying long-lived peoples researchers will discover the magical formula or secret elixir of life and share it with everyone.

Aging in Japan

There are unique features of the aging process in every society, but one of the most interesting cases is that of Japan. While it is true that Japan has experienced some of the same changes in the transition to an industrial society that have occurred in other societies, there are at least two important differences: (1) Preindustrial Japan was unlike most of the Western preindustrial societies in its cultural tradition; (2) Japan's industrialization, which has taken place entirely in the twentieth century, has been large scale and very rapid.

Palmore (1975) contends that the experience of growing old is very different in Japan than in Western European and North American societies because even though Japan has experienced extremely rapid social change and has become a highly industrialized and urbanized society, the status of the old remains high. Japan's population (104,665,000 in 1970) is just about half that of the United States, although its land area is about equal to that of Montana. In some ways the demographic structure of Japan is very much like that of other industrialized societies. The birthrate and the life expectancy at age 65 are very much like those for the United States, and although the percentage of population over age 65 was only 7.9 in 1975, it is expected to rise to about 17.7 by the year 2015 (Palmore, 1975; Maeda, 1978).

Unlike most Western societies, the Japanese have a strong cultural tradition of respect for elders that is thought to derive from an age-grading system in which the young defer to the old, and from an attitude of filial piety that is based on Confucian precepts and the ancient practice of ancestor worship (Plath, 1972; Palmore, 1975). Japan specifically enforces deference to elders by observing a national holiday, Respect for the Elders Day; by using the 61st birthday as a special occasion on which family elders are honored; using respectful language when speaking to elders; by reserving certain seats on buses and trains for elders; by sponsoring sports days for elders; and through government programs providing economic, medical, and social support (Palmore, 1975).

The Japanese family structure is also different from family structure in most Western societies, especially when it comes to the position of older parents. It has been suggested that European and North American nuclear families usually reside in separate households because of the demands for mobility and urban residence inherent in an industrial system. Japan, however, is an urbanized and industrial society in which older parents usually live with their children. In fact, in Japan over three-fourths of all people over age 65 live with at least one of their children, usually the eldest son. There is even some social stigma attached to parents who have no children living with them. The most common sentiment found among older people in Western societies is that parents should live separately from their children as long as possible, but the Japanese have no such preference for independent living units. Maeda (1978: 59) states that "independence, which is one of the most highly esteemed virtues of western societies, is not necessarily regarded so in Japanese society. It might not be too much to say that Japanese older persons are not only allowed but also expected to be dependent on their adult children, rather than to be too independent or stubborn." The three-generation family is very common in Japanese society, and more important, it is a preferred family form. Even young adults in Japan today favor the three-generation household, or at least favor living close enough to their parents so that they can support and care for them (Maeda, 1978).

Although older people in Japan are not expected to give an outward appearance of high levels of activity, they very often are responsible for much of the household work and the raising of grandchildren. Much of the housework is done by the grandmother, partly because large proportions of older men are still employed at work outside the home. In many cases the men will continue to work because of the need for income, although attitudes toward continued employment are also generally favorable (Maeda, 1978).

It might seem to be a contradiction that Japan has one of the earliest ages of forced retirement, given what has been said about respect for elders. Most businesses have a mandatory retirement age, and in almost all cases it is 60 or younger. The most common mandatory retirement age is between 55 and 59. The pensionable age under the public pension is 60 for men and 55 for women, although the system has not yet fully matured and only about one-fourth of those over 60 receive a benefit. As a result, most people try to find another job after they are retired, even though these postretirement jobs are usually much lower in status and income than their preretirement jobs. With advancing age fewer people continue to work, although the proportion still working after age 65 is much higher than in other industrialized countries (Maeda, 1978).

Aging in Japan is a fascinating topic because of the insights that can be gleaned from comparisons and contrasts with aging as it occurs in the heavily industrialized societies of the Occident. Because of Japan's symbolic respect for elders, older people in Japan would seem to be in a relatively enviable position. Plath (1972), however, warns that Western gerontologists have a tendency to romanticize the Japanese aging process and that even in Japan the reality of being old does not always match the ideal. There is also the possibility that the position of older people in Japan may undergo significant changes in years to come. Considering the drastic changes that have occurred there since the end of World War II, the position of older people has been remarkably stable. Large increases in the proportion and number of Japanese over age 65 are projected, however, and in this sense older people in Japan today are as much pioneers as the old in other societies. As Plath (1972: 150) has so aptly stated, "The aged are among the true pioneers of our time, and pioneer life is notoriously brutal."

Aging in Europe and North America

It is instructive to compare the aging processes of European and North American nations because in many ways their cultural histories and general patterns of development are very similar. Most indicators show that the United States and Canada follow European patterns. To begin with, their life expectancy patterns are extremely similar, as is shown in Table 4.2. In general, life expectancies at birth have increased by about 20 years for males and 24 years for

Table 4.2 LIFE EXPECTANCY AT BIRTH AND AGE 65 FOR SELECTED EUROPEAN AND NORTH AMERICAN COUNTRIES, ABOUT 1900 AND 1970

	1900		1970	
	Males	*Females*	*Males*	*Females*
Years remaining at birth				
Canada	—	—	69.3	76.4
England and Wales	48.5	52.4	68.9	75.1
France	45.3	48.7	68.6	74.4
The Netherlands	51.0	53.4	71.2	77.2
Sweden	54.5	57.0	72.1	77.7
United States	47.9	50.7	67.4	75.2
Years remaining at age 65				
Canada	13.0	13.7	13.9	17.5
England and Wales	10.8	12.0	12.1	16.0
France	10.5	11.5	13.1	17.1
The Netherlands	11.6	12.3	13.6	17.0
Sweden	12.8	13.7	14.0	17.1
United States	11.5	12.2	13.1	16.7

Source: United Nations, *Demographic Yearbook* (New York, 1972).

females between 1900 and 1970. The pattern is the same for increases in life expectancy at age 65, with males increasing by about one and a half years and females by four and a half years. As was shown in Chapter 2 the general pattern in the United States is one in which control of infectious diseases has brought about a reduction in infant and early-childhood mortality, so that more people live into the later stages of the life cycle. The increases in life expectancy at age 65, however, show that the number of years added to the later stages of life has been quite modest.

In most Western industrialized societies an older person is very likely to live either with a spouse or alone, but it is not at all uncommon to find older people living with relatives, either their children or a brother or sister. When an older person lives with one of his or her children, it is very often an unmarried child. The Japanese pattern of older parents living in the same household with the eldest married son is not very common in Western societies. There are, however, frequent contacts between older parents and their children. A survey of older people in Denmark, Britain, and the United States found that between 60 and 70 percent of the respondents had seen at least one of their children on the day of the survey or on the previous day (Shanas et al., 1968).

Many countries now have some system of income support for older people; many of these programs have been developed in the last two decades. In 1940, for example, only 33 countries had a program of old age, survivors, and invalidity support, but by 1975 there were 108 such programs in existence. The types of coverage, amounts of benefits, and means of administering the program are different in different countries. Retirement ages differ from one country to another, although there is a general trend toward the establishment of age 55–65 as the normal retirement age. By 1975 Israel was the only country that required a person to reach the age of 70 to be entitled to full benefits (Social Security Administration, 1976).

Most social security programs are of three types: universal, employment related, or means tested. Some countries have a program that includes elements of all three of these types. A universal program is intended to cover all persons in a country, although most programs have some limitations, such as requiring citizenship or a specific period of residence in the country. Canada, for example, has a universal system that requires a person to live there for forty adult years to become eligible for an old-age pension. In employment-related systems, such as the one in the United States, benefits are paid only to covered workers and their dependents, and eligibility is established by earning a wage for a predetermined amount of time. Nonwage earners may be covered as dependents or survivors of wage earners, with rules of eligibility varying widely from one country to another. A means-tested program may provide benefits similar to those provided in a universal or employment-related system, but a person must establish eligibility by demonstrating financial need. Australia is one country in which the entire social security system is of the means-tested type.

Although the social security systems in various countries are not easily compared, Table 4.3 presents some of the basic features of the old-age and widow's benefits programs in selected European and North American countries. The information given in this table is for the year 1975, and undoubtedly there have been many changes in the programs of these countries since then. Note that the benefit figures are given in the currency of the country and in U.S. dollars. The dollar figures have been computed using the exchange rates of December 31, 1974, and should be regarded as approximate. The foreign exchange value of the dollar has fluctuated greatly since 1974, and the listed monetary values should be interpreted accordingly.

The table shows that there are large differences in the dates at which the social security programs were established. Of course, some of these systems have been changed greatly over the years, but Denmark has had a social security system since 1891 (one of the first in the world), while the United States did not develop such a system until 1935, Japan not until 1941, and Mexico, 1942. All of the countries require that employers contribute to the social security system (from 1.8 percent to 8.5 percent of total payroll), and in every country except Sweden the workers make direct contributions to the system (from 1.5 percent to 6.0 percent of wages earned, although usually there

Table 4.3 SOCIAL SECURITY PROGRAMS AROUND THE WORLD, 1975

	Belgium	Canada	Denmark	France	Japan	Mexico	Sweden	United Kingdom	United States
Type of program	employment related	universal	universal	employment related	universal	employment related	universal	universal	employment related
Year established	1924	1927	1891	1910	1941	1942	1913	1908	1935
Employee contribution	6.0% wages, 5.75% salaries	1.8% earnings	3 kroner a week	3% earnings	3.8% men's wages, 2.9% women's wages	1.5% earnings	none	5.5% earnings	4.95% earnings
Employer contribution	8.0% payroll	1.8% payroll	6 kroner a week	7.25% payroll	3.8% men, 2.9% women	3.75% payroll	4.2% wages +10.75% over 900 k	8.5% payroll	4.95% payroll
Normal retirement age	65, men; 60, women	65	67; 62, single women	60	60, men; 55, women	65	67	65, men; 60, women	65
Minimum pension (in 1975 U.S. $)	$243	$125	$186, single; $286, couple	$64	$3.30 × years worked, +1% average earnings	$68	$169, single; $275, couple	$16 a week	$94
Widow's benefit	80% of worker's benefit	60% of worker's benefit	$225	50% of worker's benefit	50% of worker's benefit	50% of worker's benefit	40% of worker's benefit	$27 a week	100% of worker's benefit

Source: Social Security Administration, *Social Security Programs throughout the World, 1975* (Washington, D.C.: U.S. Government Printing Office, 1976).

is a ceiling on the amount of earned income that is taxed for this purpose). The dollar amounts of the benefits show that old-age pensions are very modest sums, but these figures do not indicate the value of nonmonetary goods and services provided or the varying circumstances that make each country a unique case. Some countries have widely available and inexpensive medical services, and in Japan an older couple might very likely share a household with the family of an adult child; such variations in circumstances and conditions are impossible to summarize and compare cross-culturally.

Variations in Aging in the United States

The United States is a diverse society composed of a large number of distinct peoples and cultural traditions. In addition, many of the traditions of various groups are influenced by the pressures and exchanges that result from interaction with the dominant culture. While it is legitimate to discuss aging in the United States as if it were a unified phenomenon, it is essential to temper this discussion with the realization that aging follows specific patterns in specific groups. Some ethnic and religious groups have merged so completely into the dominant culture that they are no longer recognizable as a distinct group and their sense of separate identity has been lost. But this is not the case with all racial, ethnic, and religious groups, some of which have fostered and retained separate identities and cultural practices.

Aging in Minority Groups

One of the problems in assessing the status of the aging in minority groups is that basic demographic and social data are not always available. A certain amount of information on whites and blacks in the United States is collected and published by the Bureau of the Census, as well as some information on people of Spanish heritage; but there are problems with these data. First of all, much of the census information compares "whites" (i.e., everyone who does not claim to be something other than white) and "nonwhites" (i.e., everyone who does make such a claim). While the majority of the nonwhites in the United States are blacks, the categories of nonwhites and blacks are not identical, so that "nonwhite" data are potentially misleading. One of the recommendations of the Special Concerns Session on Aging and Aged Blacks of the 1971 White House Conference on Aging was that the Census Bureau report data on blacks as a separate category rather than including them in the category of nonwhites. While it is probably more convenient for government agencies to use the dichotomous white/nonwhite categories, data in this form are of limited usefulness to researchers, and there is also something distasteful about relegating several racial minority groups to the residual category of

Table 4.4 MEDIAN AGE OF THE U.S. POPULATION, BY RACE, FOR
SELECTED YEARS, 1810–1970

Year	All races	White	Black
1820	16.7	16.6	17.2
1850	18.9	19.2	17.4
1900	22.9	23.4	19.5
1950	30.2	30.8	26.1
1970	28.1	28.9	22.4

Source: U.S. Bureau of the Census, *Historical Statistics of the United States, Colonial Times to 1970*,bicentennial edition (Washington, D.C.: U.S. Government Printing Office, 1975).

nonwhite. While the nonwhite category does not accurately represent the black population, it entirely hides other groups, such as Native Americans and Asian Americans.

While the term *nonwhite* blurs the differences among racial groups in the United States, other designations are not much better. The terms *Native American* and *Asian American* cover very diverse groups, and the Census Bureau sometimes uses the category "Spanish speaking" or "Spanish heritage," which includes Americans of Mexican, Puerto Rican, Cuban, and Spanish descent, as well as those who have migrated from Central and South American countries. It is important to remember the diverse groups that are subsumed under the umbrella categories used in the data collection processes.

In Chapter 2 the relationship between the birthrate, the death rate, and the age structure of the population was discussed, and the same elements are useful in distinguishing between the aging processes of various segments of the American population. Table 4.4, for example, shows the median ages of the white and black populations between the years 1820 and 1970. While both groups have aged over the last century and a half, the white population has aged at a faster rate. The slower rate of aging shown by the black population is a result of the slightly higher birth and death rates of blacks. The faster rate at which the white population is aging is also demonstrated by Table 4.5, which compares the percentages of the white and black populations that are over age 65. The figures cover the years from 1900 to 1970 as well as projections through the year 2010. The table shows that the percentage of both groups over age 65 has been increasing consistently since 1900; in fact, in percentage terms both groups have more than doubled their older populations since 1900. The over-65 white population has gone from 4.2 percent to 10.2, and the over-65 black population has gone from 3.0 percent to 6.9 percent. The population projections show, however, that between now and the year 2010 the

Table 4.5 PERCENTAGE OF U.S. POPULATION AGE
65+, 1900–2010, FOR WHITES AND BLACKS

Year	Whites	Blacks
1900	4.2	3.0
1930	5.7	3.1
1960	9.6	6.2
1970	10.2	6.9
	Projections	
1980	11.6	7.8
1990	12.5	8.5
2000	12.3	8.8
2010	12.5	9.5

Source: Jacob S. Siegel, *Demographic Aspects of Aging and the
Older Population in the United States*, Current Population Reports,
Series P-23, no. 59 (Washington, D.C.: U.S. Government Printing
Office, 1976).

over-65 black population may increase at a faster rate than the over-65 white population. These projections show the over-65 segment as 12.5 percent of the white population and 9.5 percent of the black population in the year 2010.

Life Expectancy in Minority Groups

Although it is true that the death rate is generally higher in the black population, the subject is considerably more complex that that generalization implies. Table 4.6 shows the life expectancies of whites and nonwhites of various ages for the year 1973. As can be seen, the figures are generally somewhat higher for whites; however, sex tends to overwhelm race as an indicator of life expectancy. While white males have a greater life expectancy than nonwhite males for most of their lives, and the same pattern holds for females, it is also true that regardless of race females have higher life expectancies than males. Nonwhite females have higher life expectancies than white males at every stage of the life cycle.

Over the course of the life cycle the differences in life expectancy between the races tend to narrow, and by age 85 both nonwhite males and nonwhite females have greater life expectancies than white males and females. By age 85, in fact, nonwhite males have a greater life expectancy than white females, the only instance in which a male has a greater life expectancy than a female. Even by age 65, however, the nonwhite male has nearly caught up with the white male (the white male has a remaining life expectancy of 13.2 years compared to the 13.1 years of the nonwhite male), although at birth the white male had a 6.5 year advantage; likewise, by age 65 the life expectancy of the nonwhite female is only about one year less than that of the white female.

The greater longevity of nonwhites compared to whites at advanced ages and the possibility that nonwhites may be able to increase this advantage are reflected in Table 4.7, which shows the death rates for blacks and whites at age 65 and over for some of the leading causes of death. These are rates per 100,000 population, which means that the figures indicate the number of people who are likely to die (per 100,000) from each specific cause in any one year. The table shows that white males have the highest death rates of all the groups for every cause of death except one (diabetes mellitus, which is also the only exception to the finding that black females have the lowest death rates of all the groups for all of the listed causes, although they are number one for diabetes mellitus). White females have higher death rates than black males for four of the seven listed causes, and higher rates than black females for all of the causes except diabetes mellitus.

Table 4.6 LIFE EXPECTANCY FOR WHITES AND NONWHITES AT SELECTED AGES, UNITED STATES, 1973

	White		Nonwhite	
Age	*Male*	*Female*	*Male*	*Female*
At birth	68.4	76.1	61.9	70.1
21	49.6	56.7	44.1	51.7
45	27.8	33.9	24.9	30.3
65	13.2	17.3	13.1	16.2
85	4.7	5.7	6.3	7.3

Source: U.S. Bureau of the Census, *Historical Statistics of the United States, Colonial Times to 1970*, bicentennial edition (Washington, D.C.: U.S. Government Printing Office, 1975).

Table 4.7 DEATH RATES FROM SELECTED CAUSES FOR WHITE MALES AND FEMALES AND BLACK MALES AND FEMALES AGE 65 AND OVER, 1973, PER 100,000 POPULATION

	White		Black	
	Male	*Female*	*Male*	*Female*
Diseases of the heart	5,447	4,055	3,814	3,125
Cancer	1,584	875	1,450	735
Cerebrovascular diseases	1,656	1,587	1,388	1,326
Influenza and pneumonia	566	369	422	236
Arteriosclerosis	395	377	243	222
Accidents	134	95	108	61
Diabetes mellitus	162	171	154	232

Source: Jacob S. Siegel, *Demographic Aspects of Aging and the Older Population in the United States*, Current Population Reports, Series P-23, no. 59 (Washington, D.C.: U.S. Government Printing Office, 1976).

Effects of Income and Place of Residence

The most startling difference between aging blacks and whites is in their incomes. Without exception, blacks report lower median incomes than whites. The lower incomes of older blacks are a direct result of their lower earnings throughout their lives; since social security benefits are related to income earned during the working years, the lower incomes of blacks will eventually be reflected in their social security checks. In addition, racial prejudice in the United States has limited many blacks to the least desirable jobs, which very often pay few if any private retirement benefits. Table 4.8 shows the median income of various types of households in 1974. The median income for a white couple, for example, was $7,315, while a black couple received only $5,075. The table also shows income per person in black and white families of all ages and in families headed by persons age 65 or over. Again, the income differentials between blacks and whites are evident.

The majority of Americans live in urban areas, so it is not surprising to find that most older people live in urban environments. This pattern of residence is found among older whites, but even larger proportions of older blacks and older people of Spanish heritage are living in urban areas. Table 4.9 lists the places of residence of these groups of older people in 1970. About 73 percent of older whites, 76.5 percent of older blacks, and 86 percent of older people

Table 4.8 MEDIAN INCOME OF FAMILIES WITH HEAD AGE 65+, FOR BLACKS AND WHITES, 1974

Household type	White	Black
Husband–wife	$ 7,315	$5,075
Male head, wife not present	10,609	5,005
Female head, husband not present	8,525	4,602
Unrelated individuals:		
Male	3,730	2,385
Female	2,959	1,998

Median income per person for all families and for families headed by persons age 65 +, for blacks and whites, 1974

	All families	
Husband–wife	$ 4,087	$2,639
Male head, wife not present	4,556	2,482
Female head, husband not present	2,496	1,148
	Family head age 65 +	
Husband–wife	$ 3,222	$1,787
Male head, wife not present	3,944	1,691
Female head, husband not present	3,410	1,275

Source: Jacob S. Siegel, *Demographic Aspects of Aging and the Older Population in the United States*, Current Population Reports, Series P-23, no. 59 (Washington, D.C.: U.S. Government Printing Office, 1976).

Table 4.9 URBAN AND RURAL RESIDENCE OF WHITES, BLACKS, AND
PERSONS OF SPANISH HERITAGE AGE 65+, 1970 (IN THOUSANDS)

	Whites	*Blacks*	*Spanish heritage*
Central cities	5,950 (33%)	812 (52%)	194 (51%)
Suburbs	4,100 (22%)	137 (9%)	77 (20%)
Small cities	3,260 (18%)	243 (16%)	59 (15%)
Total urban	13,309 (73%)	1,192 (76.5%)	330 (86%)
Total rural	5,021 (27%)	367 (23.5%)	52 (14%)

Source: Jacob S. Siegel, *Demographic Aspects of Aging and the Older Population in the United States,* Current Population Reports, Series P-23, no. 59 (Washington, D.C.: U.S. Government Printing Office, 1976).

of Spanish heritage live in urban areas. The vast majority of black and Spanish-heritage urban residents live in the central cities of urban areas, with correspondingly fewer living in the suburbs or in small cities. On the other hand, more older whites live in suburbs and small cities than in central cities. In each group a much smaller proportion of the population lives in rural areas: about 27 percent of older whites, 23.5 percent of older blacks, and 14 percent of older people of Spanish heritage.

Older blacks and older people of Spanish heritage are found in large numbers in some parts of the United States and are relatively scarce in others. Table 4.10 shows, for example, that over 60 percent of all blacks over 65 are living in the South, while only about 5 percent live in the Western region. Older blacks have been less likely than younger people to migrate from the southern states to the northern and western states. It is expected that the older blacks will be less concentrated in the South in coming years as the results of the out-migration of blacks from the South begin to show up in the older age group.

The regional distribution of older people of Spanish heritage is very different from that of other groups. First, just under 50 percent are living in the West; in fact, there are more than twice as many older people of Spanish heritage as there are older blacks in the West. The majority of the rest of the Spanish-heritage population is living in the South, with relatively few living in the Northeast or North Central regions.

The states with the largest numbers of older blacks are either southern states or those with large populations. With the exception of New York, the states with the largest numbers of older blacks are all in the South: Texas, Louisiana, Georgia, and Alabama. The states with the largest numbers of older people of Spanish heritage are California, Texas, Florida, New York, and New Mexico. California, Texas, and New Mexico have large populations of Mexican Americans, while Florida has many Cubans and New York many Puerto Ricans.

Table 4.10 REGIONAL DISTRIBUTION AND STATES WITH THE LARGEST
NUMBERS OF BLACKS AND PERSONS OF SPANISH HERITAGE AGE 65+,
1970

Blacks		Region		Persons of Spanish heritage
246,000		Northeast		31,000
281,000		North Central		23,000
936,000		South		141,000
81,000		West		188,000
1. New York	112,000		California	131,000
2. Texas	111,000		Texas	95,000
3. Louisiana	89,000		Florida	34,000
4. Georgia	88,000		New York	23,000
5. Alabama	85,000		New Mexico	22,000
6. North Carolina	79,000		Arizona	14,000
7. Mississippi	79,000		Colorado	13,000
8. Illinois	79,000		Illinois	9,000
9. Pennsylvania	75,000		Michigan	4,000
10. California	68,000		Louisiana	4,000

Source: Jacob S. Siegel, *Demographic Aspects of Aging and the Older Population in the
United States*, Current Population Reports, Series P-23, no. 59 (Washington, D.C.: U.S.
Government Printing Office, 1976).

Aging and Discrimination

The aging members of minority groups in the United States have been characterized as facing a situation of "double jeopardy" (Jackson, 1970) as a result of being old as well as being a member of a minority group, which often means that a person has a low income, lives in low-quality housing in the central parts of large cities, and so on. A study in Los Angeles (Dowd and Bengtson, 1978) found that older blacks and Mexican Americans reported lower incomes and poorer health than older whites. The same study, however, did not find blacks to have lower life satisfaction with increasing age (although Mexican Americans were less optimistic with increasing age), nor were either blacks or Mexican Americans found to be in less frequent contact with relatives or neighbors and friends as they became older. Thus, the double-jeopardy concept may apply to some elements of the experience of aging in minority groups, but it may not apply to the social and familial elements.

The same respondents were asked about their perceptions of racial and age discrimination, and it was somewhat surprising that blacks, whites, and Mexican Americans reported slightly greater awareness of age discrimination than of racial discrimination (Kasschau, 1977). The majority of all groups were aware of both racial and age discrimination, however.

Within the older American population there is a great amount of diversity: Most of the characteristics that are used by younger groups to distinguish between certain categories of people also operate in older age groups. There is, in fact, some suggestion that in some circumstances older people may discriminate more overtly than younger people. For example, because of the low pay and status of those who work in geriatric settings, many nursing homes are staffed primarily with black workers. This is especially true at the lower staff levels. Such circumstances can lead to overt antagonism between patients and staff, as in the following case (Watson and Maxwell, 1977: 112): "A black licensed practical nurse (LPN) at the Jewish home revealed through interviews that she and other black staff found it difficult to form cordial relations with their Jewish charges. She reported that some Jewish residents periodically expressed race-related hostility toward black staff." It should be remembered, however, that racism is not an affliction limited to older people but is found in varying degrees at all age levels.

A survey of the older poor in Rochester, New York, inquired into the racial attitudes of the respondents and found that older blacks hold generally positive images of whites, whereas older whites hold generally negative images of blacks. While the black respondents were generally quite favorable to the idea of joining with older whites to improve the condition of older people, large segments of older whites resisted the idea of cooperating with blacks in such an effort (Sterne, Phillips, and Rabushka, 1974).

Among a national sample of Americans over 65, there were found to be many similarities between the responses of blacks and whites, but there were also differences. Older blacks, for example, were more likely to take grandchildren or nieces and nephews to live with them (26 percent of blacks and 15 percent of whites), and blacks report that they are much more likely than whites to give their children and grandchildren advice on bringing up children, running a home, and the like (National Council on the Aging, 1975).

In the same national sample much larger proportions of older blacks than of older whites reported that they regarded crime, poor health, lack of money, lack of medical care, and poor housing as very serious problems in old age. The greater number of serious problems was found among older blacks with low incomes, thus reflecting the vulnerability of people who face a situation of *triple* jeopardy: being old, black, and poor (National Council on the Aging, 1975). Such evidence also indicates the need for gerontologists to recognize and understand the diversity that exists within older members of minority groups rather than thinking of them as homogeneous.

Aging Among Mexican Americans

Research on aging as it is experienced by the second-largest minority group in the United States, Mexican Americans, is very limited. It has been assumed that the family organization of Mexican Americans has allowed older people to assume honorific positions within an extended-family setting. But Penalosa

(1967) has noted that much writing about the Mexican American family is based on the inaccurate assumption that the contemporary family is a reflection of the traditional family. In the traditional family older members were cared for by their children, and children recognized and acknowledged their duty to support and care for their parents in old age. However, surveys of Mexican Americans in both Los Angeles and San Antonio found very few residences that contained extended families (Grebler, Moore, and Guzman, 1970). A study of older Mexican Americans in an urban area of Western Texas found that 61 percent said they did not believe that the family was obligated to support older parents. One might expect that younger Mexican Americans would have been influenced by the dominant American culture regarding the primacy of the nuclear family over the extended family, but it was surprising to the researcher that the older members also supported these ideas (Crouch, 1972). It may be that changes in values had occurred sooner in the acculturation process than had been anticipated, but it may also be that the tratition of children supporting older parents had arisen out of necessity and perhaps was never the preferred pattern of family organization (Alvirez and Bean, 1976).

There are other groups within American society that experience the aging process in a distinct manner, although precious little is known about them. It is hoped that more research can be done on these variations. Such research will surely yield significant insights into the meanings of aging.

Summary

Although there are numerous patterns of aging in various parts of the world, and although many societies have not yet been studied adequately, some researchers have been able to draw a few conclusions about aging from a comparative perspective. Cowgill and Holmes (1972) have specified 8 elements that unify the aging process in all societies and 22 ways in which it varies from society to society.

Taking a very broad, comparative view of a wide range of societies, it is possible to conclude that there is a relationship between aging and the level of industrial development. The industrially developed societies have a larger absolute number of older people and a much higher proportion of older people in their populations. The societies with lower levels of industrial development have fewer older people, even though these societies account for about two-thirds of the world's population. Furthermore, United Nation projections show that the less developed regions of the world will contain more than three-fourths of the world's population by the year 2000 and that they will also contain about 60 percent of the population over age 60. Thus, although the industrially developed regions will continue to have higher proportions of older people in their societies, the less developed regions are expected to increase their older populations by over 150 percent between 1970 and 2000.

Within the United States there are significantly different patterns of aging among different racial and ethnic groups. In general, the white population is older than the black population, although the black population will probably age at a slightly faster pace than the white population between now and the year 2010. The aging of minority populations in the United States will be greatly influenced by changes in the birthrate as well as by any changes that might occur in rates of immigration to the United States. One of the most pressing concerns of future gerontological research is a better understanding of the experience of aging in minority groups.

SELECTED REFERENCES

Sula Benet, *Abkhasia: The Long-Living People of the Caucasus* (New York: Holt, Rinehart and Winston, 1974).

Donald O. Cowgill and Lowell D. Holmes, eds., *Aging and Modernization* (New York: Appleton-Century-Crofts, 1972).

James J. Dowd and Vern L. Bengtson, "Aging in Minority Populations: an Examination of the Double Jeopardy Hypothesis," *Journal of Gerontology* 33 (1978): 427–436.

Alexander Leaf, *Youth in Old Age* (New York: McGraw-Hill, 1975).

Richard B. Mazess and Sylvia H. Forman, "Longevity and Age Exaggeration in Vilcabamba, Eduador," *Journal of Gerontology* 34 (1979): 94–98.

Erdman Palmore, *The Honorable Elders* (Durham, N.C.: Duke University Press, 1975).

PART

II Aging and the Individual

Aging can have very personal consequences, and ultimately every individual defines for himself or herself the meaning of growing older. The mental aspect of aging operates at two levels: (1) The stimuli that a person may experience are subject to sensory and perceptual changes with age, and (2) social definitions and self-definitions may undergo age-related changes. The kind of person we are and the kind of person we become throughout the adult lifespan are greatly influenced by personal definitions of aging.

To some extent, we define ourselves in relation to the roles we enact, and one of the most important roles in many people's lives is the work role. The relationship of the individual to the work role is strongly affected by age and by the ability and desire to retire. Much of contemporary social-gerontological theory revolves around the questions of how people define themselves and how aging is influenced by the type and amount of their involvement in various roles.

The Psychology of Aging

Overview. A sizable amount of evidence indicates that many people suffer a loss of efficiency in some of their senses, especially sight and hearing, as they grow older. Often such losses can be offset by mechanical aids, and most people retain effective use of their senses throughout their lives. It is possible that differences between generations in perceptual and mental functioning will decrease or disappear altogether in years to come.

A few studies have attempted to describe the personality types found among older Americans, and while it has been possible to identify some distinct types, it has been clearly demonstrated that older people do not always fit into these categories. Older people, in short, are just as diverse as younger people.

Although its basis is unknown, there seems to exist a general impression that one of the effects of aging is a decrease in mental abilities. People seem surprised when a 70 year old person is mentally alert, lucid, or unquestionably intelligent, and such a person is quite likely to be thought of as an exception to the rule. After all, it is reasoned, most older people are not mentally alert, lucid, or unquestionably intelligent. The conclusion seems simple enough: Aging must cause most people to lose some of their mental capacity. The subject is not nearly that simple, however, although one generalization seems justified at this point: Most people do not experience a noticeable decline in mental abilities with advancing age. There are a number of qualifications that must be attached to this generalization (which will be detailed throughout this chapter), but the evidence is sufficiently strong so that popular attitudes about declining mental abilities can be declared a myth.

Certain physical conditions can cause a person of any age to experience a decrease in mental capacity, and older people are more likely than younger people to be affected by some of them. But by no means are most older people suffering from one or more of these conditions. Also each younger generation in the United States has generally been better educated than the previous generation, and level of education can affect performance on many tests of mental abilities. We should thus expect that a younger cohort of Americans will usually outscore an older cohort on an IQ test. These generational differences cannot, however, be used as evidence that each individual loses some of his or her mental capacity with age. Baltes and Schaie (1974) found from their testing of people of different ages that older people usually did not score as high as younger people, but using a longitudinal format they also found that people's mental abilities did not usually decrease over time. They concluded (1974: 36) that "the differences between scores were due mainly to generational differences, not to chronological age." In other words, older people will usually score lower on a test because of the historical period in which they grew up, not because they have necessarily lost mental abilities with age. Instead, the researchers concluded that people with only average health will at least maintain their level of mental performance into the later stages of the life cycle. Actually, we really do not know the full mental potential of the older population. The intellectual capacities of older people have not been fully challenged, for example, by encouraging large numbers of people to enroll in institutions of higher education. There is every reason to believe that many older people could successfully complete college-level courses with the proper social encouragement and an appropriate intellectual climate. This is not to deny that there are changes that occur with aging and that some of these changes may hamper the full and effective use of a person's mental capacity, but it is essential to recognize the mental abilities that most older people do possess.

The Sensory Functioning of Aging Individuals

One of the fears that many people express about growing older is that their mental and sensory processes will deteriorate and they will no longer be in full control of themselves. Some of this concern can be traced to elements of our contemporary folklore that tell us that growing older means that we will inevitably suffer mental and sensory declines. Probably everyone has heard, for example, that it is much easier to learn a foreign language when we are young than when we are older, and one of the most commonly accepted bits of folk wisdom states that "you can't teach an old dog new tricks." There are other things that tend to reinforce the idea that older people are less mentally alert than younger people, such as newspaper articles and police department bulletins that warn older people to be wary of con artists because older people are thought to be easy victims of fraud. But what is the truth of the matter? Do we reach a mental peak early in our lives and then begin a long decline into senility? The answer is that growing older does not mean that we lose command of our senses or that we inevitably become mentally or physically incompetent. This generalization, however, should not be interpreted to mean that there are no age-associated declines in mental and sensory abilities.

A substantial number of studies have concluded that most people's sense organs become less efficient as they grow older. It is important to know the extent of this loss because the efficiency of our sense organs affects our ability to orient ourselves to the world and to process important information. For example, most people experience a reduction in vision as they age. Typically, a person's vision becomes less sharp between the ages of 40 and 65. A number of physical changes are responsible for the reduced vision, and one of the difficulties encountered in correcting deficiencies in the vision of older persons is that they may have more than one visual problem. Many older people have poor vision in low illumination, a problem that can usually be helped by increasing the available light in a room. But increasing the available light may cause another visual problem, since many older people are very susceptible to glare. Or the two problems may be combined: Many older people find it very difficult to drive a car at night because of the combination of low illumination and glare. Other visual problems associated with increasing age include poorer color vision and reduced accuracy of depth perception (Birren, 1964, 88–96; Fozard et al., 1977).

Most people also experience some decline in hearing as they age. The typical pattern is one in which the older person finds it more difficult to hear high-pitch tones; the higher the pitch, the greater the loss of hearing. This decline in hearing, which is caused by deterioration of the auditory system, is called presbycusis. Tests have found hearing loss to be more common in men than in women, a fact that has led researchers to question how much of the hearing loss associated with aging is the result of organic deterioration and how much may be due to environmental effects. A reasonable hypothesis would be that men may experience greater hearing loss than women because of greater exposure to noise pollution at work. If some hearing loss is caused by occupational noise pollution, then we can expect that the number of women who experience hearing loss will increase as more women enter the labor force. Also, it may be possible to control occupational noise levels and thus prevent some of the hearing loss that occurs in later life (Botwinick, 1973; Decker, 1974).

Research has also shown that some loss of efficiency in other senses, such as smell and taste, is associated with aging. Because there are some contradictory findings, generalizations on this matter should be viewed with caution. One study (Cooper et al., 1959) concluded that individuals experience declines in the four basic tastes (salty, sweet, bitter, and sour) after age 50, but other researchers maintain that any differences in the basic tastes between younger and older people may be due more to differences in taste preferences between generations rather than to a decline in the sense of taste. A similar pattern has been found in the limited amount of research that has been done on the relationship between aging and the sense of smell. Some research has shown distinct differences between younger and older age groups in their evaluation of objectionable smells, such as motor exhaust fumes. People over 65 have been found to report the odor as being less objectionable than younger people. It is not certain, however, that exhaust fumes are less objectionable to older people simply because they have a less sensitive sense of smell; again, there seem to be some generational variations in smell preferences. Younger people may define exhaust fumes as very objectionable for reasons that go beyond the sensitivity of their sense of smell, such as heightened sensitivity to all forms of urban and industrial pollution as a result of the recent concern with environmental purity. In a related example, common sense would lead us to expect that city folk would find the smell of cow manure more objectionable than rural folk would, even though rural residents might be more capable of correctly identifying the smell. In any case, research on age-associated declines in smell must be tempered by the knowledge that there may be generational conditions that influence the results (Engen, 1977).

The available research tells us that we can probably expect some loss of efficiency in our basic senses as we grow older. But the research does not indicate that we are likely to lose the use of our senses entirely. Vision and hearing loss very often can be corrected or at least improved through the use of eyeglasses, hearing aids, or medical therapy. Moreover, some of the declines in perceptual functioning that occur with age probably are not very important for most people in everyday life. The decline in the ability to hear very high-pitched tones, for example, has very little practical effect on the lives of most people. Most people, thus, will experience a decline in the efficiency of their sense organs with age, but they will retain functional use of their senses throughout their lives and never lose them.

Perceptual and Mental Functioning

As already indicated, the study of the relationship between aging and sensory, perceptual, and mental functioning is complex, and the research is confounded by some serious methodological problems. If we ask the question "Do most people experience declines in their mental abilities as they age?" the usual research answer is "yes." This answer is only superficially correct, however, and at best, only partially indicative of the true state of affairs.

One of the first problems that confronts the researcher is to define the meaning of mental functioning. This is a difficult task when dealing with a relatively homogeneous group, such as school-age children; but an adequate definition of mental functioning is almost impossible when the intent is to compare different age groups. There are obvious differences in the everyday functioning and mental patterns of people of different ages. Schoolchildren are continually exposed to evaluative testing, whereas adults are only seldom exposed to tests and therefore might be expected to suffer some decline in test-taking ability. It is also possible that older people are more resistant to test taking than younger people simply because younger people are more likely to view testing as a normal event. Nevertheless, most research on the relationship between aging and mental functioning uses standardized tests of mental functioning and compares the test results of different age groups. For example, a researcher might administer the most commonly used standardized test, the Wechsler Adult Intelligence Scale (WAIS), to 200 adults at about the same time. The researcher would then use the test scores from the WAIS to compare the intelligence levels of people of different ages, employing a cross-sectional research design.

Results of Standardized Testing

Using standardized exams and a cross-sectional research design, most researchers find what Botwinick (1973) calls the "classic aging pattern." In this pattern the association between aging and intelligence is multidimensional. Intelligence tests are usually divided into several subtests that attempt to measure the different processes that are thought to contribute to intelligence. The WAIS, for example, contains eleven different subtests grouped into two types with separate scores. Each individual, thus, receives a verbal score and a performance score on the test; these two scores can then be combined into a summary intelligence score.

In the classic aging pattern people usually maintain their verbal scores as they age, while their performance scores decline appreciably. It appears that the primary reason for the decline in the performance scores is that the performance tests attempt to measure psychomotor abilities, and speed of response is therefore a crucial test element. Many psychologists believe speed of response to be an important measurement of the functioning of the central nervous system and the thought processes. Not all of the performance decline that occurs with age can be attributed to decreases in speed of response, however, because even when time limits are removed from the WAIS, declining performance scores are linked with increasing age.

The classic aging pattern in the results of intelligence tests is found in most groups of people. It occurs in different occupational groups, different socioeconomic groups, and groups with different educational levels. A person's relative position within a given cohort seems to remain relatively constant, however; people who scored high on intelligence tests when they were young usually still score high compared with others of their own age when they are older; still, the test scores of an older cohort are usually lower than those of younger cohorts. In other words, intelligence differences within cohorts remain stable throughout the aging process even though each cohort's psychomotor skills decline with age (Botwinick, 1973).

Perceptual Changes with Age

Many of the results of research on the perceptual changes that occur with age correspond to the findings of cross-sectional research on intelligence. Some studies (Comalli, 1965, 1970) have found that children and older people are more susceptible to illlusions than middle-aged adults. A number of perceptual tests are used to measure age differences; the best known of these is the Müller-Lyer illusion. Are the lines in the following diagram equal in length?

Older people would be expected to have a greater margin of error than middle-aged people when they are asked to arrange the line segments in this illusion

into equal lengths. One researcher has argued that older people are less susceptible to other illusions because of "stimulus persistence." This means that older
people tend to react only to the first stimulus when they are presented with
a series of stimuli. This reaction is in contrast to that of younger people, who
tend to respond differently to each stimulus in a series even if the stimuli are
identical. Most people will perceive different sounds if the same word is repeated quickly several times. The stimulus persistence of older individuals
causes them to differ from the general population because they perceive fewer
changes in the sounds. The inference used to explain this perceptual pattern
is that they are less responsive to new information. If this is true, then we
would expect to find that older people are less likely to modify their behavior
in response to new experiences or new information. This line of argument has
implications for such topics as the political ideology of older people, a topic
that will be discussed in Chapter 8.

It should be remembered that there is a great distance between the everyday
lives of most older people and laboratory research into such topics as perceptual testing. Most of the perceptual research is based on research subjects who
are responding to rapid-fire sights or sounds or to intentionally ambiguous
pictures or illusions; thus, the experiments are distinct from the experiences
to which most older people are exposed in their daily lives. At the same time,
if these research reports are indicating age changes in the central nervous
system or other bodily systems, then we must continue to try to understand
them and to evaluate the significance of the findings.

Critiques of Research on Aging and Intelligence

As mentioned in Chapter 1, a cross-sectional research design allows the researcher to determine differences between age groups at only one point in time;
then these age differences are used to infer what happens as people age. As
noted before, there are many problems with inferring age changes from such
research. Most researchers therefore prefer to use a longitudinal research
design whenever possible. It is then possible to measure the extent of change
within a particular group of people. An ambitious longitudinal research design
might propose to give an intelligence test to a group of people at age 20 and
test them again every ten years for the rest of their lives. This design would
be far superior to a cross-sectional design for the measurement of intelligence
changes with age. In fact, Schaie and associates (Schaie and Strother, 1968;
Baltes and Schaie, 1974) have argued that the classic aging pattern is a myth
built upon the flaws of the cross-sectional research design. They maintain that
cross-sectional research on intelligence has been measuring generational
change rather than declines in intelligence with age. They argue that the
educational level, and therefore the measured intelligence, of the population
is increasing with each generation; therefore, what appears to be a decline in

intelligence with age is really an increase in the intelligence of younger generations. If this is true, then future generations of older people may not show the classic aging pattern in their intelligence test scores.

Terminal Drop

Another aspect of the relationship between age and intelligence is the phenomenon called terminal drop. First discovered by Kleemeier (1962), terminal drop is a decline in cognitive functioning in the period immediately preceding death. Several studies have confirmed the initial discovery (Jarvik and Falek, 1963; Jarvik and Blum, 1971; Riegel and Riegel, 1972). If the existence of terminal drop could be proven, it might make it possible to predict death as much as five years in advance. At present, however, the concept is unrefined, and some studies have failed to support the concept, while other researchers argue that it is a myth (Berkowitz, 1965; Palmore and Cleveland, 1976).

Learning

The adage "you can't teach an old dog new tricks" is often applied to humans as well as to their dogs. This piece of folk wisdom, like many others is not entirely correct. Older people can learn new things, although usually not as easily or as rapidly as younger people.

Most learning and memory studies use something like a paired-associate learning situation, in which subjects are presented with pairs of words that they must learn to associate. The subjects are shown one word; then, after a short interval (perhaps two seconds), the associated word is shown. In this situation the subject is supposed to say the associated word before it appears; that is, when a subject can correctly associate the word pair, he or she has learned the associated pair of words. A number of studies have shown that younger people perform better on these types of learning experiments than older people (Botwinick, 1973). Some researchers maintain that learning experiments place too much emphasis on speed of response and thus end up testing psychomotor skills instead of learning. Canestrari (1963), for example, found that older people improved their performance on the learning of a paired-associate list when the time restriction for response was removed. Young people also improved their performance in the self-paced learning situation, and did better in the experiment; but Canestrari documented his argument that learning experiments are measuring psychomotor skills in addition to learning abilities.

Several studies have demonstrated that paired-associates learning can be improved when research subjects use mediators, devices that help a person remember an associated pair of words by putting them in the context of a sentence or constructing a mental picture. If you were instructed to associate the words *army* and *bank,* you could use a mediator by making up a sentence such as "The army attacks the bank." In a study conducted by Hulicka and

Grossman (1967), the research subjects were instructed to use mediators. Although under these conditions the older people did not surpass the younger people in number of correct answers, they showed dramatic improvement in their scores. Without using mediators, the older people recalled only 13 percent of the word pairs, but when instructed in the use of mediators they could recall 65 percent of the pairs. What these studies demonstrate is that older people are quite capable of learning. With only very simple adjustments, they can achieve remarkable improvements. Although it is not yet possible to state precisely the relationship between aging and learning, the differences in learning capacity between the young and the old may be much less than was previously thought.

Memory

Very closely related to learning is memory. It has been known for a number of years that we experience some memory loss as we age, but that loss of recent memory is more severe than loss of remote memory. The same relationship between recent and remote memory is found among older people who are diagnosed as suffering from senile dementia or organic brain syndrome. As Botwinick (1973) has noted, however, this conclusion is based more on clinical impressions than on systematic studies using appropriate research controls. Still, most cross-sectional studies comparing the memory capacities of different age groups show a correlation between advancing age and memory loss (Gilbert and Levee, 1971; Moenster, 1972; Erber, 1974).

In the last few years some interesting experiments have attempted to increase the recent memory of older people through the use of hyperoxygenation, in which a person is given pure oxygen at high atmospheric pressures. In the initial experiments by Jacobs and associates (1969), the subjects were given 100 percent oxygen for 90 minutes, twice a day, for 15 days. After these treatments the subjects showed large increases in their memory test scores. The theory that led to these experiments was that increased oxygen might improve memory because it is known that lack of oxygen has a negative effect on learning and memory, and it was hypothesized that the memory loss of older people is due to inadequate oxygen flow to the brain. Not all of the evidence about hyperoxygenation has been as positive as the original experiment. Goldfarb and associates (1972) replicated the original experiment using a group of people who had been psychiatrically defined as suffering from brain damage, and the results did not show the memory gains of the previous study. In addition, the researchers found that most of the results of the oxygen treatment were negative, with some of the patients experiencing irritability and emotional distress as a result of the experiments.

Although most research has found some losses in recent memory with age, it was generally felt that people usually do not experience much loss in remote memory. This widely held belief apparently arose out of experiences with older people who could recall remote events of early childhood. Recent studies, however, have discovered the same general pattern of age-related loss in long-term memory as in recent memory. Schonfield (1972), for example, found that older people were less able to recall the names of their schoolteachers than younger people. Another study (Bahrick, Bahrick, and Wittlinger, 1975) confirmed this age-related pattern of remote memory when they tested people on the recall of names and faces from their high school yearbooks. While even very old people may be able to recall isolated events or people from early childhood, systematic studies show that, in general, the older a person is, the less likely that person is to be able to accurately recall verifiable bits of information.

In sum, the available research on sensory, perceptual, and mental processes shows that most people experience some declines as they age, especially in the efficiency and speed of their responses to stimuli. It is important to remember, however, that most people never completely lose the ability to use their basic senses and mental powers. People of all ages are able to learn, solve problems, act creatively, and recall recent and remote events with a remarkable degree of accuracy. None of the research shows an age at which rapid deterioration in any of the sense or mental abilities begins, nor is there any evidence that most people have much difficulty adjusting to any of the gradual changes that occur with age. The evidence is not as depressing as many people fear. While we will probably experience some slowing of our mental processes, we are not usually destined to end our lives in a state of senility or mental helplessness.

Social Stereotyping of Older Persons

Social gerontologists maintain an optimistic view of the aging process. Some are perhaps a bit romantic about the realities of growing old, preferring to see aging in its best possible light and even overlooking some the less pleasant aspects of becoming older. But this upbeat view of aging on the part of a relatively small group of professionals is in sharp contrast to the negative views of aging that are part of the accepted folk knowledge of American society. And negative attitudes toward aging are not held only by the young; older people often hold many of the same attitudes. When a Louis Harris poll asked a national sample of Americans what they thought were the worst years in a person's life, 33 percent of those between 18 and 64 years of age said that the sixties and the seventies are the worst years, while 35 percent of those over 65 held that opinion (National Council on the Aging, 1975). When the pollsters asked the same sample to identify what they believed to be the worst things about being over 65 years of age, they said that poor health was the worst thing, followed by the problems of loneliness, poor finances, lack of independence, and neglect. There were very few differences between the responses of the younger and older people in the sample. Whether this view of aging is correct or not, it appears that there is a fair degree of consensus as to the low social value placed on old age. We can say, then, that there is a wide consensus regarding the main features of growing old in American society, or a dominant stereotype of old age.

Stereotypes and Typifications

It is very common today to speak of a social stereotype, such as the stereotype of old age, but it is important to define what we mean by a stereotype, since the term is used with a variety of meanings. In popular usage the term *stereotype* usually refers to a factually incorrect image of some person or group. The term may be used to indicate that someone has committed the logical error of attributing the qualities associated with a group to a specific member of that group. We have, for example, evidence that associates hearing loss with advancing age; however, it would be illegitimate to treat every older person as though he or she suffered from extreme hearing loss when in fact any particular individual may suffer no hearing loss at all.

Many social stereotypes bear no relationship to any research evidence, or to any evidence at all, and some stereotypes may be contrary to fact, experience, or logic. Quite aside from the problem of applying the stereotype to a particular person, relying on an inaccurate stereotype can lead one to think of entire groups of people, and perhaps to interact with members of the group, in grossly inadequate ways. Stereotypes can be misused in a manner that causes one to treat others in arbitrary and insensitive ways. However, stereotyping is very closely related to the more general process of typification (McKinney, 1969).

Typifications, when used correctly, are not only useful but essential for human social interaction. As we learn the language of our society, we also learn the basic assumptions and definitions that allow us to interact with other members of that society. Part of this process involves learning to make sense of the world around us, and this is made possible by learning to think of things and people as examples of general types, or as typifications. When used in this manner, typifications are neither good nor bad, negative nor positive, correct nor incorrect.

Since typifications are social creations, they are also constantly changing; for example, we are constantly checking the typifications we use against our own experiences. If we find that a typification does not fit our experiences, we usually adjust the typification to accommodate the new information. Typifications, thus, are not rigid and unchangeable preconceptions that defy all reason and logic; instead, they are one of the tools we use to order and make sense of the mass of information and detail that we are confronted with every day. They are also essential because they allow us to interact with people whom we have never met before, and they allow us to encounter the world with the confidence that we are capable of handling ourselves in the social world—we do not have to approach everything and everyone as if we were totally naive. In short, the use of typifications gives us an ordered view of the world that allows us to interact with others in a socially competent manner.

Typifications of Old Age

When we refer to typifications of old age, we are referring to the typical ways in which people in the United States regard old age. Through research we may find those typifications accurate or inaccurate. What, then, are the typifications of old age in American society? What images of old age do most people have, and how accurate or inaccurate are those images? There are several ways to approach these questions, and there are therefore several different answers. Palmore (1971) has used American humor and joking as a way of determining some popular attitudes toward aging. He found that a slight majority of the jokes he analyzed viewed aging or older people in negative ways but that the rest were either positive or ambivalent about aging. The jokes he found that tended to be most negative when applied to older people dealt with such topics as physical ability, physical appearance, age concealment, the old maid, and mental ability. In general, however the jokes about older women tended to be much more negative than those about older men. Older women were most often the objects of derisive jokes when the subject was the old maid or age concealment. It is curious that the old maid is a subject of derisive humor when there are no comparable jokes on the subject of old bachelors.

Perhaps surprisingly, the jokes about sex in the older years were about evenly divided between those displaying positive and negative attitudes, although there might be some disagreement as to which jokes are negative and which are positive. Consider, for example, the following joke: A young male robber has frisked an older woman without finding any money and is about to give up when she exclaims, "Don't stop now—I'll write you a check!" On the face of it, the joke would seem to be negative in tone, implying that the older woman cannot secure sexual attention and must pay for such attentions. The joke also seems to imply that the younger male robber does not regard the older woman as sexually desirable. The joke may also be seen as positive, however, in that the older woman demonstrates an active interest in sexual attentions. A similar joke about an older man may be almost entirely positive: An older man married a young girl and died only a week later, with a smile on his face that it took the undertaker three days to remove. In this instance the man is depicted as being able to attract the younger female as a wife, and it is also implied that he is sexually competent. On the other hand, the joke implies that the older man is not physically capable of maintaining a marriage with a younger female. An even more positive joke involves a man who is about to marry a much younger woman and is being warned by his physician that too much sex could be fatal. But the old man shrugs and replies, "If she dies, she dies" (Richman, 1977). The joke is positive, at least in the sense that it depicts the older man as sexually competent and confident of his own capacities. Just how much jokes can tell us about the attitudes of Americans toward aging and old age is an open question, but as an element of popular culture they can be used as indicators of popular attitudes.

The national survey mentioned earlier in the chapter is another source of information about popular attitudes toward age and aging (National Council on the Aging, 1975). This survey reported that Americans view old age as a time of illness, loneliness, poverty, and dependency. Note, however, that people gave these responses when they were asked to name the worst things about being over 65 years of age. In addition, people's attitudes toward aging may not be as negative as they appear to be at first glance—"poor health" was the *only* response given by more than 50 percent of the sample.

In the same survey respondents were asked to rate "most people over 65" on a list of attributes. The respondents reported that they thought of people over age 65 as "friendly and warm" and "wise from experience." These were the most frequently reported attributes of older people, with three-fourths of the respondents saying that people over 65 years of age are very friendly and warm. In addition, 82 percent of the respondents under age 65 felt people over 65 were friendly and warm, but the total figure was reduced because only 25 percent of the respondents over age 65 thought people their own age are friendly and warm!

On the other hand, less than 50 percent of the respondents felt that people over 65 years of age are very physically active, very good at getting things done, very bright and alert, or very open-minded and adaptable, and only 5 percent thought of older people as being sexually active.

The Harris poll also provided some information on the older American population when respondents over age 65 were asked to state the most serious problems they faced. The most important finding was that less than 25 percent of the respondents cited any one problem as being very serious. This would indicate that there is no one problem that applies to even a bare majority of the older population. Only 21 percent of the older respondents said that poor health was a very serious problem. You will recall that 62 percent of respondents of all ages felt that poor health was the worst thing about being over 65, yet nearly 80 percent of those over age 65 state that poor health is not a serious problem. One-third of the general public felt that loneliness is one of the worst things about being over 65, but only 12 percent of those over age 65 report loneliness as a serious problem. The general impression is that popular conceptions of old age may be more negative than the actual circumstances of older people. In other words, people may be more fearful of aging than the experiences of older people warrant. What we also quickly discover is that stereotypes we hold are inadequate for dealing with the diversity of older Americans. The literature of social science is replete with examples of the diversity of human social behavior. We need to make generalizations and to categorize people into types in order to approach the world with a more or less stable world view, but we soon discover that individuals whom we know with even a little intimacy are more complex and atypical than our stereotypes and typifications would lead us to believe. In short, we find that the diversity of social behavior is just as important as the uniformities that we perceive and use to make sense of the mass of details we encounter every day.

Variations in Attitudes Toward Old Age

Attitudes toward old age seem to vary by age, by level of education, probably by social class, and perhaps in other ways that are not yet known. A significant amount of research has dealt with children's views of adults and older people. Most of the research concludes that children have mostly negative attitudes toward aging and old people (e.g., Kogan and Shelton, 1962). But some recent studies have questioned these findings. Thomas and Yamamato (1975) tested grade school and high school students for their attitudes toward young, middle-aged, and old persons, and their findings were opposite from those of most previous research. They found children and adolescents to hold generally favorable attitudes toward middle-aged adults and old persons, and do not hold negative attitudes toward old age. Similarly, an analysis of old age as it has been presented in children's literature over most of the last ninety years did not conclude that the images presented were usually negative, nor did the researchers find that more recent children's stories presented more negative images of old age than stories published in the late 1800s or early 1900s (Seltzer and Atchley, 1971). It had been expected that children's stories would show some deterioration of the image of old age in recent times, but this was not found to be the case.

It is entirely possible that the abstract images that people hold of old age or of older people are far different from the kinds of attitudes that would develop in a setting in which older and younger people interact with one another. Auerbach and Levenson (1977) tested some young (ages 18–22) college students regarding their attitudes toward older people and found that most of the students held positive attitudes. They then tested to see what the effect would be if some younger students took a course with some older students (age 65 and older); they found a marked decline in the young students' positive attitude toward older people. By the end of the course an overwhelming proportion of the younger students held negative attitudes toward older people, even though at the beginning of the course a great majority had reported positive attitudes. In this setting the younger students appeared to resent the older students because the older students identified with the instructors and devoted an inordinate amount of time to classwork, a circumstance that was probably exacerbated by the fact that many of the older students were enrolled only in the one course. Many of the younger students felt that the older students caused irrelevant digressions because of their tendency to allude to their personal lives and past experiences.

While it may seem surprising that attitudes toward older people would become more negative as a result of interaction with older students, this finding nevertheless demonstrates that attitudes toward older people are probably changeable. If it is possible to observe a shift from positive to negative attitudes, it is logical to expect that the opposite could also occur. Also, just because the interaction between younger and older students on a college campus led to more negative attitudes, it would not be valid to conclude that the same result would be found in other interactional settings.

Personality and Aging

The study of personality types and the dynamics of personality among older people constitute a relatively undeveloped area of research. Most studies of personality have concentrated on children and adolescents; very few have focused on adults and older adults. The lack of adult personality research may be due partly to an early-childhood bias among researchers, a bias that results from the idea that personality is set very early in life and that few personality changes occur in adulthood. A second reason for the lack of research on adult personality is that the concept of personality is difficult to study in later stages of the lifespan. A study of personality dynamics or changes of personality over a lifetime requires a painstaking longitudinal research design, which means that the researcher must collect personality inventories at different stages in the lives of a representative group of people. Because of this and other problems associated with the study of adult personality dynamics, a thorough study has not yet been done.

The few studies that have reported preliminary results show that personality tends to remain stable; that is, it does not change much over time. This is actually an overstatement of what we know about personality and aging. It would be expected that biological changes, role losses, life crises (such as the death of one's mate), and eventually the phenomenon of terminal drop all affect personality, yet such effects have not been identified. The research studies completed so far do not show many personality changes over time, but neither have they adequately answered all the questions that need to be answered (Woodruff and Birren, 1972). The one thing that seems clear at present is that there is no old-age personality, no monolithic personality type that encompasses all aging people.

While it is very difficult to research the relationship between personality and age, it is possible to approach the meaning of personality by carrying out cross-sectional studies. Cross-sectional studies of personality, however, present the same kinds of problems as cross-sectional studies in other areas of gerontology. In other words, we can execute a cross-sectional research design by trying to ascertain whether there are modal personality types among various age groups, or we can study just one age group at one point in time (e.g., study a group of people over age 65 and classify them into various personality types). The problem with these approaches is that we do not know how these people have maintained or changed their personalities; we do not know what effects different experiences and historical circumstances have had on them; and we have no way of controlling for the effects of social structure—of educational, occupational, social, and political factors. About all we can do when using a cross-sectional or one-point-in-time survey of age groups is describe the character types we find within those groups.

Reichard's Five Personality Types

Personality refers to the psychic structure of individuals, especially the ways in which they respond to the world through their feelings, impulses, and emotions. Personality ties the psychic structure of the individual to the person as an organism, as a biological being. There is also a social dimension to personality, first in the way an individual develops in response to social influences, but also in the way a society produces certain personality types as a result of unique historical circumstances as well as the various roles that must be filled within the society.

A cross-sectional study of adult personality can tell us something about the psychic structure of individuals, but it will not be able to tell us much about the social dimension of personality. It will, however, give us evidence about the changing personality structure of American society. To the extent that we find differences in personality types between various age groups, we can relate these changes to historical events and changes in the structure of the society.

One of the earliest studies that applied psychoanalytic concepts to personality and aging was published in 1962 (Reichard et al.). The researchers used a cross-sectional design to analyze the personality characteristics of 87 white males between the ages of 55 and 84. At the time they were interviewed, all of the respondents were in good health; about half were retired and half still working. The researchers compiled personality profiles on the subjects, using 115 personality ratings organized around the general categories of aggression, passivity and dependence, ego organization and impulse control, defense mechanisms, mental functioning, emotional organization, attitudes toward self, attitudes toward women, attitudes toward people in general, attitudes toward minority groups, conceptions of father, conceptions of mother, punishment as child, conceptions of wife, identification with parents, dynamic character structure, and attitudes toward aging. On the basis of this information the researchers were able to identify persons with similar personality profiles. They found the following personality types among their subjects:

1. *Mature:* This type was described as well adjusted to the aging process. These men were capable of self-control, accepted responsibility, had meaningful social relationships, had stable work histories, and had moved gracefully into old age.
2. *Rocking chair:* This type was also well adjusted to aging. These men, however, were different from the mature type because they were more heavily dependent on others both materially and emotionally. Since they had not been highly self-directed while young, they accepted readily the relaxation that came with retirement.
3. *Armored:* This type was found to be more rigid than either the mature type or the rocking-chair type. These men maintained high levels of self-control and discipline and were also well adjusted to the aging process. Self-reliance and rugged individualism were highly valued by this type.
4. *Angry:* This type was not well adjusted to aging. These men were described as hostile. They were more likely to blame others if something went wrong, and they tended to see the world as a competitive struggle.
5. *Self-Haters:* This type was also poorly adjusted to aging. Instead of blaming others for failures, these men tended to blame themselves. Their social relations were of poor quality, and they were very often depressed.

Although the researchers found only these five personality types in their study, they felt that a larger sample of respondents might reveal a greater variety of types. But even with their small sample they substantiated their major hypothesis, that the manner in which a person ages is dependent on his or her personality. The researchers did not maintain that adjustment to aging is determined by personality because there is a good deal of evidence that social and environmental factors greatly influence an individual's adaptation to aging. They were arguing that personality is an important factor in the adaptive process.

Although this study was able to outline five main personality types, not all of the men fit into one of the five types. A significant number displayed personality profiles that could not be placed in any of the recognizable personality types.

Neugarten's Four Personality Types

Another study that attempted to classify the personality types in an older population was based on information collected in the Kansas City Study of Adult Life (Neugarten et al., 1968). This study was different from the Reichard study in that it included both male and female subjects and used only 45 personality variables, many fewer than the other study. Using only respondents between the ages of 70 and 79, or only 59 people, the researchers found four personality types:

1. *Integrated:* This was a generally well-adjusted group of people, described by the researchers as mellow and mature. The researchers discovered that there were three patterns of behavior among people of the integrated type. These individuals might be "reorganizers," "focused," or "disengaged." The reorganizers were very active people who always undertook new activities when they gave up old ones. Upon retirement, the reorganizers replaced the lost work role with other activities. They were found to have a high level of life satisfaction. This group appeared to illustrate the activity theory. The focused individuals, like the reorganizers, were active, but they were more specialized. Instead of engaging in a wide variety of activities, they spent most of their time performing one or two roles. The disengaged individuals were like others of their personality type in that they reported high levels of life satisfaction. They were different, though, because they were much less active than either the reorganizers or the focused. The disengaged were content to grow older in a "take it easy" style.

2. *Armored–Defended:* Members of this group had relatively high levels of life satisfaction, but they differed from the integrated individuals in that they were less willing to accept the aging process. To some extent they preferred to struggle against the idea of aging. Two patterns of behavior were found among people of this type: "holding on" and "constricted." The holding-on pattern is exemplified by the cowboy who wants to die with his boots on. Such a person does not want to become old, or to behave as if he or she were old, but prefers to maintain middle-aged behavior as long as possible. The constricted person also does not want to become old, but this person reacts by becoming closed off from social interaction, that is, by constricting his or her activities.

3. *Passive–Dependent:* Members of this group were much less independent than either the integrated or the armored–defended individuals. They exhibited two behavior patterns: "succorance seeking" and "apathetic." The succorance seekers were heavily dependent on others, and their happiness seemed to depend on having someone to respond to them, someone who would give them emotional support. The apathetic people were more passive than the succorance seekers and usually engaged in less social activity. Apathetic people

are different from the disengaged in that their low level of social activity is not a response to the process of aging but instead is a long-established pattern of behavior that existed before they became old.

4. *Disorganized:* The final personality type discovered in Neugarten's research was the disorganized or unintegrated type. These people were described as having gross defects in psychological functioning and were often barely able to maintain themselves.

Differences Between Generations

Studies of the personality types found among a group of older persons are of limited usefulness in constructing a general psychological theory of aging because many questions are left unanswered. That certain personality types are found among older people does not tell us how these personality types compare with those found in other age groups. A large number of studies have examined age differences in a single personality trait. Older people have been compared to younger people in terms of such traits as rigidity and cautiousness. White and Foner (1968) summarized a large number of such studies and found that older people are more rigid, more restrained, more cautious, more passive, more egocentric, and less emotional than younger people. One-dimensional personality studies do not, however, give us an adequate basis for describing differences or similarities between age groups.

A few studies have tried to assess differences between age groups by using several dimensions of personality, but the results of those studies have not been uniform. Some studies have found strong personality stability throughout the lifespan, while others have found dramatic personality changes (Neugarten, 1977). In addition, the multidimensional personality studies have used cross-sectional research designs, which present a number of problems. Even if cross-sectional studies were consistent in their findings, we still would not know whether we were dealing with maturational processes or generational processes.

Although the results were not conclusive, Woodruff and Birren (1972) published a very interesting study of the personality characteristics of a group of adults over a span of 25 years. The researchers had access to the personality inventories of a group of people who were attending college in 1944. They asked these people to take the same personality test 25 years later. In general, they found that these people showed very little personality change over the 25-year period. The researchers also gave the same personality test to a group of students in 1969 at the same time that the older group retook the test. This allowed the researchers to compare the personality scores of the two age groups. They found large differences between the scores of the older (middle-aged) group and those of the younger groups. These two findings led them to conclude that personality is stable from young adulthood to middle age, but that significant personality changes occur between generations. If this is true, then we would have to argue that "generation gaps" may be very real and not just imagined differences between parents and their children. This idea was given even greater support when the researchers asked the group of middle-aged adults who were retaking the personality test to indicate how they thought they had answered the questions when they were in college. Surprisingly, the middle-aged adults thought they had answered the questions much differently when they were in college than they actually had. What was most revealing was that the answers the middle-aged adults thought they had given were very similar to those given by the current students. It seems that the middle-aged adults were familiar with the way adolescents and young adults would answer the test. This is not surprising, since most of the middle-aged adults were themselves the parents of adolescents and young adults at the time they retook the personality test. But it is very surprising to find that the adults thought they had given the answers given by current students when the adults were themselves of college age.

This study leads us to suspect that there are generational changes in personality. The middle-aged adults were more like each other than like the adolescents and young adults, and vice versa. The study also tells us that the middle-aged group was aware of the changes in the younger group and even thought that they themselves had been like the younger group when they were young adults, despite the evidence that the middle-aged adults were never like the younger group in personality.

Research such as the Woodruff and Birren study tells us that the relationship between age and personality is very complex. There is evidence that supports the idea of personality continuity, that is, that personality is rather stable over relatively long periods of adulthood. But there is also evidence that personality is strongly influenced by generational forces and thus is constantly being altered by social and historical forces.

Some longitudinal studies are now attempting to study more fully the relationship between age and personality, but the nature of the longitudinal study prohibits any quick results. Most of the studies that have reported on this subject have been able to make comparisons between personality testing only at very young ages and at middle age, but this will change as the subjects of these studies grow older. At present we must conclude that it seems most likely that personality remains more or less stable for most people throughout the lifespan, but that there are probably generational or cohort effects on the establishment of personality (Schaie and Parham, 1976). It also seems likely that there are some social effects on personality, effects that probably produce changes of one sort or another. Social influences such as marriage, divorce, childbearing, education, and death of loved ones almost surely affect personality. But how and to what extent remains unknown.

The Self-images of Older People

Most research on the self-perceptions of older people shows that most older people view themselves positively. At least in comparison with younger respondents, older people display a high degree of satisfaction with themselves and few cases of negative self-image (Trimakas and Nicolay, 1974). As would be expected, people who are financially secure and living in their own homes have more positive self-images than individuals who are poor or live in institutions. Older people do not seem overly concerned with age-related changes in their appearance. Sample surveys that ask older people to state what they most dislike about growing older find that very few mention changes in physical appearance. Concern with bodily appearance may well be heavily influenced by generational pressures, and we may find that in the future some cohorts of older people will show greater concern with their physical appearance. This does not mean that older people today are not concerned with their appearance. Most studies of institutionalized older people report that both men and women are quite concerned that their hair be cut and/or set at regular intervals and that other cosmetic amenities be provided. But this interest in proper grooming is distinct from the question of whether older people are greatly concerned with the changes that age has caused in their appearance. Older people are concerned about grooming but are not very concerned about age-related changes in appearance.

Hess and Bradshaw (1970) found that self-concept improved with age, but they also discovered that what people would like to be (their "ideal self") also increased. If this information proves to be generally accurate, we would conclude that people tend to set their personal standards higher with age; that is, the more people achieve, the more they would like to achieve.

The self-concepts of older people are related to how they feel about being old. We know that different age groups very often have different ideas as to what chronological age is young, middle-aged, or old. A number of studies have found that young people tend to think of old age as beginning at an earlier age than that at which older people think it begins. Students very often report that they think old age begins at 60, whereas older people often report that they think it begins at 70 or later. Peters (1971) found that sex and social class also influence people's perceptions of the onset of old age. Women saw old age beginning earlier than men did, and working-class people saw old age beginning earlier than middle-class people did. Drevenstedt (1976) found that both age and sex influence people's perceptions of various stages of adulthood. Young males saw both men and women achieving young adulthood, middle age, and old age at lower ages, while young females reported slightly higher ages. Older males reported lower ages for the beginning of each stage of adulthood than older females, but both older men and older women reported higher ages than either young males or young females. All the respondents, young and old, male and females, perceived women as reaching each of the stages of adulthood slightly earlier than males.

More important than age and sex differences in perceptions of the onset of the stages of adulthood is the remarkable agreement among all groups concerning the broad outline of the stages of adulthood. What is not known is how these perceptions influence people's behavior as they move through the life cycle. If most people perceive distinct adult stages such as young adulthood, middle age, and old age, what does this mean in terms of how people view themselves as they move from one stage to another, and what do they think it means in terms of how they are expected to behave, how they interact with members of other age groups, and so on? Social age may be an artificial, contrived, or arbitrary definition, but as long as age is thought of as real it will be real in its consequences. What this means is that people will behave "young" or "old" if they accept these terms as real elements of their self-concept.

The significance of self-concept lies in its relationship to life satisfaction. Life satisfaction, in turn, is closely related to well-being, the condition of being happy, free from serious worries, and socially well adjusted. Life satisfaction in an older population is often measured by the Life Satisfaction Index (Neugarten et al., 1961; Adams, 1969). Life satisfaction scores have been correlated with self-images, and it has been found that people who describe themselves as old often have low life satisfaction scores, whereas older people who are well educated, have high occupational status, are married, and have friends and a pleasant environment have high life satisfaction scores (Larson, 1978).

Summary

While it is true that many people lose some of the efficiency of their sense organs as they age, many of these declines are of only marginal significance, and other losses can be reduced or corrected in various ways. In any case, most declines in sensory functioning are tolerable, and most people of any age retain effective use of their basic senses. Our mental and perceptual abilities may, likewise, lose some of the efficiency of earlier years, perhaps because we are less likely to maintain some of our mental skills throughout the adult years, during which we face relatively few mental testing situations. Nevertheless, we can expect to retain these capacities throughout life.

The types of personalities that are found within any society are formed by a large number of factors, one of which is the factor of generation. Any given individual may show considerable personality stability over the lifespan, but there appear to be significant personality changes between one generation and the next. This being the case, we can expect to find that the personality composition of the older cohorts in a society will always be in a state of flux.

At any rate there is no evidence that age per se has any great effect on personality development, and there certainly is no evidence to indicate that older people are any more similar to each other in personality than members of any other age group.

SELECTED REFERENCES

Doris N. Auerbach and Richard L. Levenson, "Second Impressions: Attitude Change in College Students Toward the Elderly," *Gerontologist* 17 (1977): 362–366.

Paul B. Baltes and K. Warner Schaie, "Aging and IQ—the Myth of the Twilight Years," *Psychology Today,* 7, no. 10 (1974): 35–38, 40.

James E. Birren, *The Psychology of Aging* (Englewood Cliffs, N.J.: Prentice-Hall, 1964).

James E. Birren and K. Warner Schaie, eds., *Handbook of the Psychology of Aging* (New York: Van Nostrand Reinhold, 1977).

Jack Botwinick, *Aging and Behavior* (New York: Springer, 1973).

Jean Drevenstedt, "Perceptions of Onsets of Young Adulthood, Middle-Age, and Old Age," *Journal Of Gerontology* 31, no. 1 (1976): 53–57.

National Council on the Aging, *The Myth and Reality of Aging in America* (Washington, D.C.: National Council on the Aging, 1975).

Bernice L. Neugarten, ed., *Middle Age and Aging* (Chicago: University of Chicago Press, 1968).

George R. Peters, "Self-Conceptions of the Aged, Age Identification, and Aging," *Gerontologist* 11, no. 4 (1971): 69–73.

Suzanne Reichard, Florine Livson, and Paul G. Peterson, *Aging and Personality* (New York: Wiley, 1962).

K. Warner Schaie and Iris A. Parham, "Stability of Adult Personality Traits: Fact or Fable?" *Journal of Personality and Social Psychology* 34, no. 1 (1976): 146–158.

Diana S. Woodruff and James E. Birren, "Age Changes and Cohort Differences in Personality," *Developmental Psychology* 6, no. 2 (1972): 252–259.

CHAPTER **6**

Work, Retirement, and Leisure

Overview

The Meaning of Work and Retirement

Mandatory Retirement

Attitudes Toward Retirement

Women and Retirement

Age Discrimination in Employment

Adjustment to Retirement

Aging and Leisure

Summary

Overview. In an industrial society a person's occupation is very important, not only because it provides income but also because it contributes to the development of the worker's self-concept and view of the world. If the role of the worker is so important, how is it possible to have a system of retirement that does not cause the worker to undergo a transitional crisis? There is no single answer to this question, although some studies have found that some people's orientation to their work changes as they age, even before retirement (Cohn, 1979); others make the transition by reorienting themselves to family, leisure, and voluntary roles. In the United States today retirement is not universally viewed with dislike—many people are quite willing to retire, and if their retirement income will be adequate, many are anxious to retire.

The Meaning of Work and Retirement

One of the most important aspects of aging is the question of retirement. But retirement as a social phenomenon cannot be understood except in the context of work, because the meaning of retirement is largely an outgrowth of the meaning of work. Much of human life is organized around work; indeed, human existence would be impossible without work. Even societies situated in relatively lush environments must perform some work, at least to the extent of gathering the fruits and vegetables provided by nature. And most societies, even relatively uncomplicated ones, must work to transform the products provided by nature into the necessities or amenities of life.

Work has different meanings in different societies, and the meaning of work can change markedly within a particular society over time. Friedmann and Orbach (1974, p. 616) note, for example, that people in preindustrial societies performed work without much concern for a regular schedule; that is, they worked when it was necessary and were idle the rest of the time. They quote the historian E. P. Thompson as saying that the work pattern of preindustrial peoples "was one of alternate bouts of intense labour and of idleness," depending on the time of the year and the needs of family and community. One of the outstanding features of industrial society is that it has scheduled work as a regular activity. This has led to the punching of time clocks, the nine to five job, and the forty-hour week. According to social reformers and many social scientists, the creation of the industrial system of production has alienated the worker from the work process, a situation that is assumed to have been absent in preindustrial modes of production. If this is true, then the meaning of work varies from one historical period to another and probably from one society to another. And if the meaning of work is cross-culturally and historically variable, it is likely that the meaning of work varies throughout the life cycle and that work means different things for younger workers than for older workers.

Are most workers in industrialized countries alienated from their work? Certainly, some workers are dissatisfied with their work role, but this does not appear to be the case for most workers. Blauner (1966, p. 474) reviewed various attitude surveys of American workers and concluded that "the evidence shows that in the numerous samples of the labor force which have been interviewed, more than 80 percent indicate general job satisfaction." Blauner also found that workers in high-status occupations (such as professionals and managers) were more satisfied with their jobs than those in low-status occupations (such as unskilled or semiskilled operatives); however, the majority of workers in all occupations and industries were found to be satisfied with their jobs. It should also be mentioned that satisfaction with the work role is not limited to occupational settings outside the home. Lopata (1971), in *Occupation: Housewife,* found that most of the women she interviewed rated the roles of mother, wife, and housewife as very important and rated as very low such roles as career woman or worker (meaning one who works outside the home). These responses were obtained from women who had some experience working outside the home—96 percent had worked for wages at one time or another. The most reasonable conclusion would appear to be that workers, whether employed outside the home or as housewives, are generally satisfied with their occupational roles.

The fact that most people are satisfied with their occupational roles does not necessarily mean that they invariably build their lives around their jobs. Friedmann and Orbach (1974, p. 613) argue that "work does not seem to take precedence over other life areas for most workers." In fact, they say, most of the evidence indicates that job aspirations peak in the middle years of adulthood, although this peaking seems to occur later for white-collar and professional workers than for blue-collar or manual workers.

The meaning of work is an antecedent to the meaning of retirement. One might predict that workers would look forward anxiously to the day they could retire if work were meaningless or if it were looked upon with dislike; on the other hand, if most workers find satisfaction in their work, it would seem reasonable for them to dislike the onset of retirement. During the 1940s and 1950s, in fact, there was widespread opposition to retirement, and even today there is considerable concern about the injustice of older people's being "pushed-aside" or "placed on the shelf" to make room for younger people.

Mandatory Retirement

Palmore (1972) has summarized the arguments for and against a system of mandatory retirement. He says that compulsory retirement is an easy system to administer because no judgments or evaluations of particular individuals have to be made. In this sense, then, a system of universal compulsory retirement would treat everyone equally. Also, mandatory retirement at a predetermined age allows both employer and employee to plan ahead for retirement. Because workers are retired mandatorily, businesses must provide a pension system. Compulsory retirement also reduces competition among workers for jobs, allows younger workers to be hired and promoted, and allows the older worker to step aside gracefully without having to admit to any occupational inadequacies or health problems.

On the other hand, it would also be possible to have a system of flexible retirement that could serve many of the same functions as a compulsory system without discriminating against an entire group of people simply because of their age. Most people are effective workers after age 65; in fact, many older people have skills that are needed in many occupational settings. In addition, if more older people are allowed to continue working, the financial strain on social security and private pension systems will be alleviated. For people who are able and want to continue working after an arbitrary retirement age, life will be more enjoyable; and when they decide to retire they will be able to do so with the knowledge that they are in command of their own lives.

There is a widespread sentiment against a system of mandatory retirement in the United States, and in recent years Rep. Claude Pepper has led a campaign to abolish mandatory retirement at the federal level. When the National Council on the Aging (1975) asked a random sample of Americans whether they agreed or disagreed with the statement "Nobody should be forced to retire because of age, if he wants to continue working and is still able to do a good job," an overwhelming majority—86 percent—agreed. Just as significant is the fact that there was no difference between the responses of adults ages 18–64 and those of adults age 65 and over, which indicates that the issue of mandatory retirement is not viewed as relevant only to the older population.

The national survey also asked people who were 65 years of age or older and were not working whether they had looked forward to stopping work. The responses were very evenly divided between those who had looked forward to stopping work and those who had not. When these people were asked to mention the things they missed most about their jobs, about three-fourths said that they missed the money and the people at work. A majority said that they missed the work itself, the feeling of being useful, things happening around them, and the respect of others.

Even if most people are opposed to mandatory retirement because of age, and even if those who are retired report that they miss some elements of the occupational world, it does not necessarily follow that most people are opposed to their own retirement. A number of different studies have reported that most people in the United States have retired voluntarily. In the study mentioned previously, 61 percent of the retired people over age 65 reported that they had retired voluntarily, while the majority of the rest (37 percent of this group) reported that they had been forced to retire. Women were more likely to have retired voluntarily than men, as were higher income and more highly educated respondents. Whites were more likely to have retired voluntarily than blacks. The interviewers also asked these retired people what their reaction would be if they were asked to come back to work or to take on a new job that suited them well. Most of these people indicated that they were not interested in employment, either because they preferred retirement or because they were physically unable to return to work; 71 percent said they would not even consider going back to work. Only 11 percent said they would definitely consider doing so.

Even though many people have retired even when they were not required to do so, and thus are technically classified as voluntary retirees, many of these people were forced to retire by poor health. It is possible that truly voluntary retirement will become much more common in the future if workers are assured of adequate retirement incomes. Pollman (1971) found that in a group of early retirees who had been automobile workers the availability of an adequate retirement income was the number one reason for early retirement.

Poor health was the primary reason for about one-fourth of the retirees, but this reason was a distant second to availability of an adequate retirement income. This study is consistent with a number of other studies and has lead Friedmann and Orbach (1974, p. 616) to conclude that "by the middle of the 1960s American studies were consistently reporting a favorable outlook toward retirement among manual workers and many categories of white-collar workers provided they had an adequate income."

The changing attitude toward retirement in American society might best be characterized as a shift from a "push" to a "pull" phenomenon. Traditionally, it was believed that retirement represented expulsion of the worker from an occupation against his or her wishes, so that he or she was pushed into retirement. Today, by contrast, it appears that the role of retirement has achieved a degree of social legitimation, so that when adequate retirement income is available an increasing number of people are pulled into, or attracted to, retirement.

Real-life situations, of course, are often much more complex than can be depicted in survey studies, as is illustrated in the excerpt (pages 124–125) from an article that appeared in the *Los Angeles Times* on June 30, 1978.

Obviously, Sergeant Buckland is not a clear-cut case of a person being either pushed or pulled into retirement, but elements of both forces are present. He is being pushed and pulled by a relatively high retirement income, although he is also being pushed by the rumor of a future decline in retirement benefits. He is being pulled into retirement because of the turmoil surrounding his occupation, but he may also feel pushed by the legal and professional changes that have left him a relic of former times. Even though Sergeant Buckland probably represents an unusual retirement situation because of the glamor and fantasy associated with his Elliott Ness type of occupation, he probably exemplifies the ambivalent feelings that many people have toward retirement.

Attitudes Toward Retirement

It is quite possible that different occupational groups hold different attitudes and exhibit different behavior with regard to retirement. Some research (Atchley, 1971; Rowe, 1973; Rowe, 1976) has found that professional groups, such as physicians, college professors, and scientists, have distinct approaches to retirement, perhaps because they view their jobs as vocations. Many individuals in these groups have been shown to maintain their occupational involvement even after they have been officially retired. Rowe (1976) found that the majority of retired scientists in his sample continued to spend time on scientific research, and this was true no matter how long the scientists had been retired. Those scientists who were between the ages of 76 and 94 were as deeply engaged in research as those who were in the 65–70 and 71–75 age groups.

That some people will not retire from the occupational world even if they could afford to do so is illustrated by the Sixty-Five Club at the University of

"BUCK" GIVES UP BADGE, NOT THE HAT

29-Year Officer Retires to Avoid Prop. 13 Pension Cut

BY PENELOPE MCMILLAN

Carrying the gunbelt he never wore, Sgt. Charles F. Buckland walked down a long corridor to end a 29-year career with the Los Angeles Police Department—a career ending now partly because of Proposition 13.

The bony, blue-eyed policeman with one missing finger wore, as usual, his size 15 black shoes, a shapeless suit that seemed to struggle against his 6-foot, 3½-inch frame, and of course, his straw hat with the brown band.

The last of the old Robbery Division's fabled "Hat Squad"—a team of five detectives that 20 years ago did the "tough stuff" police don't boast about anymore—Buckland put the gunbelt on Lt. David Musil's desk. Very slowly, he extracted Badge 1016 from his wallet.

"SWAT took the place of men like Buckland," Robbery-Homicide Division Capt. Gene Rock said recently. "We didn't need SWAT in those days. Buckland did it all by himself."

"Put your name, rank, serial number and division assignment on that card please," Musil said efficiently. Buckland did so, and Musil said he should take his badge and ID to Personnel Records to complete the procedure.

"Normally, we have 40 or 50 retiring this time of year," Musil said. But in the wake of Proposition 13's passage, 176 officers applied for retirement this month. The rumor in the department is that future pensions will be affected by removal of cost-of-living increases and the possible abolishment of higher-paying bonus positions, such as the Investigator 3 position Buckland held. He was one of 47 in that rank alone to leave.

"It's never going to be easy to go,"

Buckland said, "but there's so much turmoil, maybe it's easier now." Buckland retires with a pension at 67% of his pay, meaning he will receive approximately $1,600 a month.

The 57-year-old officer walked back down the corridor, saying "Howdy" and "Yep," in his laconic, John Wayne-like manner to those who greeted him and who asked if Thursday was his last day.

From the time he joined the department in June, 1949, Buckland said, he always wanted to be "a hat," because they were the elite, the ones who were sent to deal with the most dangerous suspects.

"One of those guys walked in from the Hat Squad [and] you thought God had come in the room. Everybody froze," Buckland said, adding, "Of course, that kind of appealed to me. I patterned myself after 'em."

Even though the Hat Squad long since has been replaced by what he calls "sophisticated groups" because "we play by a different set of rules today," he still wears the hat, indoors and out.

"I like the shade it gives," he said simply. Like clockwork, every year he has bought two brown Stetsons for winter and two straw hats for summer. "I don't change."

Aside from achieving his goal of becoming one of the Squad, Buckland won the LAPD's highest honor, the Medal of Valor, in 1955 and over the years became the department's specialist in solving truck hijack cases. He is described by those who know him as fearless, hardworking and totally committed to his job.

"Truth of the matter is, I didn't ever figure on goin'," he said. "But look at it this way. I would like to stay. But that's bein' selfish. I have to take my wife into consideration." If Proposition 13 cuts eventually reduce pensions, that would affect her widow's benefits, he continued.

"She'll probably outlive me. That's the stats in this country."

Buckland, who is never addressed by his first name, always as "Buck" or Buckland, has been married for 36 years and lives in Highland Park. One of his two children, Charles Buckland Jr., is a patrol officer in Hollenbeck Division.

Capt. Jack Donahoe, he recalled, finally asked him to join the Hat Squad in 1958, and as far as Buckland's concerned, those were the good old days.

"They never smiled," he said. "You'd see three of 'em standing on the corner in suits, hats, no one smiling. People figured they were thugs right out of the East Coast, you know?

"In those days, when you'd develop a suspect you didn't have to get a warrant, he continued. "You just went and let yourself into his house and if he wasn't there you just sat there and waited. You didn't care how you solved the case as long as it was solved. You couldn't have a squad like that today. They just wouldn't allow it."

Laws changed, suspects got more rights, and, as Buckland put it, there were "sobsisters pleading they (suspects) were being dealt with severely. Twenty-five years ago, you sent Robbery after 'em and nobody pleaded their case."

"I'll give you a little example of what I pulled," he added and began a story of a robbery he solved, of how he and his partner dealt with the suspect.

"We don't even handcuff him," Buckland said, "and he knows there's only one reason: we're going to kill him and we don't

want marks to show. We drive out there to the N. Broadway St. bridge. We pick the guy up and by the time you have him hanging over that bridge by his heels he's talking to ya. You think they don't talk, but they do."

Retirement won't be easy, he said. "Capt. Donahoe committed suicide after he retired. My first partner, he committed suicide after he retired, my last partner that retired hung himself. I had to go over, cut him down. You can go on and on."

Buckland became silent for a moment. "I'm going to work on photography," he said. "The best thing a person can do is develop outside interests." Buckland also owns 42 acres of citrus groves in Texas and a one-third interest in a mobile-home park in Hesperia.

"For 20 years, I've been the center of every big development in the department, right? I walk out of here and if I come back Monday nobody'll even go to coffee with me. Nobody wants to talk to somebody that's retired. That's the way it goes."

Buckland reached Personnel Records and stood in line, his hands folded in front of him.

"How many years do you have on?" asked Starlette Soniega, a senior clerk, without looking up.

"Twenty-nine," Buckland said jovially. The clerk filled out a record sheet, put the ID and the badge in a small plastic bag, handed him a retirement certificate and said, still not looking at him:

"We're out of badges (retirement badges). There'll be a three- to five-month wait. We'll mail it to you."

"Well, that's it," Buckland said quietly, and walked away, adjusting his hat.

California's Hastings College of the Law. Hastings has a policy of hiring distinguished professors who have retired from other colleges and universities, and about one-third of the law school faculty is composed of people who are past the usual retirement age. These people are not honorary faculty members but full-time professors who teach a normal schedule and are paid a full salary. While some of the older faculty members continue to do research and write articles and books, others have decreased these activities in order to concentrate on teaching. The advantage that Hastings seems to have over other law schools is that it has created a mixture of younger and older faculty members, with the result that faculty members with diverse ages offer students a variety of perspectives, a diversity of experience, and a mixture of professional orientations. According to one of the faculty members, "Too many law schools have too heavy a concentration of people with too little time for the classroom." The younger professors are concerned with establishing themselves professionally by devoting considerable time to research, publication, and/or the private practice of law. The older professors, who are already professionally established, can afford to devote most of their attention to classroom teaching. The advantages provided to the law school by the presence of the Sixty-Five Club members in no way obscures the contributions of faculty members who are interested in establishing themselves by engaging in other professional activities. The older faculty members recognize the inherent advantages of a diverse faculty; as one commented, "It is useful to have some people around who are writing and practicing and the like. I wouldn't want it all one way or the other" (Stix, 1977). Hastings seems to have discovered that a faculty of various ages can provide an educational institution with complementary skills, talents, and interests.

Women and Retirement

Many areas of social science research have tended to focus on men, while giving women less attention. This is especially true of research on the work and retirement roles of women. Retirement has been viewed by many social gerontologists as an extremely important event in the aging process, but very often it has been treated as a matter of importance only for men. It has been assumed that retirement is much less of a problem for women that for men, partly because widowhood has been regarded as the major transition for women in later life (Beeson, 1975). For women who work outside the home, however, the work orientation is often greater than for men (Streib and Schneider, 1971), and many women carry a high positive work orientation into retirement. But even though the work role may be very important for many women, this does not necessarily indicate that they will be anxious about retirement or that they will have a difficult time adjusting to it or even dislike it (Atchley, 1976; Fox, 1977).

Women who do not spend most of their adult lives working outside the home are faced with a form of mandatory retirement that is very subtle but nonetheless real. The traditional role of housewife is unique in modern industrial societies because it does not come under the normal rules of retirement found in occupational settings outside the home. In American society the housewife has been largely taken for granted and regarded as an attachment to her husband. The housewife typically has no private pension plan, and unless she has worked outside the home for enough years to qualify, she is not covered by social security. She has usually been eligible for some retirement benefits because of her husband's employment—if she meets specific requirements.

In occupational terms, however, the housewife experiences a gradual retirement because of a loss of many of the former duties associated with the role. Lopata (1971, p. 72) found that "unless she is a member of the three upper social classes and involved in societally active roles, the woman sixty years of age or over focuses strongly upon the role of housewife." The women she interviewed usually defined the housewife role as including such things as cleaning house, preparing and serving meals, raising children, helping the children with their schoolwork, teaching the children moral values, and so on. By the time the children have become adults and no longer need constant attention, the housewife has been, in effect, partially retired. When a 61 year old mother of four, all of whom were grown, was asked what her housewife role consisted of, all she could state was "keeping the house clean and cooking" (Lopata, 1971, p. 72). Unlike members of most other occupational groups, the American housewife is gradually retired from the major portion of her work role, but never fully retired.

Age Discrimination in Employment

Most people are heavily dependent on wages and salaries for the economic support of themselves and their dependents. In addition, their occupation or profession determines their social status and the amount of power they can exert, as well as contributing to the development of self-concept. In an industrial society employment is a major determinant of quality of life and life satisfaction, and the tenets of a liberal society proclaim that every individual must be free to aspire to any occupation or profession for which he or she is qualified, that entrance into any field must not be blocked by arbitrary or artificial standards. While most people are aware that a person's race, sex, religion, or ethnic origin are irrelevant in evaluating whether he or she is qualified to enter a particular field of study or to perform in any employment setting, attitudes about the relevance of age are much more ambivalent. In the United States federal legislation has prohibited employment discrimination because of age since 1967, but until 1978 only people between the ages of 40 and 64 were covered by the law. In 1978 coverage was extended through the age of 70. The Age Discrimination Act makes it illegal to fail to hire someone because of age, to discharge someone because of age, or to otherwise classify workers or discriminate in wages and benefits because of age. There are some exceptions to the law, such as tenured college professors (until 1982), some business executives, air traffic controllers, law enforcement officers, and fire fighters, who can be mandatorily retired at earlier ages.

While the laws against age discrimination in employment will probably be of some benefit to people who prefer to continue working beyond the normal retirement age, at present these laws will not prevent a capable person from being arbitrarily retired at age 70. The political question remains as to why anyone of any age should be discriminated against in employment solely on the basis of age and irrespective of his or her ability to do the job.

The outlook for employment opportunities for older workers is much brighter than in the recent past. By 1990 the United States labor force will be growing much more slowly than in the last decade, and workers will be in a much better bargaining position with employers. Citibank of New York (1978) estimates that by the late 1980s the number of people entering the job market in one year will be down to about 1 million, or about half the number entering each year during the 1970s. If the American economy expands at the rate that is generally anticipated, the increased demand for labor will make older workers more valuable to employers, and the older worker may have more options available with regard to continuing employment or easing into retirement by continuing to work part time. The other side of the coin is that the decrease in the number of workers relative to the number eligible for retirement benefits may cause changes in government policies or the emergence of a new social expectation that workers will continue to work at their jobs as long as they are able to do so. In this way older workers would not only be supplying scarce labor power but would also be alleviating some of the financial burdens of private and public pension systems.

Adjustment to Retirement

Retirement has often been regarded by social researchers as something to be avoided at all costs. According to Friedmann and Orbach (1974), retirement has been blamed for a variety of physical and social ills. Some people believe retirement can be fatal, and one often hears of persons who have died shortly after retirement. It appears, however, that aside from people who retire because of poor health, there is no unusual association between retirement and death. Perhaps the fact that people in poor health often must retire—and of course have a higher-than-average mortality rate—has led to the association between retirement and death. But it certainly does not mean that retirement *causes* poor health or death. A study of early retirement among automobile workers is fairly typical of the relationship between health and retirement: Whereas workers who felt that their health was declining were most likely to plan for early retirement, those who retired early reported that their health had improved since retirement (Barfield and Morgan, 1969). Streib and Schneider (1971) also found that retirement did not lead to any deterioration of health, and when they asked respondents, "Do you think stopping work has made your health better or worse?" most replied that retirement had had no effect on their health. About one-third of the respondents said that retirement had improved their health, while only about 3 or 4 percent felt that their health was worse. An epidemiological study of nearly 4,000 rubber tire workers in the United States also found no excess of mortality after retirement (Haynes, McMichael, and Tyrola, 1978).

Physical health is not harmed by retirement, nor is there any reason to believe that mental health (Friedmann and Orbach, 1974) or social relations are likely to deteriorate because of retirement. Atchley (1976) reports that most people experience no change in number of contacts with friends after retirement, and although some people increase their friendship contacts, only a few decrease them. Most people are as active in various organizations as they were prior to retirement. Relations between a wife and a husband are not generally disrupted by retirement, although couples whose marriages were unsatisfactory before retirement may be affected more than happily married couples (Heyman and Jeffers, 1968). Men have a tendency to become involved in household tasks after retirement; Kerekhoff (1966) found that some working-class wives resented this infringement on the tasks and territory that they have always controlled.

Aging and Leisure

Leisure may be defined as time that is controlled by the individual and can be expended in a manner determined by personal preferences. Activities that are performed out of obligation or necessity thus are not usually classified as leisure activities, whereas activities chosen to fill a person's free time may be so classified. Retirement usually results in a great increase in the amount of time that can be devoted to leisure activities.

Whether retired persons can adjust adequately to the role of a career participant in leisure pursuits has been questioned by Miller (1965). He argues that American society has always valued work highly, that most people (especially males) have defined work as a meaningful activity and have derived their social identity and status largely from their occupation, and that their self-image is based on their relationship to that occupation. In other words, the work role is a central element in the lives of most people, and that role provides essential social-psychological benefits.

Upon retirement, a worker loses his or her work role, and in many cases it is expected that leisure activities will compensate for this loss. Perhaps the time-filling function of a job could be replaced by a leisure career, but what about the social-psychological components of the work role? Miller notes that leisure has traditionally been linked to the work role in the United States. By this he means that leisure activities are valued not for themselves but for the part they play in allowing people to work better. Leisure activities are given social value and legitimation because it is felt that people need a certain amount of relaxation from their jobs and that after relaxing they will be able to do a better job. If leisure activities are given social approval and acceptance because of an assumed relationship to work, then the retired person who devotes himself or herself to leisure activities may face a crisis of legitimacy. This presents a problem, Miller suggests, because the retired person may have difficulty developing a positive self-image through participation in leisure activities unless such activities are granted a reasonable degree of social approval and acceptance apart from a work role. In effect, Miller questions whether a leisure orientation can allow a retired person to lead a meaningful life and maintain a positive self-image.

It may be that leisure must be defined more clearly before one can determine the social value or degree of legitimacy assigned to participation in various activities. Gordon, Gaitz, and Scott (1976) have developed a continuum of types of leisure activity based on intensity of expressive involvement, that is, the amount of cognitive, emotional, and physical involvement required for participation in a particular activity. High-intensity activities require a greater expenditure of energy; they demand focused attention and a high level of sensory stimulation. Using these criteria, Gordon and associates have divided leisure activities into five major types.

At the lowest level of expressive involvement are activities classified as "relaxation." At this level a person is resting, napping, or just being alone. This level of activity is actually social inactivity, and while it would be acceptable as an occasional involvement, it probably would not be granted legitimacy as a career orientation in retirement.

The second level of involvement is "diversion." It includes reading, watching television, socializing and entertaining, and most hobbies and spectator sports. Although this level requires more activity than relaxation, it is not very demanding and would probably gain only slight acceptance as a career orientation for a retired person.

The third level, the "developmental" level, is more demanding than the previous two, especially with regard to cognitive involvement. This type of activity includes serious reading, traveling, participation in voluntary associations, physical exercise, and attendance at cultural events. It is quite likely that developmental activities could be regarded as an appropriate career orientation for a retired person. Most of these activities require cognitive, emotional, and physical activity, and a person could become highly involved in them.

A fourth level of leisure activity is "creativity." It includes the kinds of activities that many people pursue as full-time careers: painting, dancing, writing, analysis, and so on. But one person's occupation may be another's leisure activity. For the retired person, creative activities may present no problem of social acceptance because the possible relationship to traditional work roles is more obvious.

The last stage of expressive involvement, and the one that requires the greatest amount of cognitive, emotional, and physical activity, is called "sensual transcendence." Activities at this level include highly competitive sports and aggressive interaction, as well as intense dancing, sexual activity, and ecstatic religious involvement. At this level of expressive involvement there is probably less social acceptance and approval for the retired person because of the high degree of involvement required and the ephemeral relationship of these activities to traditional work roles.

The researchers found that even though older persons very often had more leisure, "the older the respondent, the lower the level of general leisure activity" (Gordon, Gaitz, and Scott, 1976, p. 326). Lower levels of leisure involvement were found in activities that are relatively high in levels of expressive activity, especially those engaged in outside the home. There were fewer differences between age groups in activities that are relatively low in expressive involvement, for example, watching television, spectator sports, entertaining in the home, cultural consumption, and participation in voluntary associations. The researchers concluded that "what may be given up in the later years are the strenuous and outside-the-home activities, not the moderate-intensity and home-centered forms of sociability and media-based symbolic interaction."

It is possible, as Miller (1965) has pointed out, that older people's leisure activities may be restricted by the "portent of embarrassment," the fear of embarrassment as a result of a low performance level. For example, older persons may be unwilling to play tennis if they are afraid they will not be able to play capably. Or a person may decide to give up a particular activity if he or she feels the portent of embarrassment. This is an important concept that needs to be explored further because it predicts that older people will be forced into activities with low levels of expressive involvement by fear of failure in activities that are high in cognitive, emotional, and physical involvement.

Summary

For most people, working to earn a living is a fact of life, and given the inevitability of working, it is probably fortunate that most workers are reasonably satisfied with their jobs. Most people, however, are not opposed to the idea of their own retirement by the time they approach retirement age, at least if they are convinced that they will have an adequate income after retirement.

Even though workers may look forward to their own retirement, this does not mean that they support the idea of mandatory retirement at some arbitrary age; even young adults disagree with the concept of mandatory retirement. Although the Age Discrimination Act provides legal protection for most workers until the age of 70, a truly nondiscriminatory system will not be available until discrimination is illegal at any age.

When a worker retires he or she is usually able to devote more attention and time to leisure pursuits. But if people are to gain full satisfaction from leisure participation it is essential that American society grant full legitimacy to leisure activities. Americans have always supported a strong work ethic, and leisure pursuits have been devalued in comparison to work. Perhaps the present generation of retired people will be the first to engage in leisure activities as a legitimate life style.

SELECTED REFERENCES

Richard E. Barfield and James N. Morgan, *Early Retirement: the Decision and the Experience* (Ann Arbor, Mich.: University of Michigan, Institute for Social Research, 1969).

Eugene A. Freidmann and Harold L. Orbach, "Adjustment to Retirement," in *American Handbook of Psychiatry,* 2nd ed., ed. Silvano Arieti (New York: Basic Books, 1974), 1, 609–645.

Chad Gordon, Charles M. Gaitz, and Judith Scott, "Leisure and Lives: Personal Expression across the Life Span," in *Handbook of Aging and the Social Sciences,* eds. Robert H. Binstock and Ethel Shanas (New York: Van Nostrand Reinhold, 1976), pp. 310–341.

Alan C. Kerckhoff, "Family Patterns and Morale in Retirement," in *Social Aspects of Aging,* eds. Ida H. Simpson and John C. McKinney (Durham, N.C.: Duke University Press, 1966), pp. 173–194.

Helena Znaniecki Lopata, *Occupation: Housewife* (New York: Oxford University Press, 1971).

Stephen J. Miller, "The Social Dilemma of the Aging Leisure Participant," in *Older People and Their Social Worlds,* eds. Arnold M. Rose and Warren A. Peterson (Philadelphia: F. A. Davis, 1965), pp. 77–92.

A. William Pollman, "Early Retirement: A Comparison of Poor Health to other Retirement Factors," *Journal of Gerontology* 26 (1971): 41–45.

Gordon F. Streib and Clement J. Schneider, *Retirement in American Society* (Ithaca, N.Y.: Cornell University Press, 1971).

Social Theories of Aging

Overview. Social scientists attempt to explain social organization by developing and testing theories. In the early stages of knowledge about a subject there are usually a number of distinct theories. Social gerontology has been fortunate in that several theoretical frameworks have been developed to try to explain the social process of aging. The two traditional theories, activity theory and disengagement theory, have been subjected to a wide variety of tests by social researchers. In addition, two newer theories, age stratification theory and phenomenological theory, have served as frameworks for research from fresh perspectives. All of these theories are still vibrant and productive of research ideas, and it is through the competition of such perspectives as these that social gerontology will be enriched and a better understanding of the aging process will be made possible.

As humans we are biological creatures, and as biological creatures we age. We are born, and immediately we begin moving toward death. We can say that our biological nature sets the limits of our existence, but it would be a mistake to say that the biological process of aging is the whole of human aging. There is another important dimension of aging, the social dimension.

As humans we are social as well as biological animals. We are different from other animals because we have a sophisticated symbol system, and with those symbols we have created a social world. The symbol systems we learn, especially gestures and spoken and written language, are learned through interaction with and imitation of others. In this socialization process we learn the meaning and value attached to each symbol. We learn, for example, not only that the word *aged* refers to a person advanced in years but also the social value attached to that symbol. The social value attached to a symbol can range from very negative to very positive. Because we are symbol-using animals we are able to think, to assign meaning to things, and to communicate our meaning to others; that is, we do not just accept the world as it is presented to us, but interpret everything we encounter.

The process of aging is one of the things to which people assign meaning, but the meaning of aging is not the same for everyone. As social scientists, we want to learn the meanings people assign to aging. How do different societies interpret the aging process? What are the individual consequences of the social meaning of aging? In order to answer these questions and organize our knowledge about aging, we develop theories of aging.

Social scientists have developed two major social theories of aging. The older of the two is the activity theory; the other is the disengagement theory. Both are general theories of aging that discuss the aging process at a high level of abstraction. They are often regarded as contradictory: If one is correct, the other must be incorrect.

All social theories serve as guides to further research. They organize the knowledge in a specific area and describe how the world operates in that area. In doing this, they also point to questions that are still unanswered and require more research. A social theory often indicates the applied meaning of the theory; that is, it indicates how the social world should be altered or which social policies should be developed to achieve the desired results. The activity and disengagement theories of aging give different descriptions of the social world of aging, and their suggestions for change are also very different.

The Activity Theory

The activity theory is the oldest and probably the most widely accepted social theory of aging. Because it is accepted by social scientists as well as by many of those who work with older people, we can say that activity theory is the dominant paradigm in social gerontology. [A dominant paradigm is a model that is used by most of the people working in a particular field of study (Kuhn, 1962). It supplies researchers and practitioners with a set of common assumptions and a set of rules for practice.]

Activity theory states that social activity is the essence of life, and that this is true for all people at all ages. For the aging person, activity becomes very important because the health and social well-being of the aging person is dependent on remaining active. The activity theorists argue that everyone finds the meaning of life in social interaction: It is through social interaction that we learn what is socially proper and improper, our motivations for doing the things we do, and even our self-image. In other words, our views of the world, of our place in the world, and of ourselves are all secured through social interaction and social activity. From this point of view it is self-evident that social activity is at the very core of our lives. Social activity is so important that our level of social activity can determine whether we age "successfully" or "unsuccessfully." The activity theorists maintain that people must maintain adequate levels of social activity if they are to age successfully. The activity theorists state that aging people should seek active roles. If a person is able to remain socially active, they predict that he or she will achieve a positive self-image and greater life satisfaction.

The Roleless Role

Activity theory was developed by a group of sociologists at the University of Chicago who are known as symbolic interactionists. The application of symbolic interaction theory to social gerontology began with the research and writings of Ernest W. Burgess. Burgess said that "becoming old" was a new development in American society. By this he meant that the process of growing old was being defined in a new way. For one thing, growing old was becoming a normal or typical feature of most people's lives. Life expectancy had increased so much that most people could reasonably expect to become old someday. As a result, older people in American society were becoming a much larger group both in absolute numbers and as a proportion of the total population. They were emerging as a distinct social group, but Burgess argued that the social structure of American society was not capable of absorbing them. The traditional social institutions, such as the work place, the family, and kinship networks and the community, were not accustomed to accepting older people as fully participating members. Burgess saw a situation developing in which older people were being left out, excluded from the normal day-to-day activities of the society. The old were being thrust into a state of social inactivity that Burgess termed the "roleless role" (Burgess, 1960).

The roleless role, according to Burgess, is a situation in which the older person is left with no meaningful social functions to perform. It is very much like Durkheim's (1951) concept of anomie, or normlessness. The individual is left without the support and guidance of the rest of society and is effectively prevented from actively participating in important social activities. Burgess felt that old age did not have to be a negative or roleless role devoid of socially meaningful activity. Instead, the new role of the old could include responsibilities and obligations that would lead to a meaningful existence. If this could be accomplished, old age could be as rewarding as any other stage of the life cycle.

Rose and the Need for Collective Action

But how was a new social role for older people to be created? How can a group go about giving meaning and content to an otherwise roleless role? The answers to these questions were provided by another activity theorist, Arnold Rose. Rose said that older people must begin to establish their new role through their own efforts. The first thing they must do is join together to pursue their own self-interest. Once they are organized, they can work to change the social meaning of being old. Rose felt that older people could change their role by establishing a meaningful and satisfying life style, that is, by creating a new role that is relevant to older persons. The roleless role would disappear, and the new active role of the old would replace it.

Rose felt that there are precedents for the kind of collective social action he was suggesting. He argued, for example, that the adolescent youth of American society have created a meaningful social world with its own standards of behavior, its own modes of dress, and even a distinctive language. The youth culture is very strong—many parents would say too strong—and it certainly provides a meaningful social world that is distinct from the adult world. Rose felt that older persons in American society could create a subculture that would provide meaningful roles and activities just as the youth have created a subculture that is relevant to their unique situation.

There are differences, however, between the situation of the young and that of the old. One extremely important difference is that the youth have a structure for continuous social interaction that facilitates transmission of the youth culture. Schools and voluntary youth organizations bring large numbers of young people together for long periods. There are business establishments and parts of the city (drive-in movies, fast-food restaurants, lovers' lanes, and streets for cruising) that also facilitate interaction among young people. There are means of mass communication (radio stations, youth-oriented publications, etc.) that transmit elements of the youth culture rapidly and to far-flung places. The old do not have these structural advantages, which greatly aid in the creation and perpetuation of a subculture. They have nothing comparable to the compulsory school attendance laws that bring youth together. But they do have the one essential element for the development of a new role: intensive social interaction over a long period. Rose argued that interaction among the old is taking place in many diverse settings, including retirement communities, voluntary associations, and even nursing homes. The roleless role of the old leads them to isolate themselves and become socially inactive. A new and meaningful role for them will lead to social interaction and high levels of social activity, which will permit a meaningful existence and a satisfying life.

The activity theorists maintain that the old must actively seek full integration and participation in American society. To achieve this goal they must develop the organizational structures and situations for social interaction, for it is through interaction that their new role will be created. When they are organized, they will be able to pursue their own interests in competition with other established interest groups. The activity theorists see the new social role of the old and their social advancement as dependent on the activity of older people themselves. No amount of action by others in their behalf can achieve what the old can achieve for themselves. Their interests will be served best if they transform themselves into a self-conscious group. If they are successful, they will secure their position in the established social structure.

The Disengagement Theory

Although the activity theory was the first social theory of aging, it was only with the development of the disengagement theory that the activity theory became recognized as a distinct theory. Indeed, the activity theory was given its name by the disengagement theorists, who developed their theory in conscious and explicit opposition to the activity theory. Disengagement theory was first stated in *Growing Old,* by Elaine Cumming and William E. Henry (1961), the best-known study in the history of social gerontology. *Growing Old* is not the only statement of the disengagement theory, but it remains the single most important document in the development of that theory.

The activity theorists argue that it is essential for people to remain socially active as they grow older, but the disengagement theorists contend that it is both normal and inevitable that people will decrease their level of activity and seek more passive roles as they age. In contrast to the activity theorists, the disengagement theorists do not believe that it is essential for older people to remain either other directed or goal oriented in their activities. They do not state that all older people should be confined to rocking chairs, nor do they suggest an enforced inactive role for the older people. Instead, they adopt a laissez-faire attitude that supports and approves of reduced activity on the part of older persons, and they argue that older persons usually decrease their level of activity as they adapt to the normal changes that are part of the aging process.

Functionalism and Disengagement

The disengagement theorists are heavily influenced by the school of sociological theory known as functionalism or structural functionalism. Functionalism is one of the oldest sociological theories, and variants of functional theory have been used in biology, psychology, and cultural anthropology. The leading exponent of functionalism in American sociology is Talcott Parsons, and he was the first person to apply the theory to the process of aging. Parsons, however, did not use the term *disengagement theory* and perhaps for this reason his contribution is often overlooked. Nevertheless, he played an extremely important role in the development of the theory.

According to Parsons, the United States has a tradition and social structure that favor the young and operate to the disadvantage of older persons. This emphasis on youth is supported by a system of values that Parsons calls instrumental activism, meaning that Americans have a preference for things that work, for structures and ways of operating that produce visible, usually material, results. Things that are useful in a productive sense are valued more highly than things that are not immediately useful. Technological advancements thus are valued more highly than less useful products such as art or music. The construction of a highway or a bridge would presumably be considered more important than the building of an art museum, because the highway or the bridge would be immediately useful. The value system of instrumental activism, also, favors progress and those things which seem to make the society progressive. Again, material progress is usually taken to be real progress because it is visible and useful. Americans regard color television as an advance over black and white television because it is useful, much more so than a change in the structure of the American novel or the development of a new school of poetry.

If it is true, as Parsons argues, that Americans are instrumental activists who favor pragmatic and goal-directed activities, then the structure of American society, reflecting this value preference, is going to be one that favors youth over old age. The reason for this is that instrumental activities usually emphasize physical strength and agility, and young people are stronger and more agile than older people (Parsons, 1960 and 1962).

In *Growing Old* Cumming and Henry built upon the theory laid down by Parsons. They based their statement of the disengagement theory on the findings of a study of aging in a large midwestern city. Their interviews with older adults in that city led them to conclude that "aging is an inevitable mutual withdrawal or disengagement, resulting in decreased interaction between the aging persons and others" (1961, p. 14). The disengagement theorists see people moving toward disengagement as they age; if anyone resists the process, he or she will eventually face total disengagement anyway, at death: Disengagement is inevitable.

The Age Grade System

The disengagement theorists do not view the old as forced into a roleless role; instead, they see them as going through a natural, normal, and inevitable process of social withdrawal. Furthermore, they do not regard the disengagement process as depressing or lamentable. This process is no more negative as a social event than any other life cycle event, for example, marriage. Disengagement and marriage are both social conventions that ensure that certain important social goals are achieved. In both marriage and disengagement individuals are being told to give up some of their old obligations and prerogatives so that they will be free to accept new ones. We have been disengaging throughout our lives as we moved from one stage of life to the next.

The reason we go through life disengaging from the younger stages of the life cycle and accepting more mature roles in their place is that American society has an established age grade system: It establishes different standards of acceptable behavior for members of different age groups. Infants are expected to behave differently than older children; children are expected to behave differently than adults; and so on. These variations in behavior are learned by the members of a culture and then used as a guide for their own behavior. Different standards of behavior are applied to different age groups because the various groups have different rights and obligations. If all the members of the society learn and accept the age grade system, conflict is reduced, especially potential conflict between generations. The age grade system prevents conflict between young people and old people over scarce jobs because the old are allowed and expected to retire and leave the jobs to the young. Potential conflict between middle-aged people and young people is lessened by an age grade system that allows and expects the young to remain in school and leave the jobs to the middle-aged. According to the disengagement theorists, the age grade system works to the benefit of all age groups by reducing conflict over scarce resources and ensuring that the best-qualified people are allowed and expected to fulfill the most important roles. Cumming and Henry (1961, p. 164) state that the age grade system works "to keep the young out of many key roles until they know enough to fill them, and to remove the old before what they know becomes obsolete."

The age grade system in American society allows and expects older people to decrease their social activity, and Cumming and Henry believe that this is what older people do. Older people show measurable declines in their social and psychological activities. As a group, the older people are more socially isolated than younger age groups; they have fewer social roles; they have less daily social interaction; and they adopt new social goals more relevant to their age. The age grade system allows older persons greater freedom and fewer social responsibilities, and Cumming and Henry report on the basis of their research that older people become more self-preoccupied and less responsive to social rules.

Cumming and Henry do not regard disengagement and social withdrawal as a negative development, as many of the activity theorists do. Instead, they report that many of the people they interviewed showed improved morale and greater life satisfaction as they became more disengaged. They found that very old people, those over 80, enjoy their disengagement and display a sense of tranquillity that is not found among younger people.

Why does a society need an age grade system that prescribes disengagement for older people? Cumming and Henry see disengagement as society's preparation for the death of an individual. Social withdrawal allows older people to accept death for themselves and to die without causing undue disruption. When a fully engaged person dies, he or she causes a great deal of disruption in the social relationships that have been so abruptly ended. When a disengaged person dies, the world continues with little notice of the event, since most of that person's social relationships have already been severed and most of his or her instrumental activities abandoned.

The disengagement theorists see the disengagement process as a natural adaptation to the needs of the society. They would hesitate to intervene in this social process, that is, to change it in any essential way. They are convinced that societies develop ways to meet their distinct needs and circumstances, and are not as sure as the activity theorists that growing old must mean something more than it already does.

The Uses of Social-Gerontological Theories

A social theory is not an end in itself but a means to an end. One of the goals of a social theory is to provide a guide to social research, to point to areas that are in need of research, and to provide a source of definitions and concepts that allows for the accumulation of knowledge. The goal of social inquiry is an understanding of the substance of social life, an understanding of how the world operates and what this means to us and to others. Such an understanding requires the development of social theory and the use of theory in social research. To show how this occurs we will look at two pieces of social research that have used the activity and disengagement theories as guides.

Palmore's Study

Erdman Palmore (1968) constructed a research project to answer the question "Does aging reduce activities and attitudes?" Contained within this question are four possible answers, and each of them will be relevant to both activity and disengagement theory. If Palmore discovers that people decrease their activities as they grow older and that their life satisfaction is high, then his research will support the disengagement theory. If he discovers that people do not disengage and that their life satisfaction is low, this will also lend support to the disengagement theory. If he finds that people have low levels of social activity and this is accompanied by low life satisfaction, or if he finds that people maintain high levels of social activity and have high life satisfaction, then the research will support the activity theory. Figure 7.1 diagrams the relationship between social activity and life satisfaction as predicted by the activity and disengagement theories.

Palmore used data from a study in which 127 people were interviewed 4 times. The people interviewed volunteered to participate in the study and were interviewed at different times. The first interviews were conducted during the years 1955–1959 and the fourth interviews during the years 1966–1967. There were 51 male and 76 female participants in the study, and when they were interviewed for the fourth time their average age was 78. The group studied was not a random sample: All of the participants were ambulatory, noninstitutionalized residents of one region of the United States. It was, however, a panel survey, which has the advantage of allowing the researcher to observe changes that occurred over time.

Social Activity

		High	Low
Life Satisfaction	High	Support for activity theory	Support for disengagement theory
	Low	Support for disengagement theory	Support for activity theory

Figure 7.1 *Diagram of Hypothesis Prediction for Activity and Disengagement Theories*

Palmore analyzed the results of his research by comparing changes in activities and attitudes for both men and women. He found that the men showed very little, if any, reduction in either activities or attitudes. The women, however, showed reductions in both areas, although the reductions were very small. Palmore concluded that most people do not become less active as they age, and they certainly do not show a marked withdrawal from their activities. He found, in fact, that older people may reduce their activities in some areas while at the same time increasing their activities in other areas.

Palmore also discovered that those people who were most active also had the highest levels of life satisfaction, whereas those who reduced their activities had lower life satisfaction scores. He concluded (p. 262) that:

> it may well be that disengagement theory is applicable to some and the activity theory is applicable to others; that some find most satisfaction in disengaging and others find most satisfaction in remaining active. But apparently in our panel the activity theory was most applicable to most of the participants.

Lemon's Study

A study by Lemon and associates (1972) attempted to determine the relationship between social activity and life satisfaction in a retirement community. The researchers wanted to answer the question, Is there a relationship between the amount of social activity and the degree of life satisfaction?

They used a random sample of 411 people who had purchased homes in a retirement community in California, and interviewed the people before they moved into the community. The people they interviewed were mostly middle-class white Protestants; 182 were males and 229 females. The researchers were interested in finding the answers to some specific questions, some of which dealt with the different types of activities that might be related to life satisfaction. They then constructed a research hypothesis for each type of activity:

1. Informal activity (with friends, relatives, and neighbors) is directly associated with life satisfaction.
2. Formal activity (participation in voluntary organizations) is directly associated with life satisfaction.
3. Solitary activity (leisure pursuits, maintenance of household) is directly associated with life satisfaction.

By stating the hypotheses in this manner, the researchers were attempting to discover whether the relationship between activity and life satisfaction was always the same or whether it varied, depending on the kind of activity involved. They discovered that none of their original hypotheses was correct; that is, contrary to the prediction of the activity theory, the researchers did not find that a higher frequency of activity was related to greater life satisfaction.

Since their original hypotheses did not prove correct, they tried to find out whether a more specific type of activity was related to life satisfaction. In doing this they discovered that part of their original hypothesis was correct: There is a relationship between activity with friends and life satisfaction but not between activity with relatives or neighbors and life satisfaction. Going a couple of steps further, they discovered that the relationship between activity with friends and life satisfaction was true only for females and for those over age 65. The relationship between activity with friends and life satisfaction was very weak, however, and the researchers concluded that the hypothesis was not supported. As they put it (p. 521),

> The data provide surprisingly little support for the implicit activity theory of aging which has served as the theoretical base for practice as well as research in gerontology for decades. The propositions that the greater the frequency of activity, the greater one's life satisfaction and that the greater the role loss, the lower the life satisfaction were in the main not substantiated by this research.

Unanswered Questions

The two studies just described are good examples of the relationship between social-gerontological theory and research, and they are fair representations of the research process. The activity and disengagement theories provide a set of ideas that researchers are testing and evaluating in light of the evidence they have collected. The research does not, however, give us total confidence in either theory. The study by Palmore did not support the disengagement theory, although it provided some support for the activity theory. The study by Lemon and associates did not provide any support for the activity theory. There are, quite obviously, some gaps between the theories and the research, and some changes are in order. Both the theorists and the researchers will proceed from this point, making alterations either in the theories or in the manner of their research, or (most probably) in both. In addition, since neither the activity theory nor the disengagement theory has proved entirely satisfactory, other theories will be developed that will provide alternative approaches to the study of aging. Here we will look briefly at two recent developments in social-gerontological theory.

The Age Stratification Theory

One recent development in social-gerontological theory that shows great promise is the theory of age stratification. This theory is most closely associated with the work of Matilda White Riley and her associates (Riley et al., 1971), although some of the ideas contained within it were stated by Barron (1953). In a very broad way it is possible to think of a society as divided into age classes; that is, every individual is a member of a cohort that is distinct from other cohorts in identifiable ways. As an age class, older people have been treated differently by younger people in different periods of American history. Fischer (1978, p. 37) notes that in the early period, from 1607 to 1820, old age was highly respected: "Veneration of the aged was spoken of as natural and normal." This veneration was not only verbal but it was also practiced by the ceremonious honoring of older people on public occasions and in public places. In the meeting houses of early America in which religious services were held, the seats were always assigned, not randomly but carefully, in order to indicate various degrees of dignity. In these meeting houses the most honored seats were reserved for the oldest members. In the community of Hingham, Massachusetts, for example, the best seats were reserved for the minister's wife and the widow of the previous minister, while the second-best seats were reserved for the church elders (who were usually over 70). In making the seating assignments a large number of factors were likely to be considered, including wealth, power, and race, but none was more important than age. Old age was particularly important within the context of the church because it was taken to be a good sign that the older person was among the elect, that is, that God had lengthened the days of those who were chosen for salvation.

The Dimensions of Age Stratification

The age stratification theory uses the general framework provided by studies on social classes and social stratification, that is, it focuses on differences in income, prestige, power, social mobility, class relations, class consciousness, and so on. The age stratification theory begins by viewing society as composed of different age classes or age groups. These age classes have two distinct dimensions, a life course dimension and a historical dimension. The life course dimension is very much like the stages of the life cycle; individuals are members of different age groups depending on how long they have lived. People who are members of the same age group share a general biological history, have some common experiences in terms of the roles they have performed (student, parent, worker, etc.), and are likely to have similar experiences in the future. The historical dimension refers to the age group as a distinct generation or cohort; in other words, people form an age group because they have lived through a particular historical period with its unique characteristics. The assumption is that people have something in common because they have experienced certain events (both large and small) at a particular point in their life course. We can think of large-scale events, such as depressions, wars, and natural catastrophes, that had obvious effects on the people who lived through them and had different meanings for different age groups, depending on their position in their life course. In recent American history, for example, all Americans went through the experience of the Vietnam War, and this experience is assumed to have had different meanings for various age groups—it was a different experience for the draft age group than for younger or older age groups. These two dimensions, then, are indicators of the physical and social processes that operate to define the distinctive age groups or cohorts.

A particular cohort has a natural history that defines it and sets it off from every other cohort. Every cohort experiences a "cohort flow," or what might be called its demographic history. The cohort will start with a definite size, being composed of everyone who was born between two specific dates, and this size will decrease through the years. Although the cohort will begin with a set of ascribed characteristics, it may undergo change in these characteristics. A typical cohort will begin, for example, with slightly more males than females, but over its life cycle the greater life expectancy of females will cause the cohort to change in sexual composition. By the young adult years the cohort will contain more females, and by the later stages of life it will be heavily female. The cohort will also begin with a certain racial and ethnic composition, but the different life expectancies of the members will cause the cohort to change accordingly.

In addition to changes in the demographic composition of a cohort, the members of the cohort will experience changes in the roles they fulfill at different ages. The process of disengagement from previous roles and engagement of new ones will take place under a unique set of social and historical influences. In the United States, for example, the members of the cohort that was born between the years 1910 and 1915 were making the transition from adolescent to adult roles at the time of the Great Depression, and they were undertaking parental roles at the time of World War II. In addition, many of their grandchildren were born during the post-World War II baby boom, and they were retiring at a period of economic instability and under the pressures of an inflationary economy. The age stratification theory thus teaches us to analyze the functioning of a society in terms of cohorts or age groups that make up a society at any point in time.

Applications of the Age Stratification Theory

Once age groups have been defined, the age stratification theory indicates that we should study the relationships between age groups and among members of the same age group. This approach has the advantage of allowing us to look at each age group in terms of its distinctive characteristics and history, and also to view any particular age group within the context of a set of age groups. A particular advantage of the age stratification theory is that it seems well equipped to explain long-range social change in a way that sees people as both recipients of an already constructed world and active participants in the social world. This theory would provide a basis for describing the distinctive characteristics of the various generations in a society. It could be argued, for example, that the older generation in the United States today has a particular political orientation that is a result of the events its members have lived through as well as of their advanced maturity. The political orientation of the older generation might be quite different from that of the generation ahead of them or the one behind them. If there were a significant difference between the political orientations of two adjoining generations, we would expect some conflict between those groups in political matters. Each generation would have attitudes toward many different matters, only some of which would be similar to those of other living generations.

The Phenomenological Theory

Another emerging and promising social theory of aging is the phenomenological and ethnographic case study approach that has been used by Jacobs (1975), Gubrium (1975), and Hochschilds (1975). This theory derives its basic ideas and approach from the sociological school known as ethnomethodology or phenomenological sociology.

The phenomenological theory of aging is concerned primarily with the meaning of life and growing old. The meaning these researchers are concerned with is not the meaning that social gerontologists attribute to aging but the meaning attributed to it by those who are doing the aging. Rather than constructing a theory about aging, they prefer an approach that can define and portray what growing old means to those who are active participants in the process.

The phenomenological theory is an interpretative approach, especially when compared to the disengagement theory. Whereas the disengagement theory attempts to outline a general process of aging that is applicable to everyone everywhere, the phenomenological approach individualizes the aging process; it sees everyone as ultimately assigning his or her own meaning to aging. This is not to say that everyone has a unique view of aging—we construct our meanings in interaction with other people and thus are influenced by others—but it does make everyone an active participant in the construction and negotiation of the meaning of aging. This means that as researchers we have to be sensitive to all the various settings and circumstances in which people assign meaning to the aging process.

Gubrium (1975), for example, wrote an ethnography of a nursing home, a procedure that required the researcher to live in the setting that was being studied. Gubrium tried to construct the meaning of living in the nursing home, which meant documenting the life of the setting in the terms of all the participants. In the nursing home this meant documenting what life in a nursing home meant to the patients and the residents, as well as the floor staff, administrators, visitors, and so on. Gubrium (1975: Preface) states that

Living and Dying at Murray Manor documents the way in which the "work" of everyday life in a nursing home is accomplished: how the participants negotiate their roles, goals, and needs; how they invoke their rights and duties; and how, in the end, Murray Manor emerges as an organized social entity.

Jacobs (1975) has followed the same strategy in documenting the meaning of aging in other settings, a middle-class retirement community and a high-rise retirement apartment building in an urban environment. Marshall (1975) has also used this approach to describe the legitimation of death that occurs among the residents of a retirement village. The residents of this village were an average of 80 years old, and among them death had been accepted as a reasonable and legitimate process. Most had come to define death as an acceptable, and sometimes a preferred, circumstance, although they also expressed a preference for a particular style of dying. Most wanted to die a quick and painless death. Most important, Marshall discovered that in this group of people of advanced age death had been defined as a routine occurrence, and as members of a community these people had come to want their own deaths to be as little disruptive as possible. Because of the social meaning of death that emerged in this particular setting, the "residents learn not to make a great fuss about their dying. Thrown together with a large number of others facing the same fate, they have developed a community of tacit understanding which legitimates their impending deaths" (1975, p. 1140–1141).

The phenomenological approach to aging in American society has a great deal to offer, especially in attempting to understand the meaning of the aging process and the dialectic of social definition that occurs between the society and the individual.

Summary

The sociology of aging has produced two major theories, the activity and disengagement theories, which guided much of the research in social gerontology for the first couple of decades of its existence as a field of study. The activity theory was the first to be applied to the aging process, and even today it remains one of the most, if not the most, influential theories of aging. It assumes that people of all ages are naturally active and involved in social interaction, and in fact, that humans secure their motivation and self-definition from this social interaction. Specifically, activity theorists maintain that older people must maintain adequate levels of social interaction if they are to age in a manner that gives them a high level of life satisfaction. The social problem faced by older people in American society is that they are being excluded from active participation in the social world and thus are being pushed into a "roleless role."

The social problem of the roleless role can be overcome, but only if older people join together to create a new role that has social meaning and recognition. The development of a new role for older people will allow for the participation of older people as an essential and accepted group in the established social structure.

The disengagement theory is critical of the activity theory because of its assumption that older people can achieve a high level of life satisfaction only by remaining active and fully engaged in the social world. Disengagement theorists maintain that it is normal and inevitable for people to decrease their levels of social activity as they grow old. They see aging as a gradual social disengagement, a process of social withdrawal that is a prelude to the total disengagement of death. When older people disengage from the social world by reducing their daily social interactions and decreasing the number of roles they fulfill, they are reciprocated by the wider society's withdrawing from them, a condition that grants older people a greater measure of freedom and the expectation of fewer social responsibilities. Older people are receptive to the onset of disengagement, a factor that leads to an increase in their life satisfaction in the later stages of life. The social disengagement of older people allows individuals to accept the idea of death for themselves, and the death of a disengaged person causes very little social disruption.

In the last decade the activity and disengagement theories have been supplemented by the age stratification and phenomenological theories of aging. The age stratification theory views a society as divided into age classes, which are defined by their unique experiences and by their historical situation. The age classes are used as a basis for analyzing the social relations among members of the same age class as well as relationships between age classes.

The phenomenological theory of aging searches for the meaning of the aging process as it emerges from the everyday world of those who are growing old. It attempts to learn how people assign meaning, how they accept this meaning for themselves, and how this meaning may agree or conflict with the views of others with whom they interact.

The social theories of aging are both provocative and disappointing. They are provocative in the sense that they are vehicles for the understanding of aging. They organize what we know, provide the ideas that stimulate further inquiry, and provide a path toward greater understanding of the social world of the old. They are abstract, often too abstract, but within these theories is the potential for greater knowledge about the social world in an abstract sense as well as greater understanding of ourselves and our relationship to the social world. The social theories of aging are disappointing when they fail to provide the degree of understanding of the social world and ourselves that we would like to achieve.

It is safe to say that the development of theories of aging is far from completed. This condition, of course, is not unique to the sociology of aging.

Unless we assume that all physical and social phenomena are static or unchanging (an assumption that we can quickly dismiss), we can anticipate that the development of social theory may continue but will never be completed.

SELECTED REFERENCES

Ernest W. Burgess, *Aging in Western Societies* (Chicago: University of Chicago Press, 1960).

Elaine Cumming and William E. Henry, *Growing Old* (New York: Basic Books, 1961).

David L. Decker, "Sociological Theory and the Social Position of the Aged," *International Journal of Comtemporary Sociology* 15 (1978): 303–317.

Jaber Gubrium, *Living and Dying at Murray Manor* (New York: St. Martin's, 1975).

Arlie Russell Hochschild, "Disengagement Theory: A Critique and Proposal," *American Sociological Review* 40 (1975): 553–569.

Jerry Jacobs, *Older Persons and Retirement Communities: Case Studies in Social Gerontology* (Springfield, Ill.: Charles C Thomas, 1975).

Bruce W. Lemon, Vern L. Bengtson, and James A. Peterson, "An Exploration of the Activity Theory of Aging: Activity Types and Life Satisfaction Among Inmovers to a Retirement Community," *Journal of Gerontology* 27 (1972): 511–523.

Victor W. Marshall, "Socialization for Impending Death in a Retirement Village," *American Journal of Sociology* 80 (1975): 1124–1144.

Erdman B. Palmore, "The Effects of Aging on Activities and Attitudes," *Gerontologist* 8 (1968): 259–263.

Talcott Parsons, "Toward a Healthy Maturity," *Journal of Health and Human Behavior* 2 (1960): 163–173.

————, "Aging in American Society," *Law and Contemporary Problems* 27 (1962): 22–35.

M. W. Riley, M. E. Johnson, and A. Foner, eds., *Aging and Society,* vol. 3, *A Sociology Of Age Stratification* (New York: Russell Sage, 1971).

Arnold M. Rose, "The Subculture of the Aging: A Framework for Research in Social Gerontology," in *Older People and Their Social World,* A. M. Rose and W. A. Peterson (Philadelphia: F. A. Davis, 1965).

PART III

The Social Structure of Aging

Individuals grow older, but the aging of a society is highly structured in ways that are beyond the control of any particular individual. The position of older people varies from one society to another, depending on the amount of power and wealth controlled by older people. In past decades older people in the United States did not wield a great deal of power, but it is very likely that their power will increase significantly in the next few decades.

The life style of the older people in a society is greatly influenced by their economic status, and this is determined largely by the society's economic security programs. The living arrangements of an older person generally reflect the society's family and kinship structure, and involvement with extended kin and relations between generations are influenced by the family system. In sum, even though each individual is capable of defining his or her personal view of aging, the circumstances under which he or she ages is determined largely by the more general social structure of aging.

The Political Economy of Aging

Overview. To understand any group of people it is essential to grasp that group's political and economic situation. The old in America face social, psychological, and biological problems, but their most severe problems are political and economic in nature. It would be inaccurate to portray the problems of older people as *only* political or economic, but it is important to understand the political and economic position of older people in American society.

The position of older people in American society will be greatly affected by the amount of power they have. This, of course, is largely a function of how many older people there are, but it will also be affected by how well organized they are. If older people view themselves as a political force and unite on the basis of their age to support social programs and other matters that are of particular concern to them, then they will be much more effective. In addition, as the number of older Americans grows, the need for effective organization will be even more apparent.

It is extremely difficult to determine what proportion of the national wealth should be available to the older population. Most retired people do not have large incomes from private sources; thus, the social security system and welfare programs provide a large proportion of the income of older people. There is probably almost universal agreement that older people should be able to secure the necessities of life, but how much money does it take to provide those necessities? In any case, there are wide variations in people's needs. The study of the political economy of aging is just beginning, and these issues will be subjected to much public debate before they are resolved.

All societies are characterized by differential distribution of power and wealth, with some groups usually receiving more and others less. Very often various groups in the society—including the old—find themselves competing with each other over the question of how power and wealth should be distributed. This is because power and wealth are "zero order" resources, which means that they are in limited supply. Since there is only a certain amount of power and wealth to go around, not everyone receives all that he or she would like to have. And if one group is going to increase its power or wealth, someone else must give up some power or wealth.

Although power and wealth are very much related, and tend to go hand in hand, they will be treated separately in the following discussion.

Political Power

Just how much power does the older American have? Is the power of the old increasing or decreasing, and what does this mean for the future of gray power in the United States? Although the power of older people is not great, it seems that the general direction of change is toward increased power for the old.

One of the ways of evaluating the power of the old is by studying the organizations that provide the basis for political action. We can distinguish immediately between the organizations and social movements that have been important in the history of gray power and contemporary organizations and movements. Historically, the single most important social movement that sought to improve the condition of the old in America was the Townsend Movement. Among contemporary organizations three stand out as especially important: the American Association of Retired Persons/National Retired Teachers Association (AARP/NRTA), the National Council of Senior Citizens (NCSC), and the Gray Panthers. Each of these will be discussed in the following pages, together with some of the less influential and/or more specialized organizations that directly or indirectly affect gray power.

The Townsend Movement

There is a good deal of agreement among historians and social gerontologists that the Townsend Movement is both the first major organization that used gray power to pursue its goals and the best historical example of the potential power of older people in the American political system. Before the Townsend Movement various groups and individuals had lobbied for specific forms of old-age relief. A group called the American Association for Labor Legislation had worked for many years, at both the state and federal levels, for an old-age program. So, also, had the Fraternal Order of Eagles. Partly as a result of the efforts of these voluntary associations, a majority of the states had instituted some program of old-age relief even before the enactment of the federal social security system. It was the Townsend Movement, however, that generated a widespread popular appeal for a program of old-age relief, and most of the strength of the movement came from older people themselves.

The Townsend Movement received its name from its founder, Francis E. Townsend, a retired California physician. Its official name, however, was Old Age Revolving Pensions, Ltd. The movement began in 1934, although its birth can be traced to a letter to the editor written by Townsend and published in the Long Beach (California) *Press-Telegram* on September 30, 1933. According to the legend publicized by the movement, Townsend was moved to action when he saw three old women sifting through garbage cans in search of something to eat. The story is probably a fabrication, but for whatever reason, Townsend was moved to write the letter in which he outlined the basis of what was to become the Townsend Movement. He presented his analysis of the cause of the Great Depression of the 1930s and then offered his plan, which he termed a cure for the Depression. The letter generated an immediate and overwhelming public response, with many people sending replies to the newspaper and others encouraging Townsend to formalize his plan and try to get it enacted into law. The public response was sufficient to convince Townsend of the popularity and validity of his plan, and he decided to devote all of his time to the nascent movement.

The Townsend Plan

According to Townsend, the cause of the Depression was overproduction of consumer goods combined with lack of purchasing power among consumers, which led to stagnation in the economy. He reasoned that someone needed to consume the overproduction in order to get the economy moving again, and that the group that should do the consuming was older people. He proposed that all persons over the age of 60 be retired with a guaranteed monthly income of $200, an amount they would be required to spend by the last day of every month. The federal government was supposed to issue the money to everyone over age 60 as long as those receiving the money agreed not to work and to spend all the money each month. His plan, he argued, would end the Depression and at the same time eliminate poverty among older people.

Townsend proposed to finance the revolving pension scheme through the establishment of several taxes, most of which were regressive and all of which would have failed to provide the needed revenues. Although the Townsend Plan was not economically sound, it wielded great influence for a short period because of its tremendous popular support. Holtzman (1963), in an exhaustive study of the Townsend Movement, estimates that the movement had 1.5 million active supporters by 1936. These supporters were organized into local Townsend Clubs, and between the years 1934 and 1953 more than 12,000 of these clubs were organized. There were Townsend Clubs in every state in the Union. Holtzman estimates that over 10 percent of all Americans over the age of 60 were active supporters of the Townsend Plan.

Before the movement's influence began to decline, it was successful in generating a good deal of interest and support for its ideas. In Townsend's home state, California, the Republican party endorsed the Townsend Plan to counter the EPIC (End Poverty in California) campaign headed by Upton Sinclair in his bid for the governorship. In 1935 the plan was introduced as a bill in Congress, and representatives of the plan were called to testify. The movement was even able to elect a representative to Congress from the State of Michigan.

In 1936 the Townsend Movement reached its peak as a national political issue, although even then the plan had no chance of being enacted into law. The movement decided to join with a group of populist politicians to oppose the reelection of Franklin Roosevelt, and they campaigned under the banner of the Union party. The future of the Townsend Plan was made quite clear by the resounding defeat of the Union party.

The Townsend Plan was never enacted into law, and in this limited sense the movement was a failure. In a broader sense, however, the movement was important because it demonstrated popular support for a program of old-age relief, and this support was instrumental in the establishment of the American system of social security. Although the movement suffered a slow decline and eventual collapse, it assured itself a place in American history because it was the first large-scale protest organization that sought to secure the interests of the old (Holtzman, 1963; Putnam, 1970).

The Social Security Act

It would be an oversimplification to state that the Townsend Movement was responsible for the establishment of the social security system. In the first place, the Townsend supporters were opposed to the Social Security Act of 1935 because they preferred the Townsend Plan. In the second place, the Social Security Act was developed independently of the Townsend Movement, and it is quite possible that a system of social security would have been enacted even without the influence of the movement. Third, the Social Security Act was a broader piece of legislation; it dealt with problems that were beyond the narrow provisions of the Townsend Plan.

The system of social insurance that was to become the Social Security Act of 1935 was the brainchild of President Franklin D. Roosevelt and a group of close advisers. As early as 1930, when Roosevelt was still governor of New York, he publicly announced his support for a system of social security (Roosevelt, 1938). He felt that a system of social security was necessary if workers were to be able to live out their later years with dignity and freedom from the worst forms of poverty. He was convinced that the only reasonable means for preventing the absolute impoverishment of most older Americans was the establishment of a federal system of social insurance. He envisioned a system in which people would pay in money to the government while they were still young and working so that they could receive the money as a pension when they were old and retired. He felt that it was very important that the social insurance system be supported by the contributions of the workers themselves because this would allow people to receive a pension that was a direct result of their own thrift and foresight.

As soon as Roosevelt became president, he began laying the groundwork for the establishment of a social security system. The system he had in mind would cover older people but would also help support people in times of unemployment. In 1934 he appointed the Committee on Economic Security, which was chaired by Secretary of Labor Frances Perkins. (It was also in 1934 that Townsend founded his organization, the Old Age Revolving Pensions, Ltd.) Roosevelt directed the committee to develop a simple system of social insurance that would protect nearly everyone from the hazards of unemployment and old age. On June 8, 1934, he announced that his administration would submit a comprehensive program of social insurance to Congress early in 1935.

The essence of the Roosevelt plan was that old-age relief would be a form of social insurance and the benefits the workers received upon retirement would be an "earned right" in the sense that they would be based on the contributions made during the working years. Therefore, the pensions would not be welfare or government pensions dependent on the sufferance of those in power. There was, however, another side to the desire of the Roosevelt administration to establish a system of social security. This was the administration's expectations regarding the effects the system would have on the national economy. Roosevelt stated when he signed the Social Security Act that the bill was intended to reduce the impact of any future depressions, mainly by stabilizing the boom-bust cycle that was a persistent problem in capitalist economies. The Social Security Act was thought of as a weapon against future depressions because it ensured that older Americans, a low-income group, would always have a certain amount of purchasing power. In other words, the old would become a stabilizing influence on the American economy because of the flow of money provided by the social security checks. Thus, the Social Security Act was developed by the Roosevelt administration for two reasons: It was concerned about the personal troubles of older people who faced unemployment and impoverishment due primarily to economic circumstances that were beyond their own control; it also recognized the potentially beneficial effect the social security system could have on the national economy.

Where were the old themselves during the time that the Social Security Act was being written and enacted? To the extent that they were involved (and this involvement was more indirect than direct), it was owing to the influence of the Townsend Movement. Through the movement older people had some effect on the enactment of social security, but that effect was not nearly as great as is often assumed. By joining the Townsend Movement older Americans ensured that the Social Security Act would contain old-age insurance provisions, even though the movement itself never proposed or supported a system of social insurance. The Old Age Revolving Pension plan was a method of funneling money to people over the age of 60, but it was not a contributory system of social insurance based on the concept of earned rights. Although both plans would have provided monthly income to retired people, in concept and design they were two distinct and unrelated proposals.

The development of the legislation that was to become the Social Security Act was important to the Townsend Movement because the congressional hearings on the bill gave Townsend and his supporters their first opportunity to testify before Congress. Their testimony received considerable attention from the press, and thus the Townsend Plan became widely known. However, the Townsend supporters offered their plan as a substitute for the administration's proposal, so that the issue became defined as a choice between the Townsend Plan and the Social Security Act (Witte, 1963). There was never any doubt that the Social Security Act would win in Congress, at least in a head-to-head battle with the Townsend Plan; but there was considerable doubt as to whether either program could generate enough support to pass both houses of Congress and become law. It was the Townsend Movement's success in generating national attention and popular support for the concept of old-age relief that persuaded enough senators and representatives of the need for the Social Security Act for the bill to be passed.

The Social Security Act and the Townsend Movement developed at about the same time in American history, and they had in common a desire to salvage the American economy from the Depression by establishing a system of old-age pensions. Aside from these similarities the two proposals varied widely and were independent and distinctive ideas. The Townsend Movement as a collective action on the part of older people themselves was not responsible for the origination or development of the Social Security Act but was indirectly responsible, even if unintentionally, for the eventual passage of the act by Congress.

Contemporary Organizations and Political Power

Although many contemporary organizations have large numbers of older persons among their members, and many of these organizations devote a portion of their attention to problems of old age, three organizations stand out as concerned primarily with the interests of older people. Two of these organizations, the American Association of Retired Persons (AARP) and the National Council of Senior Citizens (NCSC), are important because of their large membership. The third, the Gray Panthers, is important because of the immense amount of mass media attention it is able to generate.

The American Association of Retired Persons

The AARP is officially known as the National Retired Teachers Association/ American Association of Retired Persons (NRTA-AARP) because it began in 1947 as the NRTA. Founded by a Los Angeles educator, Ethel Percy Andrus, the association soon outgrew its original orientation. It now has about 10 million members, all of whom are 55 or older.

The AARP has prospered mainly because of some of the programs it has sponsored, especially the selling of life insurance and prescription drugs by mail. Today the organization also sells other services, such as travel planning, and serves as a disseminator of information on aging. Members receive a monthly issue of its magazine, *Modern Maturity,* a professionally produced publication that advertises the services of AARP and informs and advocates for the old in a moderate tone.

Some of the critics of the AARP maintain that the organization is little more than a nonprofit organization that funnels business to profit-seeking enterprises. One critic maintains that the services provided through AARP can be obtained at a lower price on the open market (Main, 1975). The AARP, however, devotes large portions of its resources to advocating for the old and supporting research and education in gerontology. The University of Southern California has received support from the AARP in the establishment of its Davis School of Gerontology and the Andrus Gerontology Center. In these ways, at least, the AARP differs from a typical profit-seeking organization (Pratt, 1976).

The National Council of Senior Citizens

The second largest old-age association is the NCSC, which is only about one-third the size of the AARP. The NCSC is closely associated with the labor unions; many of its members are retired union members, and it relies heavily on labor unions for leadership and monetary support. The NCSC was established in 1961 for the specific purpose of supporting the establishment of medicare. Since the passage of medicare in 1965, however, the NCSC has broadened its objectives. It now serves many of the same functions as the AARP, providing prescription drugs, travel planning services, and so on, and advocating for the old. It also publishes a monthly newsletter, *Senior Citizens News* (Pratt, 1976).

The Gray Panthers

The Gray Panthers are important not because of a large membership roll but because of the attention they have attracted from the mass media in recent years. The Gray Panthers do not aspire to be an effective mass membership, service-providing organization but instead have concentrated on increasing the visibility of public issues related to aging.

The Gray Panthers organization was founded in 1970 by Maggie Kuhn after she had been mandatorily retired because of age. The organization remains closely associated with Kuhn, who is a charismatic leader, and would have a difficult time existing without her talented presence. Despite the fact that it is a very small organization compared to AARP or NCSC, its public recognition far outstrips that of either of the larger organizations.

Part of the mass media attention devoted to the Gray Panthers derives from the organization's provocative name, and part derives from the popularity and oratorical skills of Maggie Kuhn. More important, however, is the fact that the Gray Panthers have developed a statement of principles that constitutes a radical critique of aging in American society. They propose to humanize the society at all ages, and seek to form coalitions with younger age groups to achieve common goals. The major concerns of the Gray Panthers are as follows:

establishing participatory democracy, especially in residential institutions and
social service settings.
low-cost mass transportation systems
improved medical care and a national health care program
abolishment of age discrimination in employment and compulsory retirement
a guaranteed-income program, tax reform, guaranteed employment, and national standards for private pensions
a national program of age, income, and racial/ethnic integrated housing
reduction of the military budget and unconditional amnesty for Vietnam-era
resisters and deserters
educational reform to provide low-cost programs for all age groups

There are a number of other organizations that deal with aging in American
society, most of them having fairly specific interests. Binstock (1972) lists eight
such organizations: the National Council on Aging, the Gerontological Society, the Natonal Association of Retired Federal Employees, the National
Caucus on the Black Aged, the American Association of Homes for the Aging,
the American Health Care Association (formerly the American Nursing
Home Association), the National Council of Health Care Services, and the
National Association of State Units on Aging.

The Influence of Older People

The fact that age-based groups exist is not enough to assume that they wield
great power. Perhaps even more basic than the question of power is whether
these groups express the will of older people. Are they a manifestation of the
development of a group consciousness among older people? Do older people
recognize themselves as members of an age group with special interests and
concerns and the desire to bring about social change? Are these organizations
truly old-age associations?

With the exception of the Townsend Movement, American history provides
no examples of influential age-based interest groups. Even the Townsend
Movement was as much a cure for the Depression as an economic program
for older people. The potential influence of older people in the United States
today has never been greater. But even among the interest groups that focus
specifically on the old, the extent of their potential collective power of the old
is not certain.

It appears that one of the goals of the AARP/NRTA is the development
of a group consciousness among older people. Nevertheless, it began with the
goal of securing the pension rights of retired teachers, and it has emerged as
a strong service-providing organization that considers group consciousness
and advocacy a secondary goal. In addition, this organization has been successful partly because it has had the benefit of strong leaders and not because
it is a grass roots movement. The same can be said of the Gray Panthers,

although group consciousness and advocacy are its primary goal; the organization is heavily dependent on a few leaders rather than many active followers. If the AARP and the Gray Panthers were to merge, combining mass support with a clear ideological position, the result might be an old-age association that would be recognized as a representative interest group.

Do contemporary old-age groups influence the American political system? The answer is yes, although there is some question as to the amount of power they wield. Pratt (1976) concludes that the NCSC played an important role in the passage of medicare and the 1972 amendments to the Social Security Act. The AARP has also been influential, although it is less activist than the NCSC. The influence of the Gray Panthers seems to be more in the area of public opinion that in the passage of state or federal legislation. Hudson and Binstock (1976) believe that one of the reasons for the influence of the major old-age groups on federal legislation is the potential electoral force they represent. Politicians do not want to offend older people because of their voting power. At the same time, there is some doubt that the large organizations could control the voting power of their members.

There is no doubt, however, that older people are a much more visible group than at any other period of American history. The fact that there are three major organizations and a number of smaller ones committed to the problems of aging tells us that public awareness of aging is at an all-time high. But are these forces strong enough to weld the old into a significant political group, a viable interest group capable of pursuing collective goals?

Older people may become a viable interest group in the future, but at present they are a diverse group of people who hold different attitudes and values, and their membership in organizations for older Americans is not sufficient to overcome these differences. They do exhibit a strong tendency to recognize specific political areas and issues that affect them, such as issues of health care, and the potential for collective action seems quite high in these areas (Weaver, 1976). Even in the battle over medicare, however, the old-age associations were not the strongest forces in the legislative victory, although they did play strong supporting roles. The contending foes in the fight over medicare were the American Medical Association (AMA) and the labor unions, especially the AFL-CIO. The AMA opposed medicare because it constituted a foot in the door for a national health plan and "socialized medicine." It feared that any government intervention in the field of health services would erode the position of the physicians as private entrepreneurs and force them into the role of public servants. The labor unions, especially through the organization they founded, the NCSC, were strongly in favor of medicare as a means of ensuring that the basic medical needs of older workers would be met (Rose, 1967).

Older Americans are almost certainly going to become a stronger political force in the years ahead. More associations are focusing on the problems of older Americans as well as giving their members a sense of identity. But the political influence of older people is going to increase for other reasons as well (Pratt, 1976). For one thing, the old as an interest group are not opposed by any single group that sees its interests as being in conflict with those of the old. Most groups are somewhat hesitant to oppose "the old folks," partly because of the family connection; that is, everyone has older members in his or her own family. Most Americans view the political issues of aging as legitimate areas of concern and will not oppose them. Moreover, older Americans and old-age associations are usually able to form strong coalitions in support of their interests. In the past the old-age associations have usually found strong support in the Democratic party and the labor unions (AFL-CIO), as well as several smaller professional and social-service groups. These and other factors point to the prediction that the political influence of American old-age organizations will increase in the future.

The Political Attitudes and Voting Behavior of Older People

One of the popular beliefs about aging is that people become more conservative in their social and political attitudes as they age. It is assumed that young people are flexible in their attitudes and ideas, more willing to accept new ideas and social change, and that the process of aging engenders inflexibility and resistance to new ideas and social change. This conservatism, which is a result of maturational processes, is also thought to be one of the main causes of the generation gap, that is, the conflict in values and standards of behavior that is thought to exist between mothers and fathers and their sons and daughters. As in so many other areas related to aging, these beliefs are oversimplified and inadequate descriptions of the relationship between aging and social and political attitudes.

It would be incorrect to state that there is no evidence for the generalization that older generations in the United States tend to be more conservative in their social and political attitudes than younger generations. There is, indeed, a good deal of research evidence that supports this very conclusion. On a wide variety of contemporary issues, attitude surveys find older people more likely to support the status quo and to resist social change, and to exhibit lower levels of tolerance for radical, deviant, or unusual forms of behavior. Compared with younger people, older people have been shown to hold more conservative opinions on the desirability of the racial integration of neighborhoods and schools, on sexual mores, on the use of drugs, on religious values, on law enforcement, and on a number of other specific topics (Hunt, 1960; Marascuilo and Penfield, 1966; Fengler and Wood, 1972; Glamser, 1974). These differences in attitudes are usually found to be related to age even when other differences, such as differences in social class and education, are controlled.

The generalization about aging and increased conservatism has been found in other societies, too, for example, Colombia (Webber, Combs, and Hollingsworth, 1974). One consistent exception to the general relationship between increasing age and greater conservatism on political issues occurs when the issue involves older people in a direct way. For example, older people are usually more favorable toward proposals for government programs that would provide medical or economic assistance to older people (Schreiber and Marsden, 1972).

Some social scientists have argued that the greater conservatism of older people is also demonstrated by their identification with the Republican party. Crittenden (1962) demonstrated a tendency for older people to identify themselves as Republicans, whereas younger people are less likely to be Republicans and more likely to be Democrats. The Republican party is usually regarded as more conservative than the Democratic party; it draws its support largely from business interests, whereas the Democratic party which is regarded as more liberal, draws a great deal of its support from labor unions and minority groups. It is argued, therefore, that since older people are more likely to be Republicans than younger people, this is another indicator of the relationship between age and conservatism.

If we accept the generalization that older people are more politically conservative than younger people, we are still confronted with the question of whether this greater conservatism is a result of life cycle or generational forces. In other words, when we compare the political attitudes of members of different age groups using a cross-sectional survey approach, we know that there are age-related differences but not whether the differences are caused by people becoming more conservative as they age or whether one's attitudes are related to the generation to which one belongs. To answer this question we need longitudinal studies that allow us to see attitudinal change or stability over time. Relying on longitudinal studies and cohort analysis, Glenn (1974) concludes that people do *not* become more conservative as they grow older. By this he means that people do not usually remain rigid in their political attitudes over their lifespan. People change their political and social attitudes as they age, but for most people the change is toward more liberal attitudes. Many older Americans hold somewhat conservative attitudes toward the desirability of racial integration, but these attitudes are very likely to be less conservative than they were thirty, forty, or fifty years ago. Whole societies have a tendency toward the liberalization of social and political attitudes, and older people reflect this liberalizing tendency. At the same time, older people appear to become increasingly conservative because the attitudes of the society as a whole have changed more rapidly than those of individuals. The result is that older people are very often more conservative in their attitudes when compared with younger cohorts, even though they have actually developed more liberal attitudes as they have aged. We thus have an apparent contradiction wherein people usually become more liberal in their political and social attitudes as they age, while at the same time becoming an increasingly conservative portion of the society as a whole.

It is often thought that older Americans exert a strong influence on elected officials because high percentages of older people vote in elections. Whether elected officials are more sensitized to issues that are important to older people because of this belief is not known, but they might well be. Most voter participation studies show that people between the ages of 45 and 65 are the most active participants, but high percentages of those over 65 are still voting. People over 65 are significantly more likely to vote than those under 25.

Table 8.1 shows voter participation by age in the 1972 national election. Even though the Table shows a decline in the percentage of persons over age 65 who voted, actually the percentage of persons between the ages of 65 and 74 who voted remains very high (68.1 percent), and it is only among those over age 75 that there is a marked decline in voting (55.6 percent). This decline is not due to a decline in political interest but reflects increased incidence of physical infirmities and transportation problems that prevent some older people from going to the polls on election day. There is a lot of evidence (Glenn and Grimes, 1968; Glenn, 1969) that older people are as interested in political matters as any younger age group, if not more so.

Gerontocracies

There are some examples of gerontocracies—societies that are ruled by elders —but these are usually simple societies. Even in the societies that are thought to practice gerontocracy, however, advanced age alone is usually not sufficient to make a person powerful, and usually older women are not powerful. Practicing gerontocracies thus are usually societies in which power is held by some

Table 8.1 VOTER PARTICIPATION IN 1972 NATIONAL ELECTIONS, BY AGE

Age	Number of persons of voting age	Number of persons voting	Percentage of persons voting
18–20	11,022,000	5,318,000	48.3
21–24	13,590,000	6,896,000	50.7
25–34	26,933,000	16,072,000	59.7
35–44	22,240,000	14,747,000	66.3
45–64	42,344,000	29,991,000	70.8
65 +	20,074,000	12,741,000	63.5

Source: U.S. Department of Commerce, *Statistical Abstract of the United States, 1973* (Washington, D.C.: U.S. Government Printing Office, 1973).

of the older men. Industrialized societies, in contrast, are usually not thought to be gerontocracies, even though it is widely recognized that political leaders in these industrialized societies are usually men in late middle or old age.

There are some positions of authority, such as that of Supreme Court justice, that are usually held by males of advanced age. It is common for Supreme Court justices, since they are appointed for life, to sit on the bench into their late 70s. The Supreme Court may be an exception to the rule, however; most institutions are not dominated by older individuals. Still, Schlesinger (1966) concludes that the higher the political office, the older the age at which people attain that office.

Even when positions of political leadership are held by older persons, this does not mean that the leadership will automatically be more conservative. Fishel (1969) did not find older political candidates to be more conservative on various political issues than their younger opponents. Eisele (1972) discovered that U.S. senators who had been elected two or more times, tended to become more conservative in their later terms than they had been in earlier terms.

It is well known that many revolutionary leaders are quite young. Fidel Castro of Cuba was in his early 30s when his revolution brought him to power. Thomas Jefferson was only 34 when he signed the Declaration of Independence. It is, moreover, only in societies that have recently experienced a political revolution that most of the leadership positions are filled by young adults. After a revolution the general trend is for the average age of the leaders to increase (Lasswell and Lerner, 1966). Industrialized societies, however, are usually ruled by a mixture of middle-aged males, with few leaders in important positions who are very young and few who are very old. Those who are in important political positions when they are in their late 60s or 70s usually come to those positions when they are younger and are able to maintain their power.

The Economic Status of Older Americans

Just as societies develop procedures for the distribution of power, they develop procedures for the distribution of wealth. Who gets how much of the wealth of a society is influenced by a large number of factors, but age is usually among the most important of these. This is certainly the case in the United States.

It is not easy to assess the precise distribution of wealth in a large industrial society like the United States. Most studies of the distribution of wealth focus on current income as the most important element, but for older people a yearly income figure can be a misleading indicator of economic status. In the United States in 1976 the median income for families headed by a person 65 years of age or older was $8,721. The median income for all families in the United States was $14,958. This means that families with a head over 65 received only about 58 percent of the income received by families headed by a younger person. However, families in which the head is over 65 usually have fewer members than other families, so it would be helpful to also know the income per person in both types of families. As we would expect, when we compare the per person income of families headed by persons 65 or older with that of other families, we find that the income gap narrows. In 1974 the per person income of families headed by persons over 65 was $3,054, while for all families the per person income was $3,731. The per person income in families headed by persons 65 years of age or older is 82 percent of the per person income of all American families. Even these figures do not tell the whole story: The income of older black families is, on the average, only about 50 percent of the income of white families (U.S. Bureau of the Census, Series P–60, no. 107, 1977; Series P–23, no. 59, 1976).

The lower income of older people in the United States is also reflected in the proportion of older people whose incomes are below the poverty line. In 1976, 15 percent of the people over age 65 were below the poverty level, compared with 12 percent of all persons in the United States. Again, the differences between whites and blacks over age 65 are outstanding. While 13 percent of older whites were below the poverty level, 35 percent of older blacks were below that level (U.S. Bureau of the Census, Series P–60, no. 107, 1977). Despite the large proportions of older persons who were below the poverty line in 1976, there has been a significant reduction in the poverty of those over age 65 in the last two decades, as shown in Table 8.2. The number of older persons whose income is below the poverty line has been reduced from nearly 5.5 million in 1959 to nearly 3.5 million in 1976. The poverty rate during this period has been more than cut in half. Although the poverty rate for blacks was reduced from 62.5 percent in 1959 to 34.8 percent in 1976, the figure is still more than double the total poverty rate for all races. The number of older blacks who have incomes below the poverty line has been reduced only from 711,000 in 1959 to 644,000 in 1976. Although the total reduction in the poverty

Table 8.2 PERSONS 65 YEARS OF AGE AND OLDER BELOW POVERTY LEVEL, BY RACE, 1959–1976 (SELECTED YEARS, IN THOUSANDS)

Year	Whites		Blacks		All races	
	Number	Percentage	Number	Percentage	Number	Percentage
1959	4,744	33.1	711	62.5	5,481	35.2
1969	4,052	23.3	689	50.2	4,787	25.3
1976	2,633	13.2	644	34.8	3,313	15.0

Source: U.S. Bureau of the Census, *Current Population Reports*, Series P–60, no. 107, "Money Income and Poverty Status of Families and Persons in the United States: 1976," Advance Report (Washington, D.C.: U.S. Government Printing Office, 1977).

rate for people 65 years of age and older is encouraging and indicates a genuine effort to reduce the most impoverished segment of the older population, the proportion of older blacks whose income is still below the poverty line remains incongruent with the aims of the American system of social welfare.

Older people very often have fewer expenses than younger people simply because of their age. The older family is smaller, with many household units composed of only one or two persons, which means that the family needs less spacious housing. Older individuals are eligible for medicare benefits, which reduces their financial liability for the increased medical costs associated with growing older. Some job-related expenses are reduced in retirement, such as transportation and special clothing costs. In some instances older people are given certain tax benefits that are not available to younger people, such as greater federal and state income tax deductions and reduced or delayed property taxes and the nontaxation of social security benefits.

Older people also have increased expenses in some ways. Medical expenses are much higher for older people, and only a part of these expenses are covered under medicare. And even though older families are usually smaller, not all expenses are automatically reduced by smaller family size. Some food items, for example, may be wasted simply because they are sold only in large sizes. People living alone sometimes find that they cannot use an entire loaf of bread before it must be thrown away. Many older people who live in cold climates find that they are faced with high home heating bills, partly because they are home a greater proportion of the day and partly because they have a need for a higher temperature level in the home. Older people may have increased household maintenance expenses because they do not feel capable of undertaking some household repairs and therefore must hire someone to do the work.

For these reasons, it is very difficult to make adequate comparisons between the income levels of families of different ages. Some household expenses decline with age, but others increase, and therefore simple dollar comparisons are potentially misleading. Even when we know the income levels of families of different ages, we cannot make comparisons without considering other factors.

Nonincome Assets

The financial assets of older people, especially other than money income are difficult to measure, although the 1968 Social Security survey (Bixby et al., 1975) collected information on the value of owned homes, savings accounts, stocks and bonds, and the like. This study found that about half of all older people received some income from assets, although for many the asset income was small. A large majority of married people over age 65 own their own homes; the Social Security survey found 77 percent home ownership. Most of the homes (80 percent) are free of mortgage. In addition, 71 percent of the respondents said that they held some liquid assets, usually money in banks or savings and loan associations. United States savings bonds were held by 13 percent of the respondents, and 10 percent reported that they owned some stocks and corporate bonds. Most of the respondents, however, reported that they received little or no annual income from their assets. Seventy percent of those who owned some liquid assets reported that their annual income from these assets was less than $150. Thus, even though a large number of older people own either a home or some liquid assets, most receive little or no annual income from those assets. It seems obvious that most older people are not in a financial position to independently supplement their pension and social security income, even in time of need.

For most older people, the basic source of income is social security. About 86 percent of the respondents in the 1968 Social Security survey reported that they receive social security income. About half of the respondents received income from assets, although the dollar amount of income was small. About one-fourth received some income from working, while only 12 percent received income from a private group pension, and about the same percentage received public assistance. Only about 2 percent of the people reported receiving income from a private annuity, and only 3 percent reported that they received money from friends or relatives with whom they did not live.

Inflation and Older Americans

Older people are often said to be adversely affected by inflation because they live on fixed incomes. To a certain extent this is true, especially if the major source of income is savings or a private annuity or pension benefit. Inflation causes the buying power of a fixed income to decrease. Inflation will also cause some expenses to increase, such as the property tax on a house. As the value of the house increases because of inflation, the property taxes will also increase. But the basic source of income for most older people, the social security benefit, is not a fixed income. The benefits from social security are increased as consumer prices increase. This may also be the case with some private pension programs, although it is much less likely. Nevertheless, although some people may benefit from inflation, older people are usually not in a position to benefit from inflation and are much more likely to be harmed by it.

Private Pensions

Private pensions to which a worker becomes entitled as a result of employment usually provide retirement income in addition to social security. These plans are a recent development in the United States. Very few companies provided private pensions for their employees before World War II, and most of the early pensions were usually granted at the discretion of the employer. Even if a worker received a private pension upon retirement, the pension could be reduced or even terminated at some future date. This was especially true if a company changed owners or went out of business. Very often a worker lost all rights to a company pension if he or she quit, was disabled, or was fired, no matter how long the worker may have been employed by the company. Under these circumstances it is not surprising that few retired workers today have income from a private pension.

This situation is changing, although slowly. It is estimated that in 1970 nearly 30 million workers out of a labor force of nearly 86 million were covered by private pension and deferred profit-sharing plans. This means that only about one-third of all workers were covered in 1970, but this represents twice the percentage covered in 1950, when only 10 million workers out of a labor force of 64 million were covered (Statistical Abstract of the United States, 1973).

The importance of private pensions can be demonstrated by the knowledge that a social security pension will provide only about 25 percent of a person's preretirement income, even though it is estimated that a retired person will require about 75 percent of his or her preretirement income to maintain the standard of living to which he or she is accustomed. For most workers, the private pension is the only means by which they could approach a retirement income level that would allow them to maintain their life style (Henle, 1972).

Although private pension plans were fairly common in the United States in the post-World War II period, they remained almost unregulated until 1974. Some private plans were indirectly regulated—for example, by insurance regulatory laws when they were funded through life insurance companies—but there was no consistent regulation of pension plans, and some plans were essentially unregulated. The federal government began regulating private pension plans in 1974, when the Employee Retirement Income Security Act (ERISA) was enacted.

The Employee Retirement Income Security Act provides for the regulation of most existing and new pension plans. This includes most deferred-compensation plans, including profit sharing and stock bonus plans. The act set the minimum standards that a plan must meet, such as the provisions for worker participation in a pension plan, vesting (the right of the employee to the value of the pension plan), and the right of a spouse to part of the retirement benefit if the worker dies, as well as placing limits on contributions and benefits. The act also established minimum funding standards, provided for disclosure of the essential provisions of the pension plan, prevented a plan from investing heavily in the securities of the company that established it, and formed the Pension Benefit Guaranty Corporation (an agency of the federal government) to guarantee that some pension benefits will be paid to a worker even if a plan terminates with insufficient assets.

Income Security

The American system of income security in old age assumes that the government program (social security) will provide a subsistence income and insurance against catastrophic medical expenses (medicare) but that income beyond subsistence will be secured through private means. Today social security remains the only source of income, in most cases, which means that most people have to make a severe adjustment in their standard of living after retirement. Although many older Americans accumulate some assets of value, most of those assets do not produce income and their savings are very limited. The only other generally applicable means of providing income security is through vested rights in a private pension program. Although private pension programs are covering increasing numbers of workers, and even though ERISA has established a system of safeguards to protect private pensions, there are still very large problems in providing for the income security of older Americans. Over half of all workers in private industry are not covered by pension programs; survivors' benefits remain very low; workers are sometimes restricted in their job choices because the pension cannot be transferred; and most private pension programs do not adjust their benefits to inflation after retirement, which means that most workers lose some of their purchasing power each year after retirement.

The answer to the problem of income security for older people seems simple enough: Increase the amount of money they receive, either through social security or other means. To a certain extent this is what has happened in the last couple of decades in the United States. Social security benefits have been increased a number of times, and usually the increases were more than enough to offset losses through inflation. The lack of any organized political opposition to increased benefits for older Americans has encouraged this course of action. In addition, politicians feel that their constituents support a policy of increasing social security benefits. Older retired persons favor the action because they receive more money each month. Older middle-aged people support the increases because they themselves are nearly eligible for benefits. Younger families support the benefit increases because they sympathize with the poverty of the old, because they often have parents and grandparents who need the money, and because their parents and the grandparents might have to turn to them for help. Nearly everyone seems content with improving the financial status of the old; at any rate, no one seems to object strongly.

The Potential for Conflict over the Distribution of Wealth

Will current trends continue? Will the economic status of the old continue to improve in a slow but steady incremental process? This seems likely, at least for the next few years, but probably not forever. There is potential for conflict between age groups in the question of how wealth is to be distributed. The goods and services of a society are limited; there is only so much to go around, and what one person has or consumes, another person cannot have or consume. As long as a society produces enough or nearly enough to meet or nearly meet the expectations of most people, there may be very little conflict over who gets how much. As long as a family expects to get one loaf of bread a day, and it receives a loaf a day, it may be willing to let everyone else have a loaf. At least it might not be willing to fight for a second loaf, especially against someone who has none. The example is simplistic, and it ignores a large number of other factors that operate in determining the distribution of wealth, but it underscores the key point: that the distribution of wealth in a society is related to both material needs and social expectations.

A conflict between age groups over the distribution of wealth could develop if there were significant changes in either material needs or social expectations. Such a conflict would probably occur between the working adult population and the nonworking adult population, primarily retired older people. A Marxian social theorist would predict that a conflict over the distribution of wealth would involve the owning classes versus the working classes in a capitalist society, which is always a possible outcome. It is also possible, and perhaps more likely, that a conflict would erupt between the working and nonworking groups, mainly because the non-working old are a great deal more visible than the owners of capital and the conflict would be more obvious.

Why would a conflict emerge between the working and nonworking or retired populations? One circumstance that could lead to conflict would be a serious decline in production—a depression—which would make material goods scarce. A second and more likely cause of generational conflict would be a demographic change in the age composition of the society that would make it impossible to meet the social expectations of both the working population and retired population. This type of conflict appears likely when we look at the changes in the age composition of the American adult population projected for the not-too-distant future. As noted in Chapter 2, the age composition of the adult population can be expressed as an old-age dependency ratio, which tells us how many people aged 65 and over there are in comparison to the number of people aged 18–64. This is a shorthand method of indicating how many retired adults (65 +) there will be in comparison to the number of working adults (18–64).

Table 8.3 shows the dependency ratios from 1940 to 1970 with projections to 2050. The table shows us that we can expect some significant increases in the old-age dependency ratio beginning around 2020. What the projections and

Table 8.3 OLD-AGE DEPENDENCY RATIOS FOR THE UNITED STATES, 1940–2050

1940	1950	1960	1970	2000	2020	2030	2050
.118	.133	.167	.177	.199	.260	.318	.302

dependency ratios do not tell us is the effect of this change on the possibility of conflict over the distribution of wealth in the twenty-first century. If, however, the projections are accurate (see Chapter 2), we predict that the growing number of retired older persons in the United States will be dependent on the productivity of relatively fewer adult workers by the years 2020 and 2030. If the expectations of retired workers for financial support continue to increase as they have in the recent past, along with the expectations of adult workers for increasing affluence, a generational conflict may erupt over the distribution of wealth.

A conflict between working adults and retired people is by no means assured. A number of possible occurrences could act to harmonize the material interests of the two groups:

1. The amount of economic production could increase to satisfy the expectations of both groups.
2. The projected old-age dependency ratio may not prove accurate, especially if there is an unexpected increase in the birthrate, which would provide an increased number of younger workers.
3. Mandatory retirement could be eliminated, and the number of people who postpone retirement in favor of remaining in the labor force could increase.

Any one or any combination of these factors could prevent a serious generational conflict between workers and retired people over the distribution of wealth in American society.

Summary

It is quite likely that older people will become an increasingly powerful group in the political structure of the United States, not only because of the projected increase in the number of older people but also because of the organizations that are available to pursue their interests. Although it is no longer in existence, the Townsend Movement serves as a historical model of gray power and points out that in both a direct and an indirect fashion organizations of older people can wield a great deal of influence. Today, such organizations as the American Association of Retired Persons, the National Council of Senior Citizens, and the Gray Panthers have a base on which to build political power. All three organizations favor the establishment of a system of national health insurance, and the fight for this legislation will test their strength; however, whether they win the fight this year or in some future year, as an element in the American political system groups like these will become increasingly influential.

Many people believe that the American political scene is going to become increasingly conservative in the next few decades because of the increasing age of the American electorate and the increasing influence of groups representing the political interests of older people. This scenario of the future assumes, however, that there is a relationship between increasing age and conservatism. It also assumes that the general thrust of social change is in a liberal direction, especially toward a form of liberalism that is promoted by the young. But it seems quite possible that in the future some older cohorts will prove to be more liberal than many younger cohorts. The cohort of the 1960s, those people who entered adulthood during the 1960s and were well known for their radical ideas and life styles, seems a likely candidate for demonstrating the possibility that a particular cohort might be more liberal or conservative than other cohorts regardless of age.

If older people in the United States are able to increase their political power, it might be expected that they would also be able to improve their economic condition. After all, one of the almost inevitable consequences of retirement is a reduction in income, and income figures show that older people receive less income than younger people. As Streib (1976) concludes, however, lower income is not the only item to be considered when dealing with the economic status of older people. Many older people have accumulated goods over a lifetime and may have to spend very little for such things as furniture and appliances. In addition, many older people have accepted the social attitude that retired persons should receive less income that people who are still working. As Tissue (1972) has noted, some older people adapt to a decrease in income by disengaging from the consumption patterns that are prevalent among younger people.

Even though many older people may be able to adjust to lower income levels after retirement, most people are heavily dependent on their monthly income (especially from social security payments) to supply them with the necessities of life, and a severe depression in the future could have a tremendous impact on the political and economic position of the older segment of the population.

SELECTED REFERENCES

Norval D. Glenn, "Aging and Conservatism," *Annals of the American Academy of Political and Social Science* 415 (1974): 176–186.

Norval D. Glenn and M. Grimes, "Aging, Voting and Political Interest," *American Sociological Review* 33 (1968): 563–575.

Abraham Holtzman, *The Townsend Movement* (New York: Bookman Associates, 1963).

Robert B. Hudson and Robert H. Binstock, "Political Systems and Aging," in *Handbook of Aging and the Social Sciences,* eds., Robert H. Binstock and Ethel Shanas (New York: Van Nostrand Reinhold, 1976), pp. 369–400.

Dan M. McGill, *Fundamentals of Private Pensions,* 3rd ed. (Homewood, Ill.: Richard D. Irwin, 1975).

Henry J. Pratt, *The Gray Lobby* (Chicago: University of Chicago Press, 1976).

Jackson K. Putnam, *Old Age Politics in California* (Stanford, Calif.: Stanford University Press, 1970).

Arnold M. Rose, *The Power Structure* (New York: Oxford University Press, 1967).

Gordon F. Streib, "Social Stratification and Aging," in *Handbook of Aging and the Social Sciences,* Robert H. Binstock and Ethel Shanas (New York: Van Nostrand Reinhold, 1976), pp. 160–185.

Thomas Tissue, "Old Age and the Perception of Poverty," *Sociology and Social Research* 56 (1972): 331–344.

CHAPTER 9

Social Security and Programs
for Older Americans

Overview. The federal government has become the source of most
social-service and income protection programs for older people in the
United States. In general, these programs have been very successful in

achieving the results they sought. While the aims and intentions of most of these programs are quite modest, they nevertheless provide a basic level of support for people who are vulnerable to the workings of an advanced capitalist economy and the demands of a complex industrial and urban society. The social security system, for example, has provided a base of economic security for two generations of workers and their dependents, and despite the problems that are inevitable in such a large and complex system, the program has achieved a high degree of acceptance and is a stable component of the American socioeconomic system. Today other government social-service programs are emerging that will contribute to the betterment of life in an aging society.

There are a large number of government programs that are intended to serve the needs of older Americans. Some are locally instituted and operated, some funded by the states; but the best known are the federal programs. Most of the government programs for older people are of recent origin, especially when compared with similar social services in most Western European countries. The United States is often described as a society that emphasizes individualism, independence, and self-reliance, and these values have retarded the development of many social-service programs in this country. Many of the contemporary social programs, such as social security, were established in such a way that they would not violate the individual's sense of independence and self-respect.

The government programs that supply the largest amounts of money and have the greatest impact on the lives of older Americans are the federal programs. There are actually many different programs, operated by different agencies, that benefit older Americans. Table 9.1 lists fourteen programs (operated by seven agencies) that are directly related to the needs of the older population. Other programs are not listed because they affect only a part of the older population. Examples are the food stamp program of the Department of Agriculture or the veteran's pension program of the Veterans Administration. As the table shows, the majority of the social-service programs for older people are offered by the Department of Health, Education and Welfare; these programs constitute the core of the government's aging-related programs. Of all the programs, none is of greater significance and enduring importance than social security.

Social Security

The history and development of the Social Security Act was discussed in the preceding chapter, and there is no need to repeat it here except to note that the act was signed into law by President Roosevelt in 1935. The concept of a social security system, which was already widely accepted in Europe, had been included in the platform of the Democratic party during the 1932 election campaign. It was not until 1940, however, that the first benefits were paid out, and even this date was earlier than had been planned when the bill became law.

Today the social security program is often referred to as OASDHI, which stands for Old Age, Survivors, Disability, and Health Insurance. The official title indicates the four major programs of income maintenance and health care, of which three are concerned primarily with meeting the needs of older Ameri-

Table 9.1 MAJOR PROGRAMS OF THE FEDERAL GOVERNMENT THAT BENEFIT OLDER PEOPLE

I. Department of Health, Education and Welfare
  A. Social Security Administration
    1. Old Age, Survivors Insurance (OASI)
    2. Health insurance (medicare)
    3. Supplemental Security Income (SSI)
  B. Administration on Aging
    1. Multipurpose senior centers
    2. Nutrition program for the elderly
    3. State and community programs
    4. Multidisciplinary research centers of gerontology
  C. National Institute on Aging
    1. Research on the aging process and health problems
II. Housing and Urban Development
    1. Housing for the elderly
III. Department of Labor
    1. Age discrimination in employment
    2. Older Americans Community Service Employment Program
IV. Independent Federal Agencies
  A. Action
    1. Foster Grandparent Program
    2. Retired Senior Volunteer Program (RSVP)
  B. Small Business Administration
    1. Service Corps of Retired Executives (SCORE)

Source: U.S. Congress, House of Representatives Select Committee on Aging, *Federal Responsibility to the Elderly: Executive Programs and Legislative Jurisdiction* (Washington, D.C.: U.S. Government Printing Office, 1976).

cans. The segment of social security that is not an old age program is disability insurance, an income maintenance program that pays a worker under 65 years of age a monthly cash benefit if he or she is unable to work because of a disability.

Old-age Insurance

Old-age insurance is the income maintenance program that provides workers with a monthly cash benefit for the rest of their life after they retire. This cash benefit is often called the old-age pension and is what most people mean when they say they are receiving social security. The basic idea of old-age insurance is that people pay into the system while they are young and are able to work and then, when they are older and either unable or unwilling to work, may retire with the assurance that they will still have some monthly income. While there are many different ways of organizing and operating a system of old-age insurance, and every country does it in a unique way, the basic idea is the same in every case.

Nearly all workers in the United States pay into the old-age insurance system through their place of employment and thus are eligible to receive a monthly cash benefit when they retire. The Social Security Administration reports that nine out of every ten persons who receive pay for their work are covered by social security. Housewives are not covered because they usually do not receive wages for their work (unless, of course, they work outside the home). Other workers who are not included are employees of the federal government and some state and local government employees.

The social security system has expanded over the years since its inception to include more and more categories of workers, with the ultimate aim of including essentially everyone. One of the reasons for this nearly universal coverage is that the program is mandatory, which means that most groups of workers have no choice as to whether to belong to the program or not; individuals (with the exception of members of the clergy) never have a choice. The only groups of workers that have a choice are employees of state or local governments, a classification that may include, for example, employees of a public school district as well as city, county, or state workers. In most such cases the workers do not have the right to decide whether or not they will participate in the system. The decision is usually made by the elected representatives of the government unit, that is, state representatives, county supervisors, city council members, and so on. Whether the particular unit belongs to the social security system or not, the individual worker has no choice about the matter—if the group belongs, all individuals must belong, and if it does not belong, then no individual belongs. For most workers, however, participation in the social security system is mandatory.

Once an individual has met the eligibility requirements for old-age insurance, benefits are paid as an earned right, which means that individuals can receive social security benefits regardless of how much money they have saved, the value of their homes or cars, or even the amount of nonwork income (e.g., dividends on investments or payments from a private pension or annuity program) they receive. The social security program is not a welfare program but was established to ensure a minimum monthly income after retirement; it was not intended to discourage people from providing for their own income security through individual investments, savings, and the like.

To be eligible to receive old-age insurance benefits, an individual must be at least 62 years old and have worked at a paid job (or jobs) for a specified period. The person must also be retired from active work. In most cases a person must have been employed for 10 years (or 40 quarter-years), although the number of years an individual must have worked is less for those born before 1930. Persons born in 1915, for example, could have retired in 1977 and received a monthly cash benefit if they had worked at least 6½ years in an occupation covered by social security.

To receive a monthly cash benefit under the old-age insurance program, a person must be "substantially retired." In practice this means that a person cannot receive more than a specified dollar amount of money income from employment in any one year. The amount an individual can earn and still meet the retirement test changes from year to year, rising as the level of average wages rises. In 1977, for example, an individual could earn up to $3,000 a year and still meet the retirement test. In other words, an individual could receive employment income of $3,000 and still receive the full amount of his or her monthly cash benefit from old-age insurance. If an individual receives income from employment that exceeds the $3,000 limit, then he or she will lose $1 in old-age insurance benefits for every $2 of earnings over the $3,000 limit. If, for example, an individual was receiving a monthly cash benefit from old-age insurance in 1977 and earned a total of $4,000 from employment, his

Table 9.2 MAXIMUM AMOUNTS OF YEARLY EARNED INCOME ALLOWED IN MEETING THE RETIREMENT TEST

	Annual income ($)	
Year	*Age 62–65*	*Age 65–72*
1977	3,000	3,000
1978	3,240	4,000
1979	3,480[a]	4,500
1980	3,720[a]	5,000
1981	3,960[a]	5,500
1982	4,300[a]	6,000

[a] Estimates based on automatic adjustment to rising average wages.

or her yearly total of social security benefits would be reduced by $500. Because the person earned $1,000 more than the allowed amount ($3,000), he or she would lose $1 in benefits for every $2 of earnings over $3,000 or $500.

The $3,000 ceiling applies only to income received from employment and does not affect income from any nonwork source. In 1977 Congress amended the Social Security Act, and one of the amendments involved the ceiling on earned income. Different yearly ceiling amounts were established for people aged 62–64 and 65–72. Table 9.2 shows the dollar amounts of those ceilings. Beginning in 1979 the ceiling amounts for retired persons between the ages of 62 and 64 will increase each year in which there are increases in average wages for nonretired workers. For retired persons between the ages of 65 and 72, increases in the ceiling amount have been legislated through the year 1982; after 1982 this amount will also increase automatically along with increases in average wages.

Because of the retirement test, some individuals receiving old-age insurance benefits are attracted to part-time employment. In many cases such employment allows the individual to supplement his or her income while still receiving full old-age insurance benefits. At age 72 an individual becomes exempt from the retirement test and can earn an unlimited amount from employment without any reduction in old-age insurance benefits. In 1981 the age of exemption from the retirement test will be reduced to 70.

The dollar amount of the cash benefit a worker receives when he or she becomes eligible is determined by how much that person earned while employed and the proportion of his or her working life in which he or she was employed. The monthly earnings of the worker are averaged for the period from 22 to 62 years of age; the five years in which the person earned the least are disregarded in computing the average. In 1979 the minimum monthly benefit a worker could receive under social security was $133.90; the maximum was $535.00 if the worker retired at age 65. In the past, individuals could increase their cash benefit at retirement by 1 percent per year if they delayed receiving benefits until age 72. In 1978 this delayed-retirement benefit was increased to 3 percent per year. Social security also provides a special benefit for low-paid workers. The minimum social security benefit mentioned earlier is most beneficial to workers who have worked the minimum number of years in order to receive a monthly cash benefit. However, low-paid workers who have been covered by social security for thirty years may receive a larger minimum payment ($230 in 1979), which is significantly higher than the payment based on the wages they have earned. This benefit, like all other benefits paid by the Social Security Administration, automatically increases each year in which the Consumer Price Index of the Bureau of Labor Statistics rises by 3 percent or more.

The worker is not the only person covered by social security. The worker's dependents and survivors are also insured. For example, upon retirement a worker will receive a monthly cash benefit. If the worker is married, the dependent spouse can also receive a monthly cash benefit if the spouse is at least 62 years old. The amount the spouse will receive is determined by the worker's benefit and is usually about 50 percent of that benefit. If a worker retired and received a cash benefit of $300 a month, his or her spouse could receive about $150 a month if the spouse was over 62. A divorced wife or husband who was married to the worker for at least ten years may also be eligible for benefits based on his or her former spouse's employment. An insured worker's children or grandchildren could be eligible for a cash benefit if they are under 18 years of age (under 21 years for students) and are dependent on the worker for their support. There is, however, a maximum amount that a family can receive: the total cannot exceed 188 percent of the worker's benefit. Thus, even if a retired worker had a dependent spouse and several dependent grandchildren, the total family benefit could not exceed 188 percent of the worker's benefit.

It should be noted that both a husband and a wife can be eligible to receive cash benefits based on employment. In this case both would receive 100 percent of the monthly cash benefit to which they are entitled, but in most cases neither would be entitled to a benefit as a dependent of the spouse. If one spouse had a large income and the other a small income while they were working, the spouse with the smaller income might decide to receive a monthly cash benefit as a dependent of the spouse with the larger income. This could become especially important if the spouse with the larger income died, because the dependent spouse could then receive the benefit of the deceased spouse.

Survivor's Insurance

The second component of the OASDHI program is survivor's insurance. Under the provisions of this program a worker's dependents may be eligible to receive a monthly cash benefit if he or she dies. In most cases an eligible surviving spouse can receive a monthly cash benefit equal to 100 percent of the deceased worker's benefits. If, for example, a retired male was receiving $300 a month before his death, and if his wife was 62 or over and was dependent on her husband for monetary support, then she would receive 50 percent of her husband's benefit, or $150. As a retired married couple they would thus be receiving a total of $450 a month in social security payments. If the husband dies leaving his wife as his survivor, then she becomes eligible to receive her deceased husband's monthly benefit, which in this case would be $300. Under certain circumstances a divorced wife, dependent children and grandchildren, and dependent parents can also receive survivor's benefits.

In most cases an eligible individual may receive survivor's benefits as long as he or she remains in a situation of dependency. Survivor's benefits will normally cease upon the marriage of a widow, widower, or dependent child. This particular feature of the social security program has been well publicized in newspapers and news magazines as a bureaucratic phenomenon that unintentionally prevents retired individuals from marrying. Suppose, for example, that Mary Smith is receiving a monthly cash survivor's benefit of $300, which is 100 percent of her late husband's benefit. She meets Henry Jones, who is also receiving a monthly cash benefit of $300 based on his participation in social security as a worker. Smith and Jones are considering marriage, but they are concerned about the effect the marriage would have on their social security benefits. They are not wealthy, but they figure that if they combine their monthly cash benefits from social security ($300 + $300 = $600) they will be able to meet their major needs. The problem is that they will not receive as much per month after they are married as they received individually when they were single. Mary Smith will no longer be a dependent survivor of her late husband because, upon marrying, she becomes a dependent of her new husband, Henry Jones. As such, she will be entitled to about 50 percent of his monthly benefit, or about $150. Mary Smith's monthly cash benefit thus will decrease from $300 to $150, and instead of having $600 to live on, the Joneses would receive only $450 a month. In a circumstance such as this the structure of benefits of social security could well have a bearing on whether people decide to marry or to remain single.

It should be pointed out that if Mary Smith had been receiving a monthly cash benefit based on her own employment, her benefits would not be affected by any change in her marital status. It is when a person is receiving a survivor's benefit that the question of dependency becomes an important consideration. This situation has been alleviated by the 1977 amendments to the Social Security Act. Beginning in 1979 a widow or widower who marries after age 60 will not have the amount of his or her benefit reduced.

Health Insurance

In 1965 Congress passed amendments to the Social Security Act that established a program of health insurance for older people. These amendments are known as medicare even though they are actually part of social security. The health insurance program contains two plans, both of which are only for persons over 65. The first part is a compulsory program of hospital insurance, and this program is financed by the social security taxes that are withheld from a worker's paycheck. Under the hospital insurance program, covered individuals receive protection against the costs of a hospital stay and the costs of extended care after leaving the hospital. Unlike old-age insurance, medicare does not require the individual to meet a retirement test. Individuals over age 65 who are still working full time are eligible for medicare. Not all the costs of hospitalization are paid by the hospital insurance, however. The individual must still pay a deductible amount (the first $124 in 1977) and some of the daily charges if the hospital stay exceeds sixty days. Posthospital extended-care services and posthospital home health services are also covered under the hospital insurance program, although here again the patient may be responsible for a portion of the costs, depending on the need for posthospital services.

The second part of the health insurance program is available on a voluntary basis and is known as supplementary medical insurance. Although this plan is voluntary and requires the payment of a monthly premium ($7.70 in 1977), the vast majority of those who are eligible for the program elect to participate. After a yearly deductible amount, the supplementary medical insurance program covers 80 percent of reasonable charges for physician and surgeon services, outpatient hospital services and physical therapy, limited ambulance services, and a few miscellaneous medical and health services.

These three components of the social security package, the old-age, survivor's, and health insurance programs, are intended to meet the basic income and medical needs of the older population of the United States. How adequate these programs are is a matter of political debate that will probably never be completely resolved. Nevertheless, it is generally acknowledged that these programs provide a minimum of income and health security, and no one confuses them with a utopian dream. There are gaps in the medicare program that can cause an older person to incur medical expenses far beyond his or her ability to pay. Social security payments are not large enough to provide for anything beyond the basic necessities of life. While it is difficult to cite dollar amounts that accurately reflect the benefits of a typical social security recipient, Table 9.3 gives the average monthly benefits received by recipients in different circumstances for selected years from 1940 to 1977. As is obvious from the table, the average benefits paid are, and have been, very modest.

Supplemental Security Income (SSI)

Until 1974 the benefits paid by the social security programs were the only forms of direct assistance to older Americans from the federal government. Prior to 1974 there had been a program of old-age assistance (OAA) in which the federal government provided grants to the states and the states matched those grants and established eligibility requirements. Each of the states then established and administered its own program of old-age assistance in which it made payments to older people who were in need. Beginning in 1974 the old-age assistance program was replaced by a program called Supplemental Security Income (SSI). This program, administered by the Social Security Administration, established uniform eligibility requirements throughout the nation. The program is paid entirely by federal funds and does not involve any

Table 9.3 AVERAGE MONTHLY BENEFITS PAID UNDER SOCIAL SECURITY FOR SELECTED PERIODS, 1940–1976

	1940	1950	1960	1970	1977
Retired worker without dependents	$22.10	$42.20	$ 69.90	$114.20	$242.98
Retired couple	$36.40	$71.70	$123.90	$198.90	$366.05
Widow	$20.30	$36.50	$ 57.70	$102.40	$221.95

Sources: U.S. Department of Health, Education and Welfare, *Social Security Programs in the United States* (Washington, D.C., January 1973); *Social Security Bulletin*, vol. 42 (January 1979).

contribution from the states, counties, or cities, except in the states that pay larger sums in aid to older people than SSI provides.

The difference between social security benefits and SSI is that the first is an earned right, or contributory pension system, whereas the latter is public assistance, or what is commonly referred to as welfare. Not all people are eligible for monthly cash benefits from social security, but SSI provides a minimum monthly income based on need. Unlike social security benefits, however, SSI payments are not available to individuals with resources in excess of stated amounts ($1,500 in 1974), excluding the value of a home, household goods, personal effects, an automobile, and property needed for self-support. Life insurance policies are excluded from the resource ceiling if the total face value of insurance on any one person is less than $1,501.

Under the SSI program older people can receive payments that bring their monthly income up to $130 for an individual or $195 for a couple (in 1974). Individuals eligible for SSI can also receive small amounts of other income with no reduction in payments. Although the $130 monthly payment is a paltry sum, it represents quite an improvement over the previous program. Under the old-age assistance program the national average monthly payment was only $80 a month as of December 1972. Consider, also, that prior to World War II the major form of assistance available to the indigent older person was the county farm or poorhouse.

The Costs of Social Security

As the American social security system has developed, it has become better able to meet the minimum needs of the majority of older Americans. The benefits paid by social security do not provide for a luxurious life style (nor are they intended to do so), and it is not likely that the system will ever become anything other than a *minimum needs program,* at least not in the foreseeable future. One of the restrictions on the expansion of social security is the fact that the resources from which benefits can be paid are limited.

Table 9.4 SOCIAL SECURITY TAX RATE ON WAGES, 1937–2011

Years	Tax rate (%)
1937–1949	1.0
1950–1953	1.5
1954–1956	2.0
1957–1958	2.25
1959	2.5
1960–1961	3.0
1962	3.125
1963–1965	3.625
1966	4.2
1967–1968	4.4
1969–1970	4.8
1971–1972	5.2
1973–1977	5.85
1978	6.05
1979–1980	6.13
1981	6.65
1982–1984	6.70
1985	7.05
1986–1989	7.15
1990–2011	7.65

The source of the funds from which social security benefits are paid is the social security tax on wages. From 1937 to the present the social security tax structure has changed significantly, and under the present law it will continue to change in the years ahead. Table 9.4 shows the social security tax rate from 1937, the first year the tax was collected, to the present, together with the rates legislated for the years 1979 through 2011. The table shows that the tax rate has risen significantly over the years, starting from a very modest 1 percent and increasing to the 7.65 percent rate planned for the years 1990–2011.

The future increases in the tax rate were established by the 1977 amendments to the Social Security Act in response to the financial problems the system was experiencing. By 1975 it became obvious that, year by year, more money was being paid out in benefits than was being received from taxes. The deficit was $1.5 billion in 1975, $3.2 billion in 1976, and $5.6 billion in 1977, and was expected to increase in succeeding years. Because of the changes in the tax rates, however, it is now anticipated that between the years 1980 and 2010 the income from the tax will exceed the system's expenditures. Between the years 2011 and 2025 expenditures will again exceed income, but excess income from the previous years and interest on that excess will provide a balanced budget. By the year 2025, however, the trust fund balances will have fallen to a point at which another increase in social security taxes will become necessary (Robertson, 1978). It should be remembered, however, that projections of future income and expenditures are based on assumptions about the state of the national economy and projected birth and mortality rates, and would be affected by significant changes in any of these assumptions.

It must also be mentioned that the amount of social security tax a person pays is actually double the rate listed in Table 9.4. The rate listed in the table is the amount usually deducted from the gross pay of each employee, but an equal amount is paid by each employer for each employee. For the employer the tax paid for each employee is a cost of doing business, and it makes little difference whether the tax is paid directly or is deducted from the employee's gross pay. The significance of this practice for the employee is that he or she pays income taxes on the portion of social security taxes that is deducted from the gross pay but not on the portion that is paid directly by the employer. Recently more employers have chosen to pay the entire social security tax directly, rather than having the worker pay half of the tax. In turn, the employee's gross pay is reduced by the amount the worker paid previously in social security taxes. Because of the reduced gross salaries, the employers save a small percentage on their social security taxes by using this method of payment. Likewise, the worker saves a small amount on his or her personal income tax because of the reduced amount of gross income, even though the take-home pay remains the same. In the long run the worker may receive a smaller social security benefit at retirement because the benefit is based on the worker's gross income. Social security benefits are not taxed as income when received under either of the two methods of payment of the taxes.

In addition to changes in the social security tax rate, over the years there have been changes in the maximum wages on which social security taxes are collected. Unlike income taxes, which are collected on the total amount of wages earned in a year, social security taxes are collected only on a stated amount. The maximum amount has usually been high enough so that many workers pay social security taxes on all of their yearly income. Table 9.5 shows the maximum wages that have been taxable from 1937 to the present, along with the maximum dollar amount of taxes that could have been paid in each year. In 1937 a worker paid social security taxes on the first $3,000 of earned income; any amount earned over $3,000 was not taxed. This maximum amount has been increased over the years to offset inflation, and the 1977 amendments legislated further increases. In 1981, the first $29,700 of earned income will be subject to the social security tax. After 1981, the maximum amount taxed will be increased to the extent that there are increases in the level of average wages in the United States. The combination of a rising tax rate and a rising ceiling on taxable wages has resulted in large increases in the amount of social security taxes an individual worker can pay. In 1930 an individual earning at least the maximum in taxable wages paid only $30 (or $2.50 a month) in social security

Table 9.5 MAXIMUM WAGES TAXABLE AND MAXIMUM ANNUAL TAX
FOR SOCIAL SECURITY, 1937–1981

Year	Maximum wages taxable ($)	Maximum annual tax ($)
1937–1949	3,000	30.00
1950	3,000	45.00
1951–1953	3,600	54.00
1954	3,600	72.00
1955–1956	4,200	84.00
1957–1958	4,200	94.50
1959	4,800	120.00
1960–1961	4,800	144.00
1962	4,800	150.00
1963–1965	4,800	174.00
1966	6,600	277.20
1967	6,600	290.40
1968	7,800	343.20
1969–1970	7,800	374.40
1971	7,800	405.60
1972	9,000	468.00
1973	10,800	631.80
1974	13,200	737.10
1975	14,100	824.85
1976	15,300	895.05
1977	16,500	965.25
1978	17,700	1,070.85
1979	22,900	1,403.77
1980	25,900	1,587.67
1981	29,700	1,975.05

Note: Each year after 1981 the maximum wages that are taxable will be automatically adjusted to annual increases in average wages.

taxes, whereas in 1981 an individual could pay a maximum of $1,975.05 (or $164.58 a month).

The social security tax on wages has increased faster than any other tax in the post-World War II period, yet it has encountered the least resistance from taxpayers. There are probably several reasons for this, including the facts that the social security tax started at a very low level (1 percent), still represents a smaller total amount than most people pay in income tax, and is not collected on income other than wages, such as profits, dividends, or rents. Taxpayers may also regard the social security tax as one from which they hope eventually to get their money back—an advantage not associated with other taxes. There is also the family connection. Social security taxes can be perceived as providing financial support for parents as well as ensuring that the taxpayer will not have to become dependent on his or her own offspring. Whether the social security tax will meet with greater resistance in the future remains an open question.

Who Pays for Social Security?

The social security program in the United States is a modest one, providing only minimal levels of income for the older population. At the same time, social security tax receipts and OASDHI benefit payments are among the largest components of the federal budget, amounting to about $80 billion a year. This puts OASDHI benefit payments in second place (a distant second) behind national defense expenditures. An expenditure of this magnitude deserves serious scrutiny. It raises several questions regarding who pays the tax, who benefits from the payments, and so on.

We have already seen that the social security tax is a tax on earnings from employment and that the vast majority of wage earners are covered by social security. We also know that social security was designed to be a form of social insurance. This means that an individual is investing money to protect himself or herself against a possible eventuality. You might purchase a life insurance policy to protect your survivors against the possible financial effects of your death. Social security is a form of insurance that provides for the possibility that you may live into old age, when your ability to earn income will be severely restricted. As a bonus, social security also provides income to your dependent survivors if you die. Because social security is a form of insurance, one group of people who benefit from the program are older people, and the longer a person lives, the better the return on his or her investment.

An extreme case that illustrates this feature of social security is that of Ida Fuller (Schulz, 1976). Fuller is reported to be the first person to ever receive a social security benefit. She retired from her job as a law firm secretary in 1940. By the time she retired she had paid less than $100 into social security. She lived until 1975, reaching an age of over 100, and in her 35 years of retirement received over $20,000 in social security benefits. If Fuller had had a dependent spouse or a dependent survivor, the total amount of her benefits would have been even larger. Obviously, Fuller benefited from the structure of social security, although her case is unusual because she was approaching retirement age just as social security was beginning to pay benefits.

At the other extreme, individuals can pay into social security for all of their working lives. If they die before qualifying for benefits and leave no dependent survivors, their investment proves to have been a poor one. Because social security is a form of insurance, the number of years you live after retiring determines the extent to which you benefit from the program.

Social security is not an insurance program in all respects, however. First, the social security system has the power of the government behind it, which means that it does not have the actuarial standards of private insurance programs. Specifically, this allows the social insurance program to operate without the level of financial reserves that would be required of a private insurance program. Put simply, this means that a program of social insurance can promise to pay more in benefits than it actually has on hand. The reason it can do this is that it can assume that there will always be a working population that will be paying in social security taxes to finance the benefits paid to retired workers. Without this advantage, it would take decades for the first retired workers to receive the level of benefits that have been paid through the social security program. The disadvantage of this structure of social insurance is that retired workers who have paid into the program would not be able to collect the benefits they have been promised if, for any reason, those who are still working stopped paying into the system. Thus, retired workers covered by the social security program receive benefits as an earned right, but each generation of workers accepts a promissory note from generations yet unborn to continue the program. Workers paying into the social security program today trust that their children and grandchildren will also pay into the program when they become wage earners.

Another way in which a program of social insurance is unlike a private insurance program is that it is more sensitive to long-term social changes, such as changes in the birthrate, changes in life expectancy, and inflationary changes in the cost of living. The American system of social security is currently dealing with some of the unanticipated effects of dramatic demographic changes, a topic that is explored in greater detail in the next section.

One of the most persistent criticisms directed at the American social security system is that the social security tax is regressive because those who receive the highest salaries and wages pay the lowest percentage in social security taxes. All individuals who earn a yearly income at or below the ceiling amount ($29,700 in 1981) pay the same percentage (6.65 percent) of their earnings to social security. Since individuals do not pay social security taxes on any amount over this ceiling, their tax rate decreases the more they earn. For example, an individual earning $15,000 in 1981 will pay $997.50, or 6.65 percent of his or her income in social security taxes. A person earning nearly twice as much, $29,700, would pay $1,975.05, which is also 6.65 percent of his or her income. A person who earns $59,400, however, will also pay $1,975.05; this amount is only 3.325 percent of his or her income. In other words, all individuals earning $29,700 or more pay the same dollar amount in social security taxes, but this amount represents a larger percentage of total income for individuals who earn less, even though they are least able to afford the tax.

On the other hand, the manner in which benefits are computed tends to work to the relative advantage of those who have earned the lowest incomes; that is, low-income earners receive a better return on the money they have paid into the system than those with higher incomes. Although the average yearly wage is one of the elements used in determining the monthly cash benefit at retirement, earned income for which social security taxes were not collected is not included in the computation. Individuals earning $59,400 in 1981 will not pay social security taxes on the last $29,700 of their income, but neither will this income be used in computing their social security benefits at retirement.

The amount that is paid to social security beneficiaries is basically a political question, although many countries formerly used a "replacement ratio" of 40–50 percent. More recently, a replacement ratio of 60–67 percent has been thought to be necessary (Haanes-Olsen, 1978). A replacement ratio refers to the amount of the social security benefit as compared to the amount of money a worker earned prior to retirement. In most cases a replacement ratio is computed by comparing the average earnings of workers in the year before their retirement with the amount they receive in social security benefits in the first year of retirement. Table 9.6 shows the projected replacement ratios from 1980 to 2000 for American workers with low, average, and maximum preretirement earnings. It is evident that low earners will receive a retirement income that is slightly over 50 percent of their preretirement earnings, while average earners will receive about 40 percent and high (maximum) earners about 25 percent. It should be remembered, however, that in absolute dollar amounts the high earners will receive more in social security benefits than the average earners, who in turn will receive more than the low earners.

It is also instructive to compare the replacement ratios used in the American social security system with the ratios used in other countries. Table 9.7 gives the replacement ratios of ten European countries, Canada, and the United States in the year 1975. The table shows that there are significant differences between the replacement ratios of the various countries. For the single retired worker, the replacement ratio can be as low as 26 percent (in the United Kingdom) and as high as 67 percent (in Italy). The United States is on the low end, with a ratio of 38 percent for single beneficiaries. For the retired couple, the ratio ranges from a low of 39 percent in the United Kingdom to a high of 76 percent in Sweden. The United States is very close to the average for retired couples, with a ratio of 57 percent.

Table 9.6 PROJECTED REPLACEMENT RATIOS FOR WORKERS RETIRING

Year	Low earners (%)	Average earners (%)	Maximum earners (%)
1980	59.4	46.6	29.3
1985	53.4	41.6	23.3
1990	53.7	41.8	24.1
1995	53.6	41.8	24.8
2000	53.6	41.8	25.7

Source: A. Haeworth Robertson, "Financial Status of Social Security Program after the Social Security Amendments of 1977," Social Security Bulletin 41 (1978): 21–30.

Table 9.7 REPLACEMENT RATIOS FOR SOCIAL SECURITY PAYMENTS FOR
SELECTED COUNTRIES, 1975

	Single retired worker (%)	*Retired couple (%)*
Austria	54	54
Canada	39	57
Denmark	29	43
France	46	65
Federal Republic of Germany	50	50
Italy	67	67
The Netherlands	38	54
Norway	41	55
Sweden	59	76
Switzerland	36	53
United Kingdom	26	39
United States	38	57

Source: Leif Haanes-Olsen, "Earnings-Replacement Rate of Old-Age Benefits, 1965–75, Selected Countries," *Social Security Bulletin* 41 (1978): 3–14.

Women and Social Security

Another element that has great relevance for answering the questions "Who pays?" and "Who benefits?" is sex or, more specifically, the role of women in American society. In 1975 the U.S. Senate's Special Committee on Aging released a working paper entitled "Women and Social Security: Adapting to a New Era" that considered many problems of sex discrimination in the social security system and recommended ways of dealing with those problems. The report makes it quite clear that the original Social Security Act of 1935 made assumptions about the roles of women and the structure of the family that are no longer accurate. Because of social changes that have occurred in the last forty years, certain inequities in the social security system have become apparent and are sure to become increasingly important.

Some of the problems noted in the working paper are the following:

1. In some instances women cannot generate as many benefits for their family members as men can. For example, a man cannot receive a benefit from his wife's earnings unless he can prove that he was receiving at least half his support from her. There is no such requirement for women. The Supreme Court has recently ruled that this provision of the Social Security Act is unconstitutional.

2. A divorced woman can receive benefits from her former husband's earnings if they were married for at least 20 years. A divorced husband cannot receive benefits from his former wife's earnings.

3. A couple who both worked may receive less in retirement benefits than a

couple in which only the husband worked, even though both couples had the same earnings and contributions.

4. Homemakers are not covered by social security, and an early divorce or the death of a spouse can result in the homemaker's receiving no social security benefits.

In an effort to deal with some of these problems, the 1977 amendments to the Social Security Act provided for studies to develop proposals that would ensure equal treatment of men and women under the program. There are nevertheless a number of problems that remain to be solved in this area, and for most of them there are no quick and easy solutions.

Is the Social Security Program Bankrupt?

One of the most highly publicized features of the social security system is the question of its financial stability. Some critics have warned that the system is already bankrupt or will be in the very near future. The truth of the matter is that the present system of social security is faced with some long-term financial problems that must be dealt with, but there are no problems that are beyond solution.

The most immediate financial problem faced by the system in the 1970s was the potential depletion of the trust funds, a circumstance that was once forecast to occur as early as 1981. The trust funds are the excess money that has been saved from unneeded revenues in past years to be used in years in which more money is being paid out in benefits than is being received through the social security tax. When the rate of unemployment is high, as it has been at various times in recent years, social security revenues are reduced because unemployed persons do not pay social security taxes. During hard economic times the trust funds can be used, as they are intended to be used, to cover deficits until the economy recovers and employment rates are back to normal levels. In 1975, however, the social security trust fund amounted to about $44 billion, which is less than the total amount of benefits paid out in one year's time (Munnell, 1977, p. 94). In addition, the trust fund was expected to decline every year after 1975 into the foreseeable future, which meant that eventually there would be no trust fund to make up for the program's yearly deficits. The 1977 amendments to the Social Security Act solved this short-term financial problem.

Two other problems faced the social security system in the 1970s; and these were long-term problems. The first could be fairly easily solved, as it had been created, through legislation. This problem, called overindexing (Munnell, 1977), was created in 1972, when Congress instituted automatic adjustments to prices as the means for determining increases in social security benefits. This legislation allowed the benefits to adjust automatically to changes in the cost of living. The formula used to compute benefits worked well for retired beneficiaries, but it also compensated future retirees for inflation. In essence, they were being compensated twice for every rise in the cost of living. If unabated, this overcompensation would eventually place a severe burden on the system's ability to meet its financial obligations without very large increases in social security taxes. The overindexing problem was resolved by the 1977 amendments, however, without affecting the original intent of providing retirees with automatic cost-of-living increases.

The other long-term problem is not as easy to solve. Nor is it easy to predict accurately, since it is brought on by demographic changes. The most important elements of these changes are the mortality and fertility rates, better known as the death and birthrates.

The mortality rate is fairly predictable and is not likely to change drastically in the foreseeable future. However, the general trend is for the mortality rate to decline, which means that on the average Americans are living a little longer. This has a long-term impact on social security because the cost of benefits will increase to the extent that more people live longer. Since more people are living to enjoy an extended healthy lifespan and are still quite capable of working beyond the retirement age of 62 or 65, one of the most obvious ways to alleviate the financial pressure caused by the declining mortality rate is to raise the age at which people are eligible to receive retirement benefits. Some industrialized societies, including Ireland, Norway, and Sweden have higher normal retirement ages (Cain, 1976, p. 358), and this supports the possibility of raising the retirement age in the United States.

Fertility rates have a greater impact on the future of social security, but they are much more difficult to predict accurately. We do know, however, that the general trend since the beginning of the twentieth century has been for the fertility rate in the United States to decline. In evaluating the long-term financial needs of the social security system, it is necessary to make judgments as to the probable fertility rates for years to come. This is because in establishing tax rates it is essential to know the number of retired workers receiving benefits in comparison with the number of workers. The proportion of retired persons to workers can change significantly over time if the fertility rate changes. In 1940, for example, the ratio of older persons to the working age population was 11.6 per 100, while in 1975 it was 19.2 per 100, and it is projected to be more than 30 per 100 by 2050 (Munnell, 1977, p. 102). Since social security is on a pay-as-you-go basis, an increase in the proportion of retired persons to working persons means that the social security tax rates will not be sufficient to maintain the present level of benefits.

All of the long-term problems of social security point in one direction:

Social security revenues will have to be increased still more in the future, at least by the second decade of the twenty-first century. Among the options available are the following:

1. Increase the social security tax rate so that all workers pay a larger proportion of their income to social security.
2. Increase the wage base on which the social security tax is collected for the employer, the employee, or both.
3. Collect the social security tax on all income, not just wages and salaries.
4. Contribute some of the general revenue of the federal government to the social security program.

Whichever option, or combination of options, is selected, the social security system seems likely to survive. It is certain that changes will occur in response to the problems that plague the program, but it is equally certain that the basic form and intent of the present program will survive for years to come. To date, the American social security system has been very successful, and its current problems do not obscure its success.

The Older Americans Act

Although the Social Security Act constitutes the most important piece of legislation affecting the older population, the Older Americans Act of 1965 is also important. Most people are not aware of the Older Americans Act, but they will certainly become aware of it as some of its mandated programs become established in local communities.

The Older Americans Act, as amended, contains several major sections (or "titles") that outline the intentions and objectives of the law. Title II establishes the Administration on Aging (AOA), the administrative structure for the programs and services that the act mandates. Title III provides money for the states and communities to establish agencies on aging. These agencies are responsible for planning and coordinating social services for the old in local settings and disseminating information about available social services. Title IV provides for the training of people to work in the field of aging, as well as for research and teaching on aging. Other titles of the act provide for the establishment of multipurpose senior centers to serve as focal points for the development and delivery of social and nutritional services; strategically located nutrition centers and community service employment for older Americans. Together, these various titles are intended to achieve the following objectives for older Americans:

1. an adequate income
2. good physical and mental health

3. suitable housing at a reasonable cost
4. full restorative services for those who require institutional care
5. equal employment opportunity
6. retirement with dignity
7. a meaningful existence
8. efficient community services
9. benefits of research knowledge
10. freedom, independence, and the exercise of individual initiative in planning and managing their own lives

The influence of the Older Americans Act on the lives of many older people will surely increase in years to come. Some of the programs established under the act have already proved worthwhile. The nutrition program, for example, began as an experiment, with financial aid coming from the AOA. The experiment proved successful, and in 1972 federal funds were provided to establish and operate nutrition sites around the country. The agencies providing the hot meals must also provide transportation to and from the site, information and referral services, nutrition education, health and welfare counseling, shopping assistance, and recreational activities. The nutrition sites, often located in churches, schools, or community centers, provide a social setting for interaction as well as nutritionally sound meals.

There are thousands of senior centers in the United States today. In 1975 the National Institute of Senior Centers identified nearly 18,000 such centers. When the NISC completed a sample survey of these centers, however, it was discovered that only 17 percent of them had been established before the passage of the Older Americans Act. Thus, the act has greatly stimulated the establishment of senior centers in all parts of the country (National Institute of Senior Centers, 1975).

Many of the senior centers receive financial support from the federal government either under the provisions of the Older Americans Act (Titles III and VII) or from the Office of Economic Opportunity or ACTION. Other major sources of funds are state and county governments, the United Fund, and religious organizations and private foundations.

The types of activities most often offered at senior centers are creative activities (arts and crafts, drama, music, etc.), sedentary recreation (cards and games, movies, etc.), and classes and lectures. The services most often provided include information and referral, meals, counseling, and legal, health, and employment services. Older people may attend a senior center in order to take advantage of these services, but they are just as likely to attend in order to meet people or avoid loneliness. While some researchers have concluded that senior centers do not provide people with meaningful relationships—that friendships established through a senior center tend to be secondary relationships rather than intimate, meaningful relationships—the NISC study found that many people felt they had established meaningful relationships through involvement in the centers.

Other Programs for Older Americans

A number of services are available to older Americans in many communities. Some of them are partially or fully funded by the Older Americans Act. A particular community may have several programs, while in other communities few if any of these services are available. Because of these variations, it is impossible to generalize about the programs available in any given community.

Visiting Nurse

Many communities have registered nurses who will visit older persons, especially those with chronic illnesses, on a regular schedule. In addition to providing medical services, visiting nurses often provide practical help with the normal problems of everyday life. The fees of the visiting nurse may be paid by medicare or medicaid, although this is not always the case. In some communities, homemaker or home health aid services are available. The workers who provide these services usually are not licensed but will provide routine care, including preparing special diets and managing the household, under the direction of a physician or nurse.

Meals on Wheels

This program delivers hot meals to older persons who cannot easily leave their homes. Some meals on wheels are funded by the federal government, while many others are funded and operated by local voluntary associations.

Telephone Reassurance Programs

Many communities have programs in which older persons receive daily phone calls. If a person does not answer his or her phone, someone is sent to check at that person's home in case an accident or disability has prevented him or her from securing needed help.

Transportation Services

Some communities offer free or reduced-fare rides on city buses, and some offer minibus service for weekly shopping or other activities. Door-to-door transportation is also provided at low cost through Dial-A-Bus or Dial-A-Ride services, which usually use cars or vans for nonscheduled transportation.

Day Care Centers

Many older people need services on a daily or weekly basis but do not need 24-hour institutional care. Day care centers can provide services on an outpatient basis, thus allowing people to live in their own homes. These centers allow people to enjoy the advantages of both institutional care and home living.

Legal Assistance

Some community agencies provide legal services on civil matters to older persons free or at reduced cost. Most communities have legal aid societies that provide low-cost services for people of all ages.

There are a large number of other social welfare services that are not limited to, but are relevant to, older persons. *Aging,* a publication of the AOA, provides information on many recent developments in the provision of services to older people on a continuing basis.

Summary

The basic system of income maintenance and health protection is administered by the federal government through the Social Security Administration. The components of the social security program that are of greatest benefit to the older population are old-age insurance, survivor's insurance, and health insurance. Although the program has faced some financial problems as a result of demographic changes and fluctuations in the economy, the 1977 amendments to the Social Security Act have resolved the short-term problems, and even the long-term problems will probably be solved eventually.

The Older Americans Act provides support for many social-service programs that are beneficial to an older population and in years to come will provide the basis for a significant improvement in the quality of life for older Americans.

SELECTED REFERENCES

John A. Brittain, *The Payroll Tax for Social Security* (Washington, D.C.: Brookings Institution, 1972).

Leonard D. Cain, "Aging and the Law," in eds. Robert H. Binstock and Ethel Shanas *Handbook of Aging and the Social Sciences* (New York: Van Nostrand Reinhold, 1976), pp. 342–368.

Sheila B. Kamerman and Alfred J. Kahn, "Community Services for the Aged," in *Social Services in the United States* (Philadelphia: Temple University Press, 1976).

Alicia H. Munnell, *The Future of Social Security* (Washington, D.C.: Brookings Institution, 1977).

National Institute of Senior Centers, *Senior Centers: Report of Senior Group Programs in America* (Washington, D.C.: National Council on the Aging, 1975).

A. Haeworth Robertson, "Financial Status of Social Security Program After the Social Security Amendments of 1977," *Social Security Bulletin* 41 (1978): 21–30.

James H. Schulz, *The Economics of Aging* (Belmont, Calif.: Wadsworth, 1976).

U.S. Department of Health, Education and Welfare, Administration on Aging, *Older Americans Act of 1965, as amended* (Washington, D.C.: U.S. Government Printing Office, 1976).

————, Social Security Administration, *Social Security Programs in the United States* (Washington, D.C.: U.S. Government Printing Office, 1973).

U.S. Senate, Special Committee on Aging, *Women and Social Security: Adapting to a New Era,* 94th Cong., 1st sess. (Washington, D.C.: U.S. Government Printing Office, 1975).

Aging and the Family

Overview. No area of life is more closely associated with our individual fates than our relationships with our families. We are born into families, live our day-to-day lives with them, and usually are buried and mourned by them. Very significant changes occur within our families, and our relations with family members change as we age, but we do not graduate from our families as we do from schools and colleges, nor do we retire from them as we might from a job.

Even though our family is among the most stable institutions in our lives, it is changing continuously. On the one hand, as we age, we occupy different positions in the family and kinship system; and of course as other family members age, our relations with them are subject to change. On the other hand, new members are continually entering the family (through birth) and old ones exiting (through death), which means that the composition of the family is constantly changing. In addition, the family as an institution is subject to change as a result of changes occurring in other areas of the society, historical and social changes that influence the kinds of generational relations that exist within a particular family.

As individuals we possess a unified and integrated view of our own aging, but others tend to see our aging as occurring within a specific setting; that is, others see us age within the distinct roles that we play in separate social institutions. This process is most obvious and most complex in our relationship to our family and kinship system. As we grow from child to adult, we also change our primary family identification from son or daughter to mother or father. In like manner, the niece may become an aunt, the son-in-law a father-in-law. Within the family system we occupy a large number of kin positions, vis-à-vis our relatives at any one time, but there is a definite direction to the major kin positions that we occupy. As we age we adopt new kin positions, but we also lose some of our former positions: We are no longer grandchildren when our grandparents are dead, but we may someday be grandparents ourselves.

It is easy to see that we occupy different kin positions as we age and that the continual shuffling of kin positions is a dynamic aspect of the family system. Just as important, if less obvious, is the remarkable stability of the family and kinship system, which in some ways remains unchanged despite the shuffling of kin positions. For example, the basic kin positions (father, mother, daughter, son, etc.) will be relatively unchanged despite the fact that many different people will occupy those roles. Also, the family will pass on many of its practices and rituals with only minor modifications from generation to generation. We can rest assured that the family system will survive long after we have relinquished all of our kin positions.

Change in the American family system comes from a large number of sources. One of them is the variety of ethnic groups that have lived side by side in the United States for several generations. At one time, it was commonly believed that the United States was a melting pot, a term that referred to the process whereby a large number of different cultural traditions were blended into the homogeneous soup that became American culture. More recently, however, some sociologists have argued that the United States is not a melting pot but a salad bowl (Mindel and Habenstein, 1976). In other words, it is a mixture of diverse cultures and traditions whose habits, practices, and beliefs are not as easily homogenized as was previously supposed. Rather than losing all their distinctive practices, various cultural groups have been able to maintain separate identities even while becoming integral parts of the great American salad bowl.

Whether one accepts the melting pot or salad bowl image of the American cultural system, with the subtle but important differences between the two images, it remains an acknowledged fact that the family system is a very complex and intricate one. With so many different groups with distinct racial, ethnic, religious, ideological, and geographical origins influencing the family system and being influenced by it in turn, it is impossible to do justice to the entire system. Whatever is said about the American family system has to be interpreted in this light. This is especially important because the research information is uneven, with some groups having been studied relatively thoroughly and others practically ignored. It is clear, however, that the relationship between aging and the family varies from one subcultural setting to another.

The Family in American History

By looking at the relationship between aging and the family throughout American history, it is possible to assess some of the changes that have occurred in this relationship. An appropriate starting point is the family structure and practices of the Puritan men and women who settled in New England.

The importance of the New England Puritans in the history of the American family is undisputed. The Puritans were influential in the establishment of the colonial government and economy as well as the family system. It is through these institutions that their influence persists to the present day.

Today many people lament the decline in the importance of the family in American society, and very often this decline is thought to be a result of the disappearance of the extended family. When we study the New England colonial family, we can get an idea as to how strong the family system once was and to what extent it was an extended-family system. In general, the colonial family was a very strong institution, but surprisingly, it was not a fully extended family.

The colonial family was strong in the sense that the father had great power over other family members in his household and could continue to exercise his power over his sons and his wife throughout his life. By leaving a will, as he often did, he could extend his influence over family members beyond his own lifetime. The colonial patriarch was able to exercise this power even though the extended family was not the most common family form in early New England.

Generational Relations and Male Dominance

The major source of the power of a father over his adult son was the son's dependence on the father to provide him with land to farm and a house to live in. If the colonists had desired an extended-family system, they could have required the sons to remain on the homestead. They could have built a large family house or several smaller houses to accommodate the sons' families. But they did not. The typical pattern was for the father to give each son a piece of land and a house, usually some distance from the original homestead, at the time of the son's marriage. This pattern of neolocal residence actually gave the father a great deal of power over his sons, since a son could not marry until his father was willing to give the couple a farm and a house. Even after a son was married, the father was able to maintain his influence by retaining legal title to the land on which his son lived. This usually meant that a son did not gain legal ownership of his farm until his father died and left his sons their farms in his will (Greven, 1978). Thus, the typical family pattern of the early colonists was one of neolocal residence tempered by strong patriarchal power. This pattern was a curious blend of independence and dependence; adult sons were not under the direct supervision of their fathers but were still under the control of the father if he chose to exercise his authority.

Even though most sons did not live under their father's roof after marriage, very often one son—usually the youngest—stayed on the family homestead even after marriage, and he would usually inherit the family farm and house when his father died. As an example of this pattern Greven (1978) refers to the Ballard family of Andover, Massachusetts, which included three sons. The father died without leaving a will, and the sons agreed to divide the land, with each son keeping the land he was farming and the house in which he and his family were living. It was the youngest son, John, who received the land and house worked by the mother and father. Greven (1978, p. 28) comments, "It is unclear whether John lived with his wife and their four children in the same house as his parents, but there is a strong likelihood that this was the case in view of his assuming control of it after his father's death." The sons agreed, furthermore, that their mother would continue to occupy a room in the family home and would be provided for by all three sons.

If the Ballard family was reasonably representative of the family style and structure of other New England families (and there is evidence suggesting that it was), then the family structure had many of the features usually associated with an extended family. Most of the sons established new households, usually not adjacent to the land and home of their parents; yet the land was still owned by their fathers and there was a pattern of continuing obligation and responsibility between the generations. As mentioned earlier, the father very often retain lifetime legal ownership of all of his land. It seems reasonable to conclude that there was a substantial amount of economic cooperation between father and sons and between brothers, perhaps even between father and son-in-law and brother and brother-in-law, and that the sons were usually obliged to provide continuing economic support for their widowed mother.

Some fathers spelled out in their wills, in great detail, the rights of their widow and the obligations of their sons toward their mother. For example, some extant wills accorded to widowed mothers "free liberty to bake, brew, and wash, etc., in the kitchen"; "firewood, ready cut for the fire, at her door"; "a gentle horse or mare to ride to meeting or any other occasion she may have" (Demos, 1978, p. 238). Some of these stipulations were made necessary because the father was giving legal ownership of the homestead to one of the sons, but others were courtesies and responsibilities that sons might have been expected to extend toward their mother regardless of whether they were detailed in a will. We do not know, of course, what inspired a particular father to inform his sons of their duties toward their widowed mother in his will. Did the mother prompt such statements in the will out of concern about her fate once she became the grandmother in the home of her son and daughter-in-law? Was it a sign of distrust of the sons or of the daughter-in-law? Or was the detailed will simply the father's final sermon to his sons regarding filial duty? We have no way of knowing, but whatever the reason or reasons, a significant number of early New Englanders used their wills as instruments to dictate the relations that were to be maintained between the generations after they died.

Other transactions between generations were also handled in a legalistic fashion. For example, deeds that transferred property from a father to a son sometimes stipulated that the father was relinquishing his land to his son with the understanding that the son was obliged to pay his father a set sum of money every year as long as the father lived (Greven, 1978). In this situation the father was using the gift of land to his sons as a means of providing himself with an annuity. Again, it is curious that this arrangement would take the form of a legal document. For purposes of studying early New England history, this is fortunate; but surely there were other families that practiced similar intergenerational support systems that were never formalized beyond a verbal agreement or an implicit understanding.

The operation of the colonial family system assured the older male of a continuing and powerful position in the family system. Since the economy was almost entirely agricultural, patriarchal control of the land was the ultimate source of power. Even though sons were forced to defer to their fathers, however, it is important to realize that the fathers were allowing their sons to establish households of their own. Thus, while the parents' influence over a married son might remain strong, most households were nuclear families. The classical extended family was never the preferred family arrangement, even among the earliest New England settlers (Demos, 1970).

As is obvious from our discussion, the father–son relationship was very important in the New England family. Not a great deal is known about the father–daughter or mother–daughter relationship, because upon marriage the daughter became peripheral to her family of orientation. But there is some historical evidence about the conjugal (husband–wife) relationship.

Colonial Widows

It is indisputable that the New England family system was dominated by males, but this does not mean that the female was entirely without rights or privileges. Wills left by husbands give us some idea of the position of the wife, especially the older wife. For example, consistent with the English common-law tradition, a widow was entitled to one-third of the land and movable property of the estate of her deceased husband (Demos, 1970). This practice, known as widow's thirds, was enforced by legal authorities even if a deceased husband's will left her with less. In most cases a widow was given a choice between what was stipulated in the husband's will and widow's thirds.

Although colonial widows had an established legal position, there were at least two problems with their legal rights. First, even though a widow received one-third of her deceased husband's land and could use this land to support herself, she could not sell the land. She was not allowed to sell any real estate because she did not own it; instead, she was allowed to use it for the remainder of her life; then the property passed to the deceased husband's heir (probably a son). Second, because the widow was not allowed to sell any real estate received from her deceased husband's estate, it was sometimes difficult for her to generate much income from the property. Early New England was endowed with a great amount of land, but there was a shortage of labor. A widow who was prevented from selling land in order to secure income was also in the unfortunate position of controlling land that needed labor if it was to produce income (Keyssar, 1974). Without the labor power to plant, cultivate, and harvest crops, the land was of very limited value.

It would seem that a widow with land but no one to work the land would be an ideal candidate for remarriage. New England always had more men than women because of the greater propensity of men to migrate to North America. Also, because of the harsh conditions of colonial life, as well as the risk of death in childbirth, the supply of widowers would always be larger than the supply of widows; and widow's thirds would be as large as, if not larger than, the dowry of a previously unmarried woman. Historical research finds, however, that it was fairly uncommon for widows to remarry. Keyssar (1974, p. 94) remarks that "the traditional view that colonial widows remarried easily and rapidly does not conform with any of the data. . . . Once widowed, a woman was far more likely to die a widow than to enter into a second marriage."

On the other hand, a colonial widow usually was not left destitute, since her adult children would provide her with the necessities of life. As mentioned previously, this filial obligation was sometimes stated in a deceased father's will; but even if it was not stated, adult children recognized their responsibility for the support of a widowed mother. This is an important point because, as we will see, one of the most persistent features of the American family structure has been the tendency to transfer some family functions to other social institutions; and one of the transferred functions has been the obligation of children to support their aged parents.

Community Support for People Without Families

Even in colonial New England, not all widows were supported by their children. When widows or widowers were unable to support themselves, it was usually the local community that provided them with the necessities of life. As Keyssar (1974, pp. 115–116) concluded in his study of colonial America, "Although the family had primary responsibility for the care of widows and the law sought to insure that families fulfilled that responsibility, indigent widows were not simply left to perish. The town was the secondary agency of social welfare and was expected to intervene when family support was not available." As an example, Demos (1978, p. 240) notes that New Haven, Connecticut, voted to give a man called "Old Bunnill" some public benefits, including an allowance of two shillings per week; later, when the man said that he wanted to return to England, the town paid his passage with public funds. Not all residents of the early colonies were as fortunate. Old slaves were sometimes turned out by their owners to fend for themselves when they were too old to be an economic advantage. One slave narrative said that old slaves were treated with little concern by the owners:

> As far as the owner is concerned, they live or die, as it happens; it is just the same thing as turning out an old horse. Their children, or other near relations, if living in the neighborhood, take it by turns to go out at night with a supply saved from their own scanty allowance of food, as well as to cut wood and fetch water for them; this is done entirely through the good feelings of the slaves, and not through the masters' taking care that it is done. (Fischer, 1978, pp. 64–65)

The Family Life Cycle in Colonial America

It is difficult to present a "typical" picture of the structure of family life in colonial America, but Fischer (1978, p. 56) provides the following description as indicative of the life cycle of some New England families:

Men married at twenty-five; women, at twenty-one. Normally the first baby was born within a year of the marriage; the last came when the wife was thirty-eight and her husband was forty-two. As a rule, the youngest child did not marry until the parents were sixty-four and sixty. Men and women continued to live with their unmarried children nearly until the end of their lives. Very few old people lived alone; most remained in nuclear families with their own children still around them. Scracely any of them lived in extended, three-generation households. Those who did usually had taken in a married daughter or son who had lost a spouse. When three generations lived together, it was more often the young who were in some way dependent upon the old than the old upon the young.

The colonial American family was a strong institution, based primarily on patriarchal power. People grew old in their families, with unmarried children still living at home when the parents were in their 60s. Old age did not mean retirement, nor did it usually imply dependence. In terms of power and influence, the older generation usually was in control; and the old were not on the young but the young on the old. If, however, an older person was not able to take care of himself or herself, it was expected that the family would provide aid. The community would provide financial support to widows or widowers who were without resources or family, but the usual expectation was that families would support their members in times of need.

The Decline of the Family as the Primary Source of Support for Kin

When did the family cease to be the primary source of support for kin who were in need, and how has the present system of aid for the old evolved? This is a complex question because it involves broad questions about generational relations, political economy, and the history and development of the modern systems of community and social welfare. Fischer (1978) offers an answer with a substantial amount of evidence to support it. He concludes that a revolution in attitudes occurred in the United States in the period between 1770 and 1820. He argues that the shift in attitudes was based on the idea of age equality, that is, equalization of the status of people of different ages and increasing emphasis on other status ascribers. Prior to 1770, age was an important ingredient in the determination of a person's social status, with older people being accorded greater status than younger people. But beginning about 1770, several changes occurred in American society that indicated a shift in attitudes toward age, including some observable changes in the operation of the family system. One of these was in inheritance customs. Prior to the nineteenth century, American families had favored a system of primogeniture. By the early 1800s, it was more likely that all sons would be treated equally in matters of inheritance.

Another change was the sharp decline in the practice of naming grandchildren for their grandparents that occurred between the years 1790 and 1830. The 1800s also saw the founding of old-age homes, first for the affluent and eventually for the poor; those for the poor were public institutions operated by state and local governments. The establishment of these homes was an important development because their existence indicated a decline in the position of the older members of a family. Compare, for example, the strong position of older males in the early New England colonies. Their power increased with age, so that the oldest male was the most powerful member of a family. Women were not as fortunate as their husbands, but even from the grave a man could ensure that surviving members of the family would care for his aging wife. The appearance of old-age homes is good evidence for the decline of age as an element in family power. There have always been some people who have faced the misfortune of being left without close kin to offer them aid and support in their old age; this was true in early colonial New England as well as in later periods of American history. But the United States was experiencing a much more pervasive decline in the influence of age on the family system.

There are a number of suggestions as to why age was losing its power and influence. The United States was undergoing rapid industrialization and urbanization, and this gave young people new opportunities and alternatives to the agricultural way of life. Even agricultural families were being separated when younger generations moved west as land became scarce in the settled communities. However, the decline in the influence of age is thought to be a result of the change in attitudes that produced two complementary ideas: the obsolescence of old age and the cult of youth (Fischer, 1978; Achenbaum, 1974).

Advancing age had once been glorified, perhaps even romanticized, and now it was being viewed in a much more negative light. The medical problems associated with growing old were attracting more attention. Businesses were concerned about increasing their efficiency; older workers were viewed as hindrances. It was in this new atmosphere that the glorification of youth took root. Social changes in attitudes toward age foreshadowed a significant change in the status of older people as well as in relations between generations.

The Emergence of the Affectional Family

The American family structure has changed in many ways over the past 200 years, but the most important of these changes may be the least visible. The basis of family organization has changed from the functional interdependence of generations to the affectional ties between family members. The typical colonial family was bound together by a series of mutual dependencies, usually culminating in strong patriarchal authority. Today there is much less functional interdependence between generations but a much greater degree of affection. Streib and Thompson (1960, p. 454) captured this kind of change in an interview with a 70 year old man. When they asked him whether he thought there was less affection in contemporary family relationships, he said, "There is more affection today. I am not saying I didn't hold my parents in high regard, because I did. But it was that I respected and kind of feared them, too, I guess. I thought that they had all the answers. Now take my kids: they know more than I do and they know they do, but they love the old man and even let me spoil my grandkids."

Because the family is built around affectional ties, it has become a more restricted unit in terms of meaningful affectional relations. For most people, family means a husband and a wife, their parents, their children, and their grandchildren. People will acknowledge kinship with cousins and aunts and uncles, nieces and nephews, but in actual practice even relationships between siblings are fairly limited.

There are several implications for older people in the changing structure of the family. One is that larger numbers of people will be left with no familial support. Another is that it is no longer socially necessary that a child support an aging parent, and parents might be much less likely to expect or even desire financial aid from their children because of the danger that such aid might interfere with their affectional relationships. Finally, since parents and their children are not likely to be engaged in an interdependent economic relationship, the fate of one is usually independent of the fate of the other.

The Family Life Cycle Today

Americans are taught to be very conscious of time, dividing it up into months, days, hours, minutes, seconds, and so on. We come to regard it as a resource, like money, and even associate the two: "Time is money." We are told to use our time wisely, to save time by using one method instead of another, and even, on occasion, that "time is on our side." Being so conscious of time, we usually know our age, and we come to think of the aging process in terms of our chronological age. But chronological age is only a crude indicator of aging.

Satchel Paige, the Hall of Fame baseball player and social commentator, is supposed to have asked, "How old would you be if you didn't know how old you were?" There are several possible answers to his question. Perhaps what Paige had in mind was functional age; that is, an individual would not be too old to perform any task until he or she was no longer able to perform it. A baseball pitcher would not be too old to play at the age of 35, only when he could no longer pitch effectively.

There are ways of knowing how old we are, without referring to chronological age. One of these is to note our position in our family and kinship system.

Just by knowing our familial generation—children, parents, grandparents, great-grandparents—we know how old we are in relation to the family system.

Sociologists have used the family life cycle as a major organizing theme. Individuals are born into a family of orientation, which is usually composed of a mother, a father, and their children. Upon reaching adulthood, the individual becomes a mother or father in another nuclear family, the family of procreation. There is a natural movement of individuals from the family of orientation to the family of procreation, and this movement represents the beginning of a new generation. Even within these nuclear families, however, there are distinct stages that are often used to describe the family life cycle.

One of the best-known and most frequently used models of the family life cycle is the one provided by Duvall (1971). She views the cycle as consisting of eight stages:

1. a married couple without children
2. the childbearing stage
3. a couple with preschool children
4. a couple with school-age children
5. a couple with teenagers
6. a couple with children leaving home
7. the empty nest: a couple in middle age with adult children
8. an aging couple

As is obvious, this description of the family life cycle is child oriented: that is, the married couple is defined primarily in terms of the ages of the children. If we think of these eight stages as they are related to our families of orientation and procreation, we can see that each individual would typically enter his or her family of orientation at stage 2 and exit at stage 6. If the exit from the family of orientation coincided with the time of marriage, then the individual would immediately enter stage 1 of his or her family of procreation. This would result in an individual's moving through thirteen or fourteen stages (depending on whether one was left outside of a nuclear family by widowhood) during a lifetime. Table 10.1 shows the movement of the hypothetical individual through the family life cycle and the approximate chronological ages at which each stage is experienced.

The Nuclear Family

One of the outstanding features of the American family system is the relative impermanence of the nuclear families. Table 10.1 shows that the typical person leaves the family of orientation when he or she reaches young adulthood. It is not usually very long before that person enters a new nuclear family, the

Table 10.1 HYPOTHETICAL COORDINATION OF THE FAMILY LIFE CYCLE AND THE INDIVIDUAL FAMILY CAREER

Years of age	0–2½	2½–6	6–13	13–20	20–23	23–24	24–26	26–32	32–38	38–45	45–48	48–65	65–75	75+
Individual family career stage	1	2	3	4	5	6	7	8	9	10	11	12	13	14
Family life cycle stage	(2	3	4	5	6)	(1	2	3	4	5	6	7	8	9)
		Family of orientation							Family of procreation					

family of procreation. At this point the family of orientation becomes somewhat secondary to the family of procreation. In terms of family structure this means that adult children become less attentive to their parents as they themselves begin the parenting process. The family of procreation is, by its nature and function, a child-oriented family. At least, it is child-oriented until the children leave the family to establish their own family of procreation. Older adults are left in the family of procreation; but in reality, once the children have left, the family consists only of the husband and wife until the death of one of the spouses. At this point the nuclear family that came into being at the time of marriage is dissolved. Table 10.2 indicates this process by showing the percentages of adults at various ages who form what the Bureau of the Census calls primary individual households. A primary individual is a person who maintains a household but lives with no relatives—usually a single individual living alone. The table shows that the numbers of primary individuals are fairly low until about age 55, when these households begin increasing in number. Most of the increase after age 55 can be attributed to the death of a spouse, which leaves the widow or widower as the only member of a household. Such households are not classified as families. Males are not nearly as likely as females to form primary individual households, even after age 65. About 12.5 percent of American males between the ages of 65 and 74, and about 21.1 percent of the males over age 75 live by themselves. About 36.0 percent of the females between the ages of 65 and 74 and 48.5 percent of those over age 75 live alone. Most of those who are not living alone are, of course, married.

Although we are born into a family of orientation, this family usually dissolves during our adult life. All the children born into that nuclear family exit, and eventually one of the spouses dies. As a functioning unit, that nuclear family is gone, although it is preserved symbolically through photographs and memories. Upon marriage, individuals establish a new nuclear family that could last until one of the spouses dies.

Table 10.2 MALES AND FEMALES LIVING OUTSIDE OF FAMILIES, BY AGE, MARCH 1977 (PRIMARY INDIVIDUALS)[a]

Age	25–29	30–34	35–39	40–44	45–54	55–64	65–74	75+
Males	13.6%	10.4%	8.3%	6.4%	7.2%	8.2%	12.5%	21.1%
Females	8.8%	4.9%	3.5%	4.2%	7.8%	18.7%	36.0%	48.5%

[a]"Persons who are not family members (that is, are not recognized as living with any relatives) are 'unrelated individuals.' Unrelated individuals are of two types—primary and secondary. A 'primary individual' is a person maintaining a household with no relatives in the household. A 'secondary individual' is a lodger, partner, guest, or resident employee with no relatives in the household or group quarters" (p. 51).

Source: U.S. Bureau of the Census, *Current Population Reports*, Series P-20, no. 323, "Marital Status and Living Arrangements: March, 1977" (Washington, D.C.: U.S. Government Printing Office, 1978).

The family life cycle concept is important because it offers a perspective for studying changes in family relations throughout a lifetime. For example, how does the parent–child relationship change over the various stages of family life cycle and the individual family career? When a person becomes a parent for the first time, he or she is in stage 2 of the family of procreation and stage 7 of the individual family career—there is a large gap in family experience between the parent and the newborn child. Much later in the lives of both the parent and the child, the parent may be in life stage 13 and the child in life stage 12. The gap has narrowed and may even disappear entirely. This movement through the individual family career stages surely has an effect on all the relationships found in the family and kinship system.

From the day a child is born until the day he or she enters school, the family is the most important influence on him or her. In school, the child is influenced by peers as well as by adults such as teachers; this reduces the influence of the family. The movement away from the family continues through adolescence, a period in which one's age mates are very important.

Shulman (1975) argues that young single adults are less likely to be highly involved with their kin groups because their major concerns lead them to associate with age mates who share those concerns. Adolescents and young single adults have among their primary concerns preparation for and establishment of a career, companionship, and mate selection, all of which usually occur outside of a family context. Mate selection, of course, must occur outside of the family.

After the period of estrangement from the family, people reengage with their family and kinfolk. Aldous (1967) feels that in the period immediately after marriage but before the birth of their first child a couple will maintain some distance from kin because of the fragile nature of the new conjugal relationship. When the first child arrives, however, the relationship is firmly established and the presence of the child is indisputable evidence that a new nuclear family has been established. Also, kinship aid is needed.

Intergenerational Relations and Exchange

It is the middle-aged family that is most involved in family affairs, mainly because the middle-aged husband and wife maintain intergenerational contacts in two directions, that is, with their parents and with their children and grandchildren.

The exchange of goods and services is often regarded by family sociologists as a good indicator of the strength of intergenerational relations and the kin network. Notwithstanding the emphasis in American society on socializing children for independence and establishing of independent households upon marriage, most research has discovered a vibrant system of exchange between generations. Not surprisingly, a significant amount of financial aid passes from parents to their married children in the early years of the children's marriages. However, the exchange relationship between the generations is much more complex than this. Hill and associates (1970, pp. 78–80) concluded that in three-generational families the middle generation bridges the exchange system. In terms of giving and receiving aid, "The married child generation with its pressure of children on resources was most needful and received most help. Whereas the relatively affluent parent generation was least in need of help and received least." The middle-aged parents help their children, but they find that their parents also have needs that must be met.

The needs of the grandparent generation are usually somewhat different from those of the young married generation. The grandparent generation is in need of help with problems of illness, household management, and emotional gratification. It is the middle generation that responds to the differing needs of both the younger and older generations. This structure of generational relations places a strain on the middle generation, which is doing most of the giving and the least receiving. It is said that "'Tis better to give than to receive," but most evidence shows that people expect exchange relationships to be somewhat balanced between giving and receiving. What the middle generation receives for all of its giving to the younger and the older generations is familial prestige and status. Hill (1970, p. 79) states that "parents who give to both younger and older generations more than they receive from either are in a patron-like status, while grandparents who give much less than they receive find themselves in a dependent status."

Generational Independence

The pattern that seems to be typical of American society is one in which children are dependent on their parents in many ways but become less so with age. The period of greatest independence from parents may be young adulthood. The apex of familial involvement is reached during middle age, when a couple may render aid of various kinds to both younger and older generations. When people grow older, they tend to give less assistance and to receive more. But even though older people may receive more aid than they give, this does not mean that they are dependent on their children. At every stage of the American family life cycle there is a great deal of emphasis on achieving and maintaining independence. It is important that the pattern of intergenerational support and aid not interfere with the overriding concern for independence.

Independence is highly valued at all stages of the family life cycle, and it has led to the description of intergenerational relations in the United States as "intimacy at a distance" (Shanas et al., 1968; Treas, 1975). This means that most people want to maintain intimate ties with family members while at the same time preserving the independence and autonomy of the nuclear family. When older persons are no longer able to maintain their independence they will turn to members of their family for help, but they will usually remain independent as long as possible (Neugarten, 1975).

Because of the strong emphasis on independence in our society, even family members want to avoid being financially dependent on kin. Older people may want and expect help from their children when the need arises, but the desire for aid stops short of expecting financial aid. Seelbach (1977, p. 423) reported that when older Americans were asked who should support old people financially, "Large majorities of both sexes (76.7% of the women and 80.3% of the men) saw financial support to be the responsibility of the government rather than offspring." This overwhelming preference for support by the government rather than by offspring does not imply that older people absolve their children of all filial responsibility, including financial responsibility, if the need arises. Wake and Sporakowski (1972) found, however, that even when older parents are in need of financial aid they are very hesitant actually to solicit such support from their children.

It seems to be widely believed in American society that older people are deserted and ignored by their children, that they are estranged from their kin network. All of the evidence indicates that this opinion is entirely false, that children usually aid their aging parents in a variety of ways and that they do so because they feel affection and filial responsibility. Most children voluntarily aid their aging parents when they are in need; when aging parents are estranged from their children, it is usually a long-term estrangement and not something that developed once the parent reached an advanced age (Blenkner, 1965; Schorr, 1960).

Whereas adult children very often provide various kinds of services for their aging parents, it is relatively uncommon for children to give their parents financial aid. Most estimates of the frequency of cash contributions to parents by adult children are that it occurs in less than one case out of ten (Schorr, 1960). But it must be remembered that older parents are attitudinally opposed to receiving cash aid. As early as 1948, Fried and Stern reported that aged parents did not want financial assistance from their children for a wide variety of reasons: that receiving support from one's children is humiliating and erodes parental authority, that the support of older people should be a responsibility of the government, that contemporary social expectations require older people to remain independent and economically self-sufficient. Many older people are more interested in receiving love and affection from their children, and many older people are not willing to risk endangering an affectional relationship in order to receive financial assistance. The conclusion reached by Streib (1965,

p. 472) is that " from the standpoint of the older generation, the maintenance of close affectional ties is of paramount importance. Parents are unwilling to jeopardize close family ties with their children by expecting financial assistance from them."

Although older people want love and affection from their descendants, they prefer not to receive money and also not to live with them in the same household. Nye and Berardo (1973, p. 528) have reported that "a study of older people revealed that an overwhelming majority were not at all eager to reside in the same household as their children and grandchildren, but preferred instead to live apart from the younger generations for as long as they were capable of doing so. It appears, therefore, that most Americans are not in favor of three-generational living."

The Grandparent Role

The family and kinship position that is most often associated with older people is that of grandparent. This role has undergone a great deal of change in the last few decades, and it may well be that social impressions and attitudes toward grandparents may not have kept up with these changes. Everyone is aware, for example, of the image of the grandfather who is supposed to smoke his pipe in his rocking chair while telling stories about the old days and the grandmother who divides her time between baking cookies and pies and crocheting in her rocking chair. This romantic view of grandparents is far removed from the contemporary grandparent, who may be in his or her late 40s or early 50s, live in the suburbs, work most of the day to earn a living, and spend very little time whittling or making blueberry muffins.

While most Americans probably find the grandparent role comfortable and satisfying, apparently about one-third of all grandparents do not (Neugarten and Weinstein, 1968). A study of grandparents found that the role had different meanings for different people. The largest number saw the position of grandparent in terms of biological renewal or continuity; that is, the grandchildren represent the future of the family line. Others saw grandparenthood as a chance for emotional fulfillment; this was especially true for those who felt that they missed some or most of the fulfillment of parenthood because they had been too busy. Some grandparents view themselves as resource persons who provide their grandchildren with help either through teaching or by giving them financial assistance. A few grandparents were found who viewed the role as an opportunity to accomplish things vicariously by anticipating the achievements of their grandchildren. But the study also found that over one-quarter of the grandparents derived very little satisfaction from the role, usually because they were emotionally remote from their grandchildren.

The study also reported that grandparents approach their role in several different ways, a diversity that was expressed in the five types of grandparent they discovered: the formal grandparent, the funseeker, the surrogate parent, the reservoir of family wisdom, and the distant figure.

The formal grandparents are those who follow the traditional role: that is, they are indulgent toward their grandchildren and may provide some aid to the parents, such as baby-sitting, they leave the parenting to the parents and do not interfere in the rearing of the grandchildren.

The funseekers maintain a very informal relationship with their grandchildren and engage in the fun and games of childhood. The relationship between grandparent and grandchild is based on a sense of equality rather than on the traditional lines of authority in the family, and both appear to derive genuine enjoyment from it.

The grandparent who acts as a surrogate parent is usually a grandmother who takes care of her grandchildren while their parents are at work. The grandparent who serves as a reservoir of family wisdom is usually a grandfather who follows traditional lines of family authority. The grandfather's position is based on the possession of special skills or resources on which the younger generation depends.

Finally, the distant figure grandparent is not actively involved in family affairs—that is, does not maintain a close relationship to the grandchildren— but is present for holidays, special occasions, and ritualistic observances.

While some people are much more involved in the grandparent role than others, most research indicates that this role is of limited significance for most people. As Wood and Robertson (1976) conclude, grandparents find the period when their grandchildren are small most rewarding. After the grandchildren reach adolescence, they establish their independence from all the adults in the family, and even though many people may live long enough to become great-grandparents, this is regarded as little more than a symbolic role. Even the role of grandparent is seldom thought to contain much substance:

> While grandparents verbally attribute a great deal of significance to the role of discussions and interviews, the behavior of most grandparents in the role is relatively limited. It is true that most of them baby-sit, take their grandchildren to the zoo, movies, and so on, read to and play with them, give them gifts, and remember their birthdays, but for most grandparents these activities occur only a few times a year. (Wood and Robertson, 1976, p. 301)

Robertson (1977, p. 170), however, found that even though the activities in which grandmothers are most likely to engage are babysitting, home recreation, and drop-in visits, they nevertheless enjoy the role and were happy about becoming a grandmother. "When asked which role they enjoyed most, parent or grandparent, 37 percent preferred grandparenting, 32 percent parenting, and 25 percent equally enjoyed both roles. On the whole, grandmothers report that grandparenting is an easier role."

The grandparental role has been given a boost in the United States with the establishment of National Grandparent's Day on September 9, 1979. It was the first time that grandparents had been granted an annual day of observance, a status equal to that of Mother's Day and Father's Day. Grandparent's Day has been designated as the first Sunday after Labor Day.

Three-generational Living Arrangements

The preference for independence also influences the living arrangements of older parents and their adult children. One survey found that most adults in the United States feel that it is a bad idea for parents to share a home with their adult children. But, when people are presented with a hypothetical choice between having an ailing parent live with a daughter and placing the parent in an institution, a much larger proportion say that the parent should move in with the daughter (Wake and Sporakowski, 1972).

In fact, very few American households (less than 3 percent) contain three generations (U.S. Bureau of the Census, 1973). Less than one-quarter of older people live in two-generational households (Shanas et al., 1968). There is a tendency for older people to maintain their own households independently of their children, and this is true of nonmarried as well as married parents. Stehouwer (1965) reported that 78 percent of married couples over age 65 live by themselves. Only 2 percent live with a married son or daughter. When a married couple over age 65 live with one of their children, it is usually with an unmarried child, and this occurs in about 15 percent of the cases. As would be expected, it is much more common for older divorced or widowed parents to live with their children. Even so, only about 45 percent of nonmarried parents live with a child or grandchild, and in more than half of these cases an unmarried parent lives with an unmarried child. About 54 percent of nonmarried older people live alone (47 percent) or with a sibling or a nonrelative (7 percent). Thus, even though nearly half of all nonmarried older parents live with a child or grandchild, most of these individuals are unmarried themselves, so that many of these situations may be viewed as cases of children living with a parent rather than vice versa.

It is not much more common for a widow to live with kin than for a widower to do so, despite the popular notion that it is usually widows who move in with their children. The U.S. Bureau of the Census found that in 1970 less than 5 percent of households contained a parent of a husband or wife when the husband or wife was the head of the household (U.S. Bureau of the Census, 1973). In addition, rather than establishing intergenerational households, older people tend to maintain independent households (Carp, 1976).

What we know about the structure and functioning of the American family system, and especially about relations between generations, leads to the conclusion that the system is based on what seem to be contradictory values, interdependence and independence. The wider kin system is based on the interdependence of the generations, while the nuclear family values its autonomy and independence. The result is that relations between generations are determined more by feelings of affection than by compulsory obligations. Most adult children have a sense of filial responsibility, but the strength of the relationship between parents and offspring is based on mutual concern derived from genuine love and affection. Children are expected to be willing to give their parents financial support and to share their homes with them if necessary; but older people do not want financial aid and prefer to live independently. Members of the various generations want family members to be geographically close, but not so close as to stifle generational autonomy. All of these contending elements of the family system are summarized by the phrase most commonly used to describe the ideal state of relations between the generations: "intimacy at a distance." The phrase seems to be a contradiction in terms, a self-negating concept, but it captures very well the tension found in generational relations. It appears that the American family system operates like a yo-yo, sometimes near, sometimes distant, but always connected by a string.

The Conjugal Relationship

The American family system is sometimes described as a conjugal system. This means that the family is built around the husband–wife relationship. Other family systems are called consanguineal, which means that the family is built around blood relationships. In a consanguineal system, for example, a son would be expected to follow the wishes of his parents over the objections of his wife. In a conjugal family system the situation is reversed; a husband would be expected to follow the wishes of his wife even over the objections of his parents. The example is perhaps more simple than real-life family situations, but it illustrates the primary distinction between conjugal and consanguineal family systems.

If the American family system is a conjugal one, it is very important to know the quality of the conjugal relationship over the life cycle. The two most famous studies of marital satisfaction at various stages of the family life cycle are the Blood and Wolfe (1960) study, which found that the quality of the conjugal relationship decreases with age and the Rollins and Feldman (1970) study, which found that marital satisfaction declines in the early stages of the family life cycle but that this trend is reversed in the later stages.

There are a number of reasons for distrusting both of these descriptions of the conjugal relationship. First, all studies of marital satisfaction have used a cross-sectional research design (see Chapter 1 for a discussion of research designs); a longitudinal or cohort analysis design would be more appropriate for observing the marital satisfaction of couples over time. Second, comparisons of various age groups or of people at various stages of the life cycle are influenced by factors that could seriously bias the findings. For example, some couples get divorced; some people become widows or widowers; others are involved in second or third marriages. All of these types of influences tend to alter the nature of the population at different stages of the family life cycle, especially the later stages. Third, even though there may be some observable differences in marital satisfaction over the life cycle, the differences may be unimportant in theoretical terms. In their study, Rollins and Cannon (1974, p. 280) concluded that since "92 percent of the variation in marital satisfaction is unrelated to family life cycle, then it seems unwise to be overly concerned with preventing the effects of family life cycle changes on marital satisfaction." If the family life cycle is responsible for only about 8 percent of the change in marital satisfaction, it would certainly be unwise to devote too much attention to the phenomenon or to warn couples of an inevitable decline in marital satisfaction as they age.

Some studies, in fact, have found that the conjugal relationship improves with age. Deutscher (1968) interviewed couples between the ages of 40 and 65 who had raised children and launched them into the adult world. He asked them about the quality of their postparental life and found that the overwhelming majority rated it as good as or better than earlier stages of family life. A very small minority stated that they found postparental life worse than previous stages. For many, postparental life brought new freedom. "It is a time of freedom—freedom from financial responsibilities, freedom to be mobile (geographically), freedom from housework and other chores, and finally, freedom to be one's self for the first time since the children came along" (p. 264). The high quality of older conjugal relationships is confirmed by Stinnett, Carter, and Montgomery (1972). They found that 95 percent of their older respondents (aged 60 to 89) rated their marriages as happy or very happy and that a majority felt that their marriages had become better over time. Even more supportive of the idea that the quality of conjugal relationships increases with age were their responses when asked what had been the happiest period of their marriage. About 18 percent said that the young adult years were the happiest and about 27 percent that the middle years were the happiest, but a whopping 55 percent reported that the present time was the happiest.

Divorce

Divorce statistics for the United States show very clearly that the divorce rate peaks in the mid-20s and declines steadily with advancing age. (See Figure 10.1.) Table 10.3 shows that divorces occur at relatively early ages; only 11 percent of the divorces of men and 9 percent of those of women occur after the age of 49. Stated another way, about 90 percent of all first divorces occur

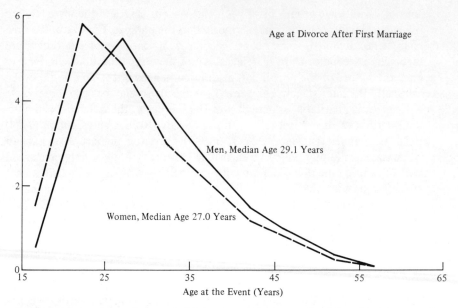

Figure 10.1 *Ages of Men and Women at Divorce after First Marriage in the United States, 1975*

Source: U.S. Bureau of the Census, *Current Population Reports*, Series P-20, no. 297, "Number, Timing, and Duration of Marriages and Divorces in the United States: June, 1975" (Washington, D.C.: U.S. Government Printing Office, 1976).

before the age of 50. If divorces serve to separate the couples who are least happy with their conjugal relationship, then older marriages should turn out to be happier when a cross-sectional research design is used—the unhappiest marriages would be excluded from the cohort.

Romantic Love in Later Years

It is often assumed that older marriages are less satisfactory because of the demise of romantic love. Couples usually get married because they are in love, but the arrival of children and the everyday pressures of making a living and running a household transform the conjugal relationship into one based on pragmatic concerns and practical realities. Greenfield (1965) argues that Americans use romantic love as the basis for courtship and marriage because they are very practical and rational in the construction of their lives. He argues as follows: If everyone based every major decision on self-interest, few people would get married and even fewer would have children. The long-term result of a self-interested approach to life would be the destruction of society itself.

Table 10.3 AGE AT DIVORCE FOR PERSONS BORN BETWEEN 1900 AND 1909

	Men		Women	
Age	Number	Percentage	Number	Percentage
14–19	13	2	52	5
20–24	72	9	157	16
25–29	127	16	183	19
30–34	155	20	159	16
35–39	130	17	156	16
40–44	106	14	104	11
45–49	71	9	72	7
50–54	43	6	43	4
55–75	56	7	48	5
Total	773	100	974	99

Source: U.S. Bureau of the Census, *Current Population Reports*, Series P-20, no. 297, "Number, Timing, and Duration of Marriages and Divorces in the United States: June, 1975" (Washington, D.C.: U.S. Government Printing Office, 1976).

A society cannot survive long without new members, most of whom are children. And without families the economy would collapse, since the family is the basic unit of consumption. This problem is resolved by the workings of romantic love. Love causes people, especially young adults, to temporarily abandon their pragmatic and self-interested approach to life. Once they have fallen in love, they get married, have children, and buy houses, food, shoes, and so on, and society survives. Once people are married and producing offspring, however, practical concerns become paramount. These require rational thought, and romantic love would be dysfunctional. In this scenario, therefore, romantic love is confined to the early years of courtship and marriage and is unnecessary in the later years.

Stinnett, Carter, and Montgomery (1972) did not find that romantic love disappears in the later years of marriage. When they asked their respondents to name the most important factor in marital success, almost half (48.6 percent) said "being in love." This was by far the most typical response, with the more practical elements of a marriage being cited by relatively few people. Likewise, Knox (1970) compared three groups of people of different ages on romantic versus realistic conceptions of love. Surprisingly, he discovered that people who had been married more than twenty years had a romantic conception of love, as much or more so than high school seniors. It was the third group, those who had been married less than five years, who took a realistic view of love. While there are a number of possible interpretations of these patterns, it would clearly be erroneous to assume that romantic love disappears from marriage after the early years.

Aging and Sexuality

The topic of aging and sexuality is important to gerontologists because it occupies such an ambivalent position in the mores and folkways of American society. Of course, ambivalence toward sexual behavior does not arise only in regard to aging; it is a persistent feature of American culture. Many parents do not want their children to know too much about sexual behavior for fear that such knowledge might lead to premature sexual activity. Because we have extended the period of dependent childhood to include adolescence, American youths are biologically capable of competent sexual behavior but are expected to refrain from sexual activity. As any textbook on the sociology of the family will document, not only do teenagers know about sexual behavior but rather large proportions of the teenage population engage in sexual activity. We find a somewhat analogous situation with regard to sexual behavior at the other end of the life cycle. There appears to be an attempt by society to deny the existence of sexual competence among older people, but research has shown that it exists.

Why does the United States have an ambivalent attitude toward sexuality at the younger and older ends of the life cycle? There is no sure answer, but many researchers argue that sexual behavior has traditionally been socially sanctioned as a means of procreation, not recreation. Sexual behavior is sanctioned only insofar as it leads to the conception and birth of children, which means that it is sanctioned from the time of marriage until menopause. Sex as recreation, or even as an expression of affection and a contribution toward a stable conjugal relationship, is not fully legitimate, or at least not as legitimate as sex for purposes of procreation.

The problem with the traditional American view of sexuality is that the biology of sex does not always coincide with the social definition of appropriate sexual behavior. This is true for adolescents, but it is also true for older adults.

The known biological status of sexuality among older adults is based on three major studies: those by Kinsey and associates (1948, 1953), Masters and Johnson (1966, 1970), and Duke University (Newman and Nichols, 1960; Pfeiffer, 1974, 1977; Pfeiffer, Verwoerdt, and Wang, 1968, 1969). Each of these studies has unique methodological problems that make it impossible to draw final conclusions, yet each has increased our knowledge about the relationship between sexuality and aging. One of the overriding problems of sex research in the United States is the nature of American attitudes toward sexuality. Sex is a touchy subject; not everyone will respond to survey questions regarding their sexual behavior, and those who respond may under- or overestimate the extent to which they engage in certain behaviors. There is always some doubt regarding the accuracy of responses to survey questions, even when the questions are not about sexual behavior. It has been known for some time, for example, that people are not always accurate when asked their age (Palmer,

1943); a recent study (Skogan, 1974) found that about 20 percent of those who had reported crimes to the police failed to report the same crimes when asked about them in a criminal victimization survey. If people are even more reluctant to talk about sexual behavior, the problems of accuracy could be magnified.

The Kinsey studies were the pioneering studies in American sexual behavior, but their contributions to the study of sexual behavior in older people were hindered by the small number of older respondents. Nevertheless, they reached two major conclusions:

1. Late adolescence is the period of greatest sexual activity for men. After that there is a gradual decrease in sexual activity over the life cycle. The study did not find an age at which men's sexual activity suddenly ceases. It noted, however, that the rate of impotence for men at age 60 is only 20 percent, whereas at age 80 it is 75 percent.
2. Women experience a gradual decline in sexual activity between the ages of 20 and 60. However, the researchers noted that the decline in female sexual activity may be due to decreased sexual capacity of aging males.

Masters and Johnson's research was more informative about the relationship between aging and sexual behavior. They directed more attention to the subject, and they also gathered laboratory data on the anatomical and physiological aspects of sexuality. They found that, in general, both men and women over 60 years of age experience a decrease in the physiological reaction to sexual stimulation. Men over age 60 are slower than younger men to develop an erection and achieve ejaculation and women over age 60 are slower to respond to sexual stimulation, although the ability to reach orgasm does not decrease. Masters and Johnson's findings agree with those of the Kinsey studies, especially with respect to the decreased sexual capacity of the male in contrast to the female.

The Duke University studies of sexual behavior are unique because they derive from a longitudinal study, so that continuities and changes have been measured over the years since 1954, when the studies began. They support two generalizations about aging and sexual behavior: "Sexual activity and coital activity are by no means rare in persons beyond age 60, and patterns of sexual interest and coital activity differ substantially for men and women of the same age" (Pfeiffer, 1977, p. 136). The study started with 254 men and women ranging in age from 60 to 94. As is often the case in a longitudinal study, the number of respondents decreases with each successive retest. At the beginning of the study about 80 percent of the men who were not impaired reported that they were sexually interested, and ten years later their sexual interest was nearly as high as before. Even though sexual interest was present, however, their sexual activity had decreased significantly over the ten-year period. At the beginning of the study 70 percent said they were regularly active sexually, but ten years later only 25 percent said they were still sexually active. Among the unimpaired women in the study, only about one-third reported sexual interest at the beginning of the study, and this level of interest did not change over the ten-year time span. Only about 20 percent reported that they were sexually active at the start of the study, but the proportion did not decline over the ten-year period. The researchers came to the following conclusion:

> our data indicated that the median age of cessation of intercourse occurred nearly a decade earlier in women than in men (ages 60 and 68, respectively). Interestingly enough, the overwhelming majority of women attributed responsibility for the cessation of sexual intercourse in the marriage to their husbands; the men in general agreed, holding themselves responsible. (Pfeiffer, 1977, p. 137).

The Duke studies thus found a decrease in sexual activity with advancing age, a finding that is consistent with earlier studies that found decreases in activity from early adulthood on. However, these studies also report high levels of sexual interest among men, even after declines in activity have occurred. Finally, the Duke studies found some evidence for a "use it or lose it" approach to sexuality: Those who have been sexually active in their younger years are more likely to remain so in the later years.

It should be remembered that the general pattern of sexual behavior among aging persons does not account for all individual variations. Research studies repeatedly uncover individuals in their 80s or 90s who have high levels of sexual interest and some who maintain sexual activity into old age. It is by no means certain that with advancing age sexual capacities will decline to the point of impotence, or that all interest in sexual activity will be lost. In addition, it is impossible to know the effect on people's behavior of negative social attitudes toward active sexual behavior among older people. It is conceivable that American society could increase the levels of sexual activity among older individuals by adopting more favorable attitudes toward sexual behavior.

Summary

In certain respects the American family system performs fewer functions for individual members today than in earlier times. The colonial family, for example, was male dominated, and the father was able to extend his influence over his sons until his death. Nevertheless, the father provided his sons with the necessities of life, that is, a house in which to live, a piece of land to farm, and so on. Under this arrangement a male might not gain a powerful position in his family until he was fairly advanced in years—in other words, until his father died—but then he could wield considerable power within the family until his own death. In the colonial family, thus, there was a strong relationship between power and advanced age, although this relationship was more or less restricted to males. However, most sons accepted responsibility for the care of their widowed mother, and even deceased fathers were able to ensure that they would do so by making the provisions of their wills contingent upon faithful exercise of filial duty toward their widows.

By the end of the eighteenth century the power of family elders had been eroded by the wide acceptance of the concept of age equality. With the coming of industrialization and the beginning of urbanization, the younger generation was no longer as dependent on the older generation for the necessities of life. The idea of the obsolescence of old age and its complement, the cult of the young, were born. Old age was no longer held in high social esteem, but youth was glorified.

While the traditional family has lost some of its functions, it has gained new ones. Most important, the family has become a source of affectional and emotional support for its members. In an industrialized and urbanized society the affectional function is as essential as economic functions were in former times.

In modern American society a new family life cycle has been established, a cycle that structures the family positions that we occupy at different ages. The stages of the family life cycle also structure relationships between generations and provide a basis for analyzing exchanges of goods, services, and emotional support between generations.

While most Americans maintain strong family ties, so that the American family system could be called a modified extended-family system, there is also a desire for generational autonomy and independence. In other words, each generation wants to be free to establish an independent household, to raise children without interference, and to be financially self-supporting. This desire for independence pervades the family structure and is characteristic of every generation, young or old. While older people would like to believe that their children would provide financial aid if the need arose, they nevertheless hope that the need will never arise and probably would not solicit aid even if it was needed.

It is often assumed that the relationship between marital partners becomes dull and routine after a number of years and that most people are eventually faced with an empty-shell marriage. There is, however, no evidence that this is always the case; indeed, there is some evidence that the marriage relationship improves with age. If it is true that older couples are happy, perhaps even "in love," this may be partly explained by the fact that many unhappy couples have been divorced.

There seems to be a strong prejudice against sexuality in the later years of life, and most studies confirm that sexual behavior decreases with age. Sexual interest remains high in many people of advanced age, however, and it is quite possible that this interest will be matched by activity if social attitudes toward sexual behavior among older people improve.

SELECTED REFERENCES

W. Andrew Achenbaum, "The Obsolescence of Old Age in America, 1865–1914," *Journal of Social History* 8 (1974): 48–62.

Frances M. Carp, "Housing and Living Environments of Older People," in eds. Robert H. Binstock and Ethel Shanas, *Handbook of Aging and the Social Sciences* (New York: Van Nostrand Reinhold, 1976), pp. 244–271.

John Demos, *A Little Commonwealth: Family Life in Plymouth Colony* (New York: Oxford University Press, 1970).

John Demos, "Old Age in Early New England," in *The American Family in Social-Historical Perspective*, 2nd ed., ed. Michael Gordon (New York: St. Martin's, 1978), pp. 220–256.

Irwin Deutscher, "The Quality of Postparental Life," in *Middle Age and Aging*, ed. Bernice L. Neugarten (Chicago: University of Chicago Press, 1968), pp. 263–268.

David Hackett Fischer, *Growing Old in America*, exp. ed. (New York: Oxford University Press, 1978).

Philip J. Greven, Jr., "Family Structure in Seventeenth-Century Andover, Massachusetts," in *The American Family in Social-Historical Perspective*, 2nd ed. ed. Michael Gordon (New York: St. Martin's, 1978), pp. 20–37.

Reuben Hill, *Family Development in Three Generations* (Cambridge, Mass.: Schenkman, 1970).

A. Keyssar, "Widowhood in Eighteenth-Century Massachusetts: A Problem in the History of the Family," *Perspectives on American History* 8 (1974): 83–119.

Bernice L. Neugarten and Karol K. Weinstein, "The Changing American Grandparent," *Middle Age and Aging: A Reader in Social Psychology*, ed. Bernice L. Neugarten (Chicago: University of Chicago Press, 1968), pp. 280–285.

Joan F. Robertson, "Grandmotherhood: A Study of Role Conceptions," *Journal of Marriage and the Family* 39 (1977): 165–174.

Isadore Rubin, *Sexual Life After Sixty* (New York: Basic Books, 1965).

Alvin Schorr, *Filial Responsibility in the Modern American Family* (Washington, D.C.: U.S. Government Printing Office, 1960).

Nick Stinnett, Linda Mittelstet Carter, and James E. Montgomery, "Older Persons' Perceptions of Their Marriages," *Journal of Marriage and the Family* 34 (1977): 665–670.

Gordon F. Streib and Wayne E. Thompson, "The Older Person in a Family Context," in *Handbook of Social Gerontology*, ed. Clark Tilbitts (Chicago: University of Chicago Press, 1960), pp. 447–448.

Lillian E. Troll, Sheila J. Miller, and Robert C. Atchley, *Families in Later Life* (Belmont, Calif.: Wadsworth, 1979).

Sandra Byford Wake and Michael J. Spirakowski, "An Intergenerational Comparison of Attitudes Towards Supporting Aged Parents," *Journal of Marriage and the Family* 34: (1972): 42–48.

CHAPTER 11

Social Problems and Older People

Overview. Much of the research in social gerontology has taken a social-problems approach, which means that it attempts to demonstrate that certain social conditions have negative consequences for some older people. The social problems of an older population are those acts, events, and settings which are socially produced and yield ill effects for a significant proportion of older people. In some instances the older people are perpetrators, while in others they are victims. In a broader sense, however, most social problems arise out of interactions between the participants.

Social problems are those problems which are defined by a society as solvable. Or, using the medical analogy, social problems are those social pathologies which are perceived of as curable (Mills, 1943). It is for this reason that social problems are usually closely related to the development of social policy and the establishment of programs for prevention and control of the "pathologies" in question.

Many facets of the aging process are thought of as problems, and a fair number of the problems of aging are social in nature. The social problems that are the subject of this chapter, however, are always present in a society but are not usually regarded as natural, normal, and inevitable. Crime, for example, is a social problem, and although this problem is not limited to older people it is a social problem that affects the old.

In relation to social problems older people may be either actors or victims. As actors, they may engage in deviant behavior such as crime or alcohol or drug abuse. As victims, they may be robbed, assaulted or discriminated against.

Aging as Deviant Behavior

Growing old is not deviant behavior in the same sense that being criminal is deviant behavior. It is normal, natural, and inevitable. There are, however, certain similarities between much deviant behavior and the process of growing old. Deviants and older people are, almost by definition, minority groups. If a contemporary form of deviant behavior were to become so widely practiced that it was no longer restricted to a minority, it would cease to be deviant and would become socially expected. This is because human behavior is not inherently good or bad, socially approved or disapproved, but is defined as either acceptable or unacceptable by the society as a whole. Deviant behavior, thus, can become socially acceptable behavior, and socially acceptable behavior can become deviant behavior. In the last decade the smoking of cigarettes and the smoking of marijuana have been moving in opposite directions on the continuum of socially acceptable and deviant behavior. Whereas cigarette smoking has become less acceptable, marijuana smoking has become less deviant. If marijuana smoking were engaged in by a majority of the population, it would be socially acceptable and not deviant.

Older people will never become a majority. Even if life were prolonged to such an extent that a majority of the population was over age 65, older people would not become a majority because the social definition of old age would change. Being a member of a minority group is not sufficient for a person to be classified as deviant; the very rich and the very powerful are minority groups, yet members of these groups are not usually thought of as deviant. Deviant behavior must violate the approved standards of behavior of the majority or at least violate the approved standards of behavior of some of the most powerful individuals and/or groups in a society. In this sense old age can be regarded as deviant behavior; that is, older people are thought of as violating approved standards of behavior.

Is it possible that a society could define old age as deviant behavior even if the process of growing old is normal, natural, and inevitable? It is possible in a society with a future- and consumption-oriented system of values. In the United States aging may be devalued because of a preference for the new, the modern, the young, all of the characteristics that are the opposites of old age. It would probably be inaccurate to say that the old are discarded as readily and as thoughtlessly as an old pair of shoes, but the mental preference for the new over the old may well extend to humans as well as to material objects.

It is an overstatement to say that Americans value only the new and the modern; after all, many people collect stamps, coins, cars, baseball cards, and other items that are known to increase in value with age. It is often reported, moreover, that various subcultures in American society have great respect for the old. It is not easy to know just what place old age occupies in the minds of most Americans. Palmore (1971), for example, analyzed jokes about old people and concluded that the majority depicted aging or old age in a negative way. At the same time, not all of the jokes depicted old age or aging negatively, and some were positive. Palmore also found that the aging of men and women may be evaluated somewhat differently. The jokes veiewed the aging woman more negatively than the aging man. Martel (1968) analyzed the content of popular fiction in American magazines over a long period and found that in recent times the magazines have presented young adulthood in the most favorable light. Northcott (1975) analyzed prime-time major-network television shows and found that both the young and the old are seriously underrepresented. He also found that American television tends to portray middle-aged adults as the most competent: Middle-aged people are the ones that other people turn to in times of crisis; they are the problem solvers.

The idea that old age may be viewed as deviant behavior is supported by a poignant analysis by Sudnow (1967) based on his observation of a hospital emergency room. Sudnow reports that many medical catastrophies are so routine to emergency room personnel that they are regarded as ordinary events. This is especially true of events that involve older people. For example, older people who have suffered heart attacks are frequently encountered in emergency room work. If a heart attack victim dies in the emergency room, the death is also regarded as normal and routine. But heart attack deaths are not normal events outside the emergency room. If a person worked in a jail, he or she could expect criminal acts to be viewed as routine and normal events. A person working in a mental hospital could accept insanity as a routine and normal occurrence. In all of these settings the deviant behavior becomes an expected occurrence; but the settings themselves are not normal ones in which most people interact on a daily basis.

Even though emergency room personnel come to accept heart attack victims and even death as a normal event, this is only true when the victim is fairly old. Sudnow reports that when a young child dies in the emergency room even emergency room staff members, who are accustomed to tragic events, are emotionally affected. The death of a young child is sad even for people who never knew the child. But people accept routinely the death of an older person. Older people thus represent a deviant group from whom deviant behavior is a normal and expected event. It is no more surprising for an older person to die than for a criminal to commit a crime. Life is the normal expectation for most people, especially young children, but it seems that older people are defined as a deviant group for whom life is not entirely normal, at least not more so than death.

A closely related instance of the stigmatized status of old age is the manner in which the label "senile" may be applied to older people. Baizerman and Ellison (1971) argue that senility is so poorly understood and so vaguely defined that it is applied to older persons almost indiscriminately. Since *senility* is a psychiatric term, it can be used in a more legalistic manner than the concept of old age as a deviant status. A diagnosis of senility transforms the deviant status of old age into the medical and legal status of mental incompetence. It would be unfair to say that the diagnosis of senility is commonly abused by family members who want to divest themselves of a problem or by psychiatrists who neither want nor know how to deal with the emotional problems of an older person. There is not enough evidence indicating that this is the case. The potential for this type of abuse is nevertheless present and will remain so as long as senility remains poorly understood. But most important for the current discussion is the fact that old age as a deviant status and senility as a psychiatric definition are so dangerously close in common usage that older people could be abused as a result.

Because of the deviant status of old age, older people may be inaccurately defined as physically ill. Karcher and Linden (1974) found that large numbers of older people are being forced into a "sick" role; for example, many older people are housed in nursing homes with extensive medical facilities, even though they do not need such facilities. The researchers also suggested, although they could not document their argument, that many older people are defined as sick because this allows families to rid themselves of older relatives in a socially acceptable way. A family might think it unacceptable to institutionalize an older member simply because of the inconvenience of caring for him or her, but if the older member can be labeled "sick," then he or she can be institutionalized for health reasons. Again, as in the case of senility, it would be difficult to make the label stick if old age were not regarded as a deviant status. It is hard to imagine a middle-aged adult being institutionalized without compelling evidence of physical or mental infirmity. Yet if old age is a deviant status, this can give credence to the need to institutionalize an older person, perhaps without strong evidence of such a need. In support of this argument Miller, Bernstein, and Sharkey (1975) reported that they had clinical evidence that older persons are sometimes placed in nursing homes for reasons other than physical or mental health, especially when there were sexual conflicts in the family.

Posner (1974) provides evidence that older people are expected to occupy a deviant status in a home for the aged; in fact, she argues that the deviant status of the aged is an organizing principle in the home. She found that the nursing home staff and the patients themselves assumed that the patients were supposed to behave in ways that the society outside the institution would regard as deviant and abnormal. The consequence of the expectation of deviant behavior was that a resident had to appear incompetent in order to receive any of the valued goods and services of the home. In other words, to receive attention it was necessary to appear incompetent, usually in ways that had little to do with the reason the patient had been admitted to the institution.

In summary, growing old in American society is somewhat akin to learning a deviant role. Even though nothing could be more normal, natural, or inevitable than growing old, it is apparently expected that older people behave in deviant ways, at least with regard to illness and death.

Deviant Behavior by Aging Individuals

Quite apart from the stigma of old age, some older people engage in more conventional types of deviant behavior. Some criminals are old, some alcoholics are old. In this section the emphasis is on older individuals who engage in these types of behavior.

Suicide

A deviant behavior that is common in the older population is suicide. Not all types of older people have high rates of suicide, however; most of the suicides are committed by white males over the age of 65. The suicide rate of white males over 65 is four times greater than the rate for the population as a whole.

As a result the over-65 age group has a high suicide rate compared with younger age groups; even though older people account for only about 10 percent of the United States population, they account for 25 percent of the suicides (Resnik and Cantor, 1970). It is well known that not all suicides are officially listed as suicides, since it is impossible to determine whether some self-destructive acts were accidents or intentional suicides. But as with all age groups, it is safe to say that the suicide rate among older people is somewhat higher than the known rate. It is not known, however, what proportion of suicides by older persons are classified as accidents or even as deaths from natural causes.

What is most puzzling about the relationship between suicide and aging in the United States is that the increase in the suicide rate with age is restricted to white males. White females over age 65 do not show any increase in their suicide rate; in fact, after age 65 it declines slightly. Even nonwhite males show a slight decline in their suicide rate after age 65. Since only white males show a marked increase in the suicide rate with advancing age, it obviously is not possible to draw any definite conclusions about the general relationship between suicide and aging.

It is interesting to compare the suicide rates of older males and females in various societies. Two generalizations can be made about suicide and age on the basis of such comparisons:

1. Older males always have a higher suicide rate than older females;
2. Older males always have a higher suicide rate than the society as a whole.

Beyond these two generalizations there exist large differences in the rates and patterns of suicide in different societies. Two societies, Japan and Israel, are somewhat different from most other societies in that the suicide rates of males and females (especially older males and females) are nearly identical.

Table 11.1 shows the suicide rates in selected societies for all persons over age 15. Although the rate for the older population is often higher than the rate for the whole society, the relationship between the two rates is nearly the same from one society to another; that is, if the suicide rate for the whole society is relatively low, then the rate for older people in that society is also relatively low, and vice versa. As the table shows, there are significant differences between the suicide rates of different countries, which means that there are cultural factors that affect suicide rates. Religious, familial, political, and economic factors are no doubt related to suicide rates.

Different societies also report that victims use different means to commit suicide. In the United States, for example, males usually use firearms or explosives to destroy themselves, whereas females usually poison themselves. In Israel, males commit suicide by hanging themselves while females poison themselves, and neither males nor females use firearms very often (Shichor and Bergman, 1979).

Table 11.1 STANDARDIZED SUICIDE RATES (AGES 15 AND OVER) IN SELECTED COUNTRIES, 1965–1969 (PER 100,000 PEOPLE)

	Males	*Females*
Mexico	4.44	1.20
Greece	6.38	2.77
Italy	10.19	4.04
The Netherlands	11.78	6.87
Yugoslavia	11.97	4.16
Israel	12.74	8.42
England and Wales	14.71	9.42
Norway	14.75	4.40
Canada	20.63	7.45
United States	22.98	8.44
Japan	24.71	18.38
France	30.20	9.74
Denmark	31.84	17.01
Sweden	36.81	13.84
Finland	47.98	12.07
Hungary	58.46	22.34

Source: World Health Organization, *World Health Statistics Report*, 29, no. 7 (1976): 396–413.

There are some known relationships between suicide by older people and their social environment. Bock (1972) found that older white males in the United States are more likely to commit suicide if they are not married, and this is true whether they are single, divorced, or widowed. Marital status does not fully explain the higher suicide rate of older males, however, because even males who are married at the time they commit suicide have a higher-than-normal suicide rate. Bock found that males who are involved in community activities have lower suicide rates, and involvement in community activities seems to hold the greatest potential for a reduction in the suicide rate.

Resnik and Cantor (1970) have identified several groups of older individuals who are likely to commit suicide; those who have experienced the loss or death of close relatives; those who have suffered psychiatric or physical maladies; those who are putting their effects in order in preparation for death; and those who threaten or have previously attempted suicide. Ruzicka (1976) analyzed the suicide rates of various societies and concluded that

1. suicide rates are always higher for men than for women;
2. suicide rates increase with age for men but tend to peak in middle-age for women and then decline.

Figure 11.1 shows the changes in the suicide rate throughout the male lifespan for five countries. In all five countries the suicide rate increases with age and is highest at the latest stages of the life cycle. The figure shows that

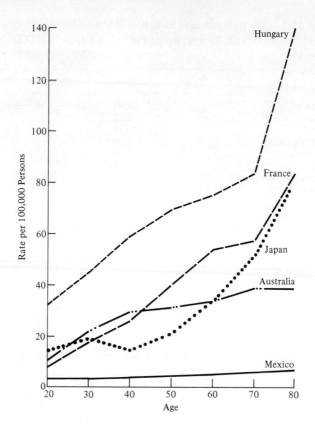

Figure 11.1 *Age-specific Male Suicide Rates in Five Countries*

Source: World Health Organization (1976), *World Health Statistics Report*, vol. 29, no. 7: 404.

even though suicide rates generally increase with age, there are significant differences in the number of suicides from one country to another. Hungary has high suicide rates at all ages and an unusually high rate after age 65. France and Australia have rates lower than Hungary, although the life-cycle pattern is fairly similar. Mexico shows a slight increase in suicide with advancing age, but compared with other societies it has very low suicide rates at all ages. Japan has a pattern that is distinct from the other four societies, because the rate in middle-age is lower than during young adulthood; however, in Japan there is also a dramatic increase after about age 60.

Crime

Another type of deviant behavior engaged in by some older people is crime. It should be noted at the outset that the crime rate for older people in the

United States is very low. The general pattern shown by the FBI's Uniform Crime Reports (1975) is for criminal behavior to decrease with age. Indeed, the crime reports show that very little crime is committed by persons over age 50. People over 65 constitute about 10 percent of the population of the United States, but they account for only 1 percent of criminal arrests. In 1975 persons between the ages of 25 and 29 were arrested nine times more often than persons over age 65.

The older people who are arrested are not usually arrested for committing violent crimes. The most common reasons for the arrest of persons over age 65 are drunkenness or driving under the influence of alcohol; these two offenses account for over 50 percent of all arrests of older people. People over 65 account for less than 1 percent of arrests for violent crimes (murder, rape, robbery, aggravated assault) and less than 1 percent of arrests for property crimes (burglary, larceny, motor vehicle theft).

Table 11.2 shows the distribution of criminal arrests for four age groups: under 25, 25–39, 40–64, and 65 and over. The oldest age group is underrepresented in all crime categories, but the largest single cause of arrest in this age group is drunkenness. Drunkenness does not fit the age pattern of violent or property crimes, which decrease with age; arrests for drunkenness increase until the age of 65, after which they decline. Most of the people age 65 who are arrested are men; very few are women.

The finding that most arrests of older persons are alcohol related is consistent with studies that have found high rates of alcoholism among males over 65. Alcoholism seems to be especially prevalent among elderly widowers (Zimberg, 1974). The exact rate of alcoholism in the older population of the United States is not known, although most estimates range between 2 and 10 percent (Schuckit and Miller, 1975). Several studies have concluded that older alcoholics began drinking relatively late in life, and at least one study found the vast majority of older alcoholics to be white males (Schuckit, 1977).

Drug Abuse
Although drug abuse in the United States is usually associated with adolescents and young adults, the potential for drug abuse among the old is very high, since a large proportion of prescription drugs are used by older people.

Table 11.2 PERCENTAGE OF CRIMINAL ARRESTS, BY AGE, 1975

	Under 25	25–39	40–64	65 and over
All crimes	56.9	25.1	16.7	1.2
Violent crimes	59.5	29.2	10.5	0.7
Property crimes	79.0	15.0	5.4	0.6
Drunkenness	23.9	30.7	42.0	3.3

Source: U.S. Department of Justice, *Uniform Crime Reports*, 1975.

One study found that people over 65 received one-fourth of all prescription drugs sold in 1967, with the drugs most frequently prescribed for older people being tranquilizers (Valium and Librium) and a nonnarcotic analgesic (Darvon) (Peterson and Thomas, 1975). The fact that older people have access to prescription drugs does not mean that their drug use is not legitimate and appropriate, but the potential for abuse is obvious. Even if abuse is not intended, the availability of large quantities of drugs raises the possibility of inadvertent abuse. Some researchers have found, for example, that older people living in congregate housing have a tendency to share drugs with each other even if the prescriptions have expired (Raskin and Eisdorfer, 1976).

Inadvertent drug abuse can also occur when older people consume more than one drug at the same time. This situation can intentionally or unintentionally occur and can happen in two ways. First, a person may have received prescriptions from two or more physicians, each of whom is not aware that the patient is taking other drugs. Second, a person may mix a drug prescribed by a physician with a self-prescribed drug that has been purchased over the counter. This abuse of drugs can involve not only barbiturates (e.g., sleeping pills) but also laxatives, aspirin compounds, bromide, antihistamines, and anticholinergics, which are found in a number of nonprescription medications. In addition, drug abuse can result when some drugs are mixed with alcohol (Schuckit, 1977).

In view of the potential for drug abuse among older persons, it is surprising that drug abuse is not more prevalent than it is. In a study of acute drug reactions (overdoses) in a Florida community it was found that the old are not overrepresented among drug abusers. Most of the drug abuse found in this study was by older females, and this was true of both white and black populations. An interesting discovery made by this study was that when older people were admitted to the hospital because of an acute drug reaction, the reaction was caused by legally available drugs, not illicit substances. This pattern was far different from that of young people, who were admitted because of overdoses of illegal drugs. Over 80 percent of the acute drug reactions among older persons were caused by sedatives and tranquilizers, and only about one-third of these individuals were admitted to the hospital because of what were thought to be suicide attempts (Peterson and Thomas, 1975).

Most of the available evidence indicates that there is some drug abuse among older persons, although the rate of abuse is lower for this group than for most younger age groups. Perhaps the biggest drug problem among older people is inadvertent abuse, which may be due to the greater access of the old to a large volume of prescription drugs as well as the heavy use of over-the-counter drugs by older people.

Deviant Behavior Directed Against Older People

Crime

One of the most obvious forms of victimization of the old is criminal behavior directed against them. There is a great deal of public concern about the potential for criminal victimization of the old. Older people often reside in urban areas with high crime rates, usually the central-city areas. Many older people live alone and are physically unable to defend themselves against criminal acts. For all of these reasons older people are potentially vulnerable to victimization.

In 1973 the United States Department of Justice conducted a survey of the general population that asked people whether they had been the victims of crimes. The survey was a great advance over official crime statistics, since it covered instances in which a person was victimized but did not report the crime to the police as well as crimes that were reported. The survey also provided information on the victim of the criminal act, such as the age, place of residence, marital status, and income of the victim. Prior to the victimization survey, which was carried out in many of the nation's largest cities, very little was known about the victims of crimes. Since the survey was based on random samples of residents in those cities, the researchers were able to estimate the actual volume of crime, not just the volume of crime reported to the police. This was especially important with regard to crime directed against older people, because it was thought that they failed to report many instances of criminal victimization directed against them because of fear or lack of knowledge of the criminal justice system, or simply because they felt that it would do no good. Previously reported crime statistics which showed relatively low rates of victimization of older people were thought to be understating the actual rate.

The victimization survey found that people over age 65 are not a highly victimized group, at least compared with younger age groups. Table 11.3 shows the rates of criminal victimization for all persons over age 12 and for people over age 65. Older people are, of course, sometimes the victims of crimes, but their rates of victimization are generally lower than those of younger age groups. People between the ages of 12 and 24 are the most highly victimized. The exception to this rule is personal larceny with contact, especially the subcategory of purse snatching. Although the overall rates for these crimes are quite low, they are the only categories in which older people experience higher rates of criminal victimization than the total population.

The evidence, thus, contradicts the commonsense notion that older people are a highly victimized group, that criminals concentrate on the old because

Table 11.3 CRIMINAL VICTIMIZATION RATES FOR PERSONS OVER AGE 12 AND OVER AGE 65, 1973 (PER 1,000 POPULATION)

	Persons over age 12	Persons over age 65
Crimes of violence	34	9
Rape	1	0
Robbery	7	5
Assault	26	4
Crimes of theft	93	23
Personal larceny with contact	3	4
Purse snatching	1	2
Personal larceny without contact	90	19
Burglary	93	55
Household larceny	109	48

Source: U.S. Department of Justice, *Criminal Victimization in the United States,* 1973 (Washington, D.C.: U.S. Government Printing Office, 1976).

of their defenselessness. This is very encouraging. It means that the mass media have exaggerated the criminal victimization of the old and that older persons can restrict their activities less and engage in more activities without undue concern. It is especially encouraging that the rates of violent crimes against older people are much lower than the rates for the total population.

Surveys of the degree of fear felt by members of various age groups in the United States show that older adults are not significantly more fearful of criminal victimization than younger people. The differences between men and women are much larger than the age differences, with females reporting far higher levels of fear than males (Lebowitz, 1975). Where people live also has a great deal to do with their level of fear. Those who live in large cities report the greatest fear, while those who live in rural areas are the least fearful. This relationship, which is not surprising, holds true for all age groups, but the differences in fear are greater for older adults than for young or middle-aged adults.

Sundeen and Mathieu (1976) report the same general conclusion from their survey of the fear of crime in southern California. They questioned older people in three different settings: a central city area, a suburb, and a retirement community with guarded walls. As expected, those living in the central-city area had the greatest fear of criminal victimization, followed by those living in the suburb; those living in the guarded retirement community had the least fear. Where greater fear of criminal victimization is found among older people, it may be a result of factors other than age. The older population is disproportionately female, with large numbers residing in central-city areas, and both of these factors are associated with increased rates of fear. Antunes and associates (1977) argues that the greater fear of older people may be related to the fact that attacks on them are more likely to occur in or near their homes and that the attacks are usually by strangers; both of these facts may increase the anxiety of older people even though victimization rates are lower for them than for younger people.

It is to be expected that fear of criminal victimization will have some effect on the attitudes and behavior of those who are fearful. Sundeen and Mathieu (1976) found that people who lived in areas that they considered high-risk areas were more likely to take precautions against victimization, such as obtaining weapons and staying home. Sundeen (1976) reports that older people who live in areas of the city with higher rates of criminal victimization also have a lower regard for the effectiveness of the criminal justice system and harsher attitudes about the need for prison sentences and criminal punishment.

Exploitation

Some practices, which may not be clearly criminal, are intended to exploit older adults. The Federal Trade Commission identifies the following deceptive schemes as ones that are often directed at older people:

1. *Health claims:* very often peddlers try to sell miracle medicines, especially "cures" for arthritis and rheumatism.
2. *Extra-income claims:* frequently ads in the classified sections of newspapers promise excellent profits from easy spare-time work, usually requiring an investment for the purchase of a vending machine.
3. *Lands in the sun:* people looking for a retirement setting are sometimes induced to purchase land they have not seen through a mail order land developer.
4. *Dancing instruction, book publishing, and correspondence schools:* these have all been used in deceptive or dishonest ways to relieve older adults of their money without giving them fair value, sometimes using high-pressure techniques to make the sale.

Medicaid and Medicare Abuse

The Special Committee on Aging of the United States Senate has spent considerable time and effort documenting some of the abuses faced by older Americans by practitioners in medicaid and medicare programs (1976).

The Special Committee on Aging identified "medicaid mills" as one of the central problems of the provision of medical services to older people and the poor. The "mills" are usually located in store front settings in the dilapidated parts of town. The services are provided in minimally equipped facilities attended by doctors who are young, without a private practice, and very often graduates of foreign medical schools. Some of the doctors could not support themselves before medicaid but now have ample yearly salaries from the mills.

The most common abuses of the mills, as noted by the investigators, were the following:

1. *Ping-ponging:* sending a patient to a number of different practitioners in a mill even though there is no medical need for these referrals. The mill can then bill medicaid for each practitioner visited.
2. *Ganging:* treating all the members of a family even if only one was at the clinic for a specific reason.
3. *Upgrading:* the practice of treating a patient for a simple illness (such as a common cold) and billing the treatment as something more serious (such as acute bronchitis).
4. *Steering:* directing a patient to a particular pharmacy, presumably by prior arrangement between the physician and the pharmacy.
5. *Billing for services not rendered.*

The Senate committee decided to send investigators, posing as patients, into some of the medicaid mills. The results were as follows:

> Perfectly healthy staff members collected literally bushels full of prescriptions. Despite the fact that investigators were instructed to refuse X-rays, more than 100 were received. Investigators received numerous other questionable tests in view of their feigned ailment, usually a cold. These included 18 electrocardiograms, 8 tuberculosis tests, 4 allergy tests, hearing tests, glaucoma tests, and 3 electroencephalograms. Investigators were asked to give, and did give, a tremendous number of blood samples and literally gallons of urine. They were told repeatedly (no less than 11 times) to return for full-scale testing. They received 7 pairs of glasses without ever asking to see an optometrist. The eyeglasses were not only unnecessary, they were totally useless; the refractions on the 7 glasses were bizarre, with no consistency at all. Investigators were repeatedly "ping-ponged" to neurologists, gynecologists, internists, psychologists, psychiatrists, heart specialists, podiatrists, dentists, chiropractors, opticians, ophthalmologists, occulists, and pediatricians. (U.S. Senate, Special Committee on Aging, 1976, p. 44)

Housing and Institutions

There is nothing more important to people than the immediate environment in which they live—their community, their neighborhood, and their residence. In general, people expect to be able to exercise a certain amount of choice in this area, and this expectation does not diminish with age. Even though most people will not be institutionalized, many express the fear that in old age they will lose the ability to determine their place of residence, their style of life, and so on. In essence, people fear that because of physical or mental deterioration they will be forced to live in an extended-care facility.

When people reach late middle age or retire, they are often faced with the question of whether to voluntarily change their place of residence. For some, the house they are living in may be too large for the reduced size of their family, may be located in a deteriorating neighborhood that is not as desirable as it once was, or may require more upkeep and maintenance than they are willing or able to perform. If an older couple or individual decides to move, a number of options are available. Older people may remain in the region in which they have been living or migrate to another area (such as the South or the West); they may choose between segregated and age-integrated environments.

It was noted in Chapter 2 that older people, as compared with other age groups, are not highly mobile. There are nevertheless large numbers of older people who relocate their residences each year. Some move short distances, while others make long-distance moves. Between the years of 1965 and 1970, for example, about 28 percent of Americans over the age of 65 relocated their residences at least once. Most of these moves (64 percent) were local; only about 20 percent were to another state (Wiseman, 1978).

Some of the older people who move only a short distance are making only minor adjustments in their living environments. For example, some people who have lived on a farm nearly all of their lives move into a nearby rural town when they retire. Even though this is a significant change in their life style and economic activities, they are still in close contact with many of their friends, neighbors, and family members. Similarly, Wiseman and Virden (1977) found that older residents of Kansas City, Kansas, tended to move to close-by suburbs because they wanted to live in a better environment while remaining near relatives.

Retirement Communities

Those older people who move a long distance are probably responding to a different set of values than those who move locally, and are perhaps seeking a greater change in life style. Upon retirement, for example, some people may desire to avoid the loss of status and purpose that they fear will occur if they remain in their preretirement setting. If they seek a more leisure-oriented life style for their retirement years, they may want to find a setting in which leisure is accorded a relatively high social value and opportunities for leisure activities are enhanced by the presence of others of like mind and circumstances (Heintz, 1976). These are the people who become residents of planned retirement communities, communities that might restrict residence to people over a specified age, usually 52 or 55.

Many people view the rise of the American retirement community as an unnatural development. For example, Bultena and Wood (1969, p. 210) state that "the segregation of older persons in special communities has been widely condemned as invidious and undemocratic and as an extension of undesirable trends in American society in which older persons increasingly have been removed from participation in instrumental activities and isolated within the social structure." Jacobs (1975, p. 71) described a retirement community that he had observed and studied as an unnatural community: "If one had lived for seventy years in the outside world, one saw or at least knew of all kinds of people. It is no idle proverb that 'it takes all kinds to make a world.'" The lack of a heterogeneous population in terms of social class, age, ethnicity, and the like indicates to Jacobs that the retirement community is an alien world. "The lack of activity and the other usual signs of life such as litter, moving autos or persons, animal excrement, or background noises is eerie."

Whether retirement communities are natural or unnatural settings is an arguable point, but most of the evidence suggests that people who choose to live in them are reasonably happy with their decision, just as those who decide against living in such settings might be miserable under the same circumstances (Bultena and Wood, 1969; Carp, 1972). And most people who live in retirement communities want to keep them the way they are, a point that has been demonstrated in a number of places when older residents have expressed the fear that they are being invaded by young people. For example, in Sun City, a planned retirement community in Riverside County, California, there was a move to adopt a zoning ordinance banning anyone under the age of 18 from living in Sun City. The unincorporated city of over 7,000 residents had been established by a real estate development company as a retirement community in 1962. The company had established the rule that at least one member of the household had to be at least 50 years old and no member could be under 18. The age limits were simply informal guidelines that had been determined by the development company, however, and the rule had never been given the force of a law. In 1977 some of the residents became concerned about the fact that families with children were buying houses in Sun City, and over 4,000 of the residents signed a petition to adopt the zoning ordinance. A newspaper reporter investigated the situation and concluded that there were probably three, and at the most five, residents of Sun City who were under the age of 18 (Siegel, 1977). The incident, nevertheless, demonstrated the degree of concern on the part of the older residents that the community remain childless and that it retain its character as a retirement community.

Extended-care facilities

While people exercise free choice in moving to a planned retirement community, those who move into an extended-care facility, such as a nursing home or the "old folks' home," usually are forced to do so by circumstances beyond their control. While many people are fearful of institutionalization, it is by no means the most likely fate of an older person. Figures from the U.S. Bureau of the Census indicate that less than 5 percent of people over 65 are institutionalized, and this figure rises only to about 10 percent for people over 75. However, about 20 percent of older people will spend some time in an extended-care facility at some time in their lives (Palmore, 1976); and in the city of Detroit it was discovered that in 1971, 20 percent of all deaths of people over 65 occurred in nursing homes (Kastenbaum and Candy, 1973). These figures indicate that while most people will never live in an extended-care facility, the quality of care available in the nursing-home setting is of great concern to older people because as many as one in five will spend some time in such a setting.

There are many types of extended-care facilities in the United States today. Some offer services that are not available in others; some are proprietary institutions while others are nonprofit organizations; and certainly some are better than others. Because of the diversity in the types of institutions and the vast differences in the quality of care available, it is difficult to make generalizations that apply to all extended-care facilities.

Patients' Rights

It is widely recognized that some older people are abused in extended-care facilities. The potential for abuse has been chronicled by Mendelson in her book *Tender Loving Greed*. Some states have enacted legislation to attempt to correct some of the abuses. An example is a California law that became effective in 1975. It specifies that any person may request that the state's Department of Health make an unannounced inspection of a nursing home for possible violations of the Health and Safety Code, and that this inspection must be completed within ten days. In addition, the law provides a statement of patients' rights that applies to every person admitted to a nursing home. The patient's rights, which may be denied only for good cause and only by his or her attending physician, are as follows:

1. To be fully informed of his rights and of all rules and regulations of the nursing home governing patient conduct.
2. To be fully informed of the services available in the facility and of the charges for services.
3. To be fully informed by a physician of his medical condition;* to have the opportunity to participate in the planning of his medical treatment and to refuse to participate in experimental research.
4. To refuse treatment to the extent permitted by law and to be informed of the medical consequences of refusal.
5. To be transferred or discharged only for medical reasons, or for his welfare or that of other patients or for nonpayment for his stay, and to be given reasonable advance notice.
6. To be encouraged and assisted throughout his period of stay to exercise his rights as a patient and as a citizen, free from restraint, interference, coercion, discrimination, or reprisal.
7. To manage his personal financial affairs, or to be given at least quarterly an accounting of financial transactions made on his behalf if the facility accepts this responsibility for him.
8. To be free from mental and physical abuse and from chemical and (except

in emergencies) physical restraints except as authorized in writing by a physician for a specified and limited period of time, or when necessary to protect the patient from injury to himself or to others.

9. To be assured confidential treatment of his personal and medical records.
10. To be treated with consideration, respect, and full recognition of his dignity and individuality, including privacy in treatment and in care for his personal needs.
11. Not to be required to perform services for the facility that are not included in his plan of care for therapeutic purposes.
12. To associate and communicate privately with persons of his choice, and to send and receive his personal mail unopened.*
13. To meet with and participate in activities of social, religious, and community groups at his discretion.*
14. To retain and use his personal clothing and possessions as space permits, unless to do so would infringe upon rights of other patients.*
15. If married, to be assured privacy for visits by his/her spouse and if both are patients in the facility, to be permitted to share a room.*
16. To have daily visiting hours established.
17. To have members of the clergy admitted at the request of the patient or person responsible at any time.
18. To allow relatives or persons responsible to visit critically ill patients at any time.*
19. To be allowed privacy for visits with family, friends, clergy, social workers, or for professional or business purposes.
20. To have reasonable access to telephones both to make and receive confidential calls.

A patient's rights as set forth in Section 72523(a) may be denied for good cause only by the attending physician. Denial of such rights shall be documented by the attending physician in the patient's health record.

The patient's rights followed by an asterisk (*) may be limited by a physician where their exercise is not medically advisable.

The fact that legislation was needed to correct some of the abuses that have been found in extended-care facilities does not mean that all facilities are abusive toward their patients. Gubrium (1975), for example, carried out an excellent study of a nursing home. In his preface he noted that

life in a nursing home has come to mean decay, cruelty, and dehumanization. Such stereotyped images derive in part from journalistic exposés and local campaigns to "clean up those hovels." Although it is true that some aspects of life in nursing homes match these stereotypes, life at Murray Manor is filled with intimate social ties, the celebration of small accomplishments, agonizing losses, boredom, conspiracies, anger, pride, humiliation, trust, love, hope, despair—in short, all the complexities that occur when a group of people spend their daily lives together.

Gubrium does an excellent job of depicting the vibrant social world of the nursing home by showing the kinds of social interaction that occur between clients as well as that between clients and nursing-home staff members. Even though people who are unfamiliar with the internal dynamics of the nursing home may assume that the clients are homogeneous, Gubrium shows that there are important and recognized differences that the clients and the staff accept and acknowledge as meaningful. Some of these differences are imposed on the clients from the outside; for example, clients are classified according to the level of skilled nursing care they require, a classification that is essential for meeting the staff–patient ratios required by state law, determining the rate of payment according to medicare, and so forth. However, the clients themselves make the distinction between those people who are merely residents— that is, people who need personal domiciliary care but not skilled nursing care —and patients who are in need of some level of skilled nursing care. Gubrium (1975, pp. 25–26) quotes one resident who understands the essential differences between being a patient and being a resident:

> We're all residents down here—all in our right minds—and know what we're doing and where we're going. And, most everybody on this floor has the privilege to go and come as they feel like it. We're not locked up. I can go any time I want and any place I want. But you get upstairs, you'll find out. It's quite different. Then you will truly see the inside of the institution. There's some pitiful cases up there. Very pitiful.

Social Conditions for Nursing-home Patient Abuse

There is no doubt that patient abuse occurs in some nursing homes, although the usual reaction of the general public is to condemn the individuals who are responsible for the abusive behavior. While individual responsibility for abusive acts is certainly warranted, Stannard (1973) has shown that some of the social conditions that exist in nursing homes allow patient abuse to occur. Despite the facts that most nursing home staff members are strongly opposed to patient abuse and that individuals who are responsible for abuse are fired from the job, abuse does occur. Stannard (1973, pp. 334–335), for example, found that abusive behavior might occur, "when a patient assaulted an aide or was perceived as deliberately making her job more difficult than it had to be. Kicking, biting, punching, or spitting at an aide, were, in the aides' minds, inexcusable and punishable behavior." The nurses and other aides were often unaware of the abuse because the aide was usually alone with the patient when the abuse occurred. And even though the nurses usually held very low opinions of the skills and character of the aides, when a patient, a relative of a patient, or an employee of the nursing home reported instances of patient abuse the nurses usually debunked the report.

Thus, the nurses argued that the patients who made such complaints were troublemakers or crazy and did not have to be taken seriously. Similarly, they felt that relatives who took up a patient's case were ignorant of the situation in the home, dupes of a crazy patient, or crazy themselves, and did not have to be taken seriously. When an employee made such an allegation, the nurses and owner imputed ulterior motives to him and in so doing debunked his claim; or they received it skeptically and did nothing. (Stannard, 1973)

The reasons that abusive behavior toward nursing home patients occurs can be tied to the general social attitudes toward old people in institutions; that is, the low social status of dependent older people places them in institutions that are themselves of low social status. They pay very low wages and salaries to workers, who come from the lower social classes and educational backgrounds. The workers are supervised by professionals, semiprofessionals, and administrators who are among the less successful members of their professions. Stannard (1973) concludes that

> work in custodial mental hospitals and nursing homes does not bring professional recognition and is regarded as a step down by their professions in general. Once in these institutions, they find themselves with patients they cannot help, confronted by staff problems which make it difficult or impossible to achieve the goals expounded by their professions.

Thus, even though the abuse of nursing-home patients can be tied to the actions of individual staff members and occurs in specific nursing homes, it should be recognized that there are broader social conditions that make possible (even probable) the kinds of abuses that are so widely lamented yet persistently present.

Summary

Older people are affected by many of the same social problems that affect other age groups, although some social problems affect older people much more than younger people. In the first place, in some senses just being older is regarded as being deviant in a youth-oriented society. This is an important consideration because the deviant status of old age may legitimate abusive behavior toward older people. In other words, the tendency to treat older people as inferior and incompetent is accepted because they are considered deviant.

Some older people are actively involved in socially disapproved behavior, and very often these behaviors are age related. Suicide among white males in the United States increases sharply with age, for example, while criminal behavior decreases with age. Also, even though the older population has access to a great quantity of potentially dangerous drugs, they are not prone to drug abuse, and most abuse of drugs by older people is inadvertent.

Older people are also victims. Some older people are the victims of criminal acts; but just as important, the fear of being victimized may cause older people to restrict their activities and place themselves under self-imposed "house arrest." Older people may also become victims as a result of their need for certain services, such as health care and extended-care facilities.

SELECTED REFERENCES

E. Wilbur Bock, "Aging and Suicide: The Significance of Marital, Kinship, and Alternative Relations," *Family Coordinator* 21 (1972): 71–79.

Jaber F. Gubrium, *Living and Dying at Murray Manor* (New York: St. Martin's, 1975).

Charles J. Karcher and Leonard L. Linden, "Family Rejection of the Aged and Nursing Home Utilization," *International Journal of Aging and Human Development* 5 (1974): 231–244.

Barry D. Lebowitz, "Age and Fearfulness: Personal and Situational Factors," *Journal of Gerontology* 30 (1975): 696–700.

Erdman Palmore, "Total Chance of Institutionalization Among the Aged," *Gerontologist* 16 (1976): 504–507.

David M. Peterson and Charles W. Thomas, "Acute Drug Reactions Among the Elderly," *Journal of Gerontology* 30 (1975): 552–556.

Judith Posner, "Notes on the Negative Implications of Being Competent in a Home for the Aged," *International Journal of Aging and Human Development* 5 (1974): 357–364.

Marc A. Schuckit, "Geriatric Alcoholism and Drug Abuse," *Gerontologist* 17 (1977): 168–174.

Charles I. Stannard, "Old Folks and Dirty Work: The Social Conditions for Patient Abuse in a Nursing Home," *Social Problems* 20 (1973): 329–342.

Richard A. Sundeen and James T. Mathieu, "The Fear of Crime and its Consequences Among Elderly in Three Urban Communities," *Gerontologist* 16 (1976): 211–219.

U.S. Department of Justice, *Criminal Victimization in the United States,* 1973 (Washington, D.C.: U.S. Government Printing Office, 1976).

U.S. Senate, Special Committee on Aging, *Fraud and Abuse Among Practitioners Participating in the Medicaid Program* (Washington, D.C.: U.S. Government Printing Office, 1976).

CHAPTER 12

Religion, Death, and Dying

Overview

Religion and Aging
   Involvement and Participation in Religious Organizations
   The Personal Meaning of Religion and Religious Activities in the Home
   Religion and the Meaning of Life and Death

Death and Dying
   The Stages of Dying
   Fear and Denial
   The Legitimation of Impending Death
   The Hospice
   Funerals
   Grief and Widowhood

Summary

Overview. The famous social theorist Emile Durkheim believed that all
societies distinguish between the spheres of the sacred and the profane, the
sacred being concerned with the transcendental matters and the profane
with the here and now. Much of the analysis of aging concerns itself with
the relationship of the individual to the profane, and it is in this sphere
that aging individuals are often depicted as undergoing social
disengagement. There is, however, no reason to assume that aging leads to
a decreased concern for the sacred. Indeed, to the extent that religion
serves to increase a person's confidence in transcendental concerns—for
example, by providing explanations of life and death—it would be expected

that the approach of death would lead to increased awareness of the sacred sphere.

Even if it were true that older people are likely to show increased concern for transcendental matters, these concerns could be expressed in a nonreligious manner or setting. Butler (1968, p. 487), for example, believes that older people exhibit a tendency to undergo the mental process called life review:

> I conceive of the life review as a naturally occurring, universal mental process characterized by the progressive return to consciousness of past experiences, and, particularly, the resurgence of unresolved conflicts; simultaneously, and normally, these revived experiences and conflicts can be surveyed and reintegrated. Presumably, this process is prompted by the realization of approaching dissolution and death, and the inability to maintain one's sense of personal invulnerability.

Older people are closer to the fact of death and therefore are more likely to undergo the life review, Butler believes. Retirement from the work force and any other processes of social disengagement provide the older person with more time in which to engage in life review.

It is often assumed that older people are more religious than they were when they were younger; this assumption apparently stems from the commonsense notion that those who are relatively closer to death will have a heightened interest in religious matters. Research to date, however, has demonstrated that the relationship between religion and aging is quite complex and is not easily reduced to any general rule. At least one analyst has concluded that there is no coherent body of literature on the interrelationships between religion, death, and aging" (Heenan, 1972, p. 173). While it is true that much basic research remains to be done on the subject, a few studies have provided some insight into this area.

Religion and Aging

Perhaps one of the reasons why the topic of aging and religion is not more fully developed is that there are a number of problems associated with researching the question of how religious behavior is affected by the aging process. In the first place, it is essential to separate religious behavior into at least the following categories: (1) involvement and participation in religious organizations; (2) the personal meaning of religion and religious activities that occur within the home; and (3) the contribution of religion to the adjustment of individuals to the process of aging and their confrontation with the existential problems of life and death. While there are obvious relationships between these categories, it is essential to treat them as separate phenomena in the research process.

Involvement and Participation in Religious Organizations

Much of the research on religion and aging has revolved around the question of how often older people participate in the activities of established religious organizations. A recent national sample of Americans revealed that people over 65 were not much more likely than younger people to have attended a church or synagogue within the past year. Whereas 77 percent of those age 65 or over said they had attended, 74 percent of those under 65 said they had done so. The group aged 55–64 had the largest proportion of attenders, while after age 65 there were slight declines in church and synagogue attendance (National Council on the Aging, 1975). In fact, much of the research on religious participation and advancing age has concluded that religious attendance drops off among older people. The decline in religious attendance has been associated with the tendency of some older people to decrease their participation in all voluntary associations, and may also be affected by physical impairments and transportation problems.

The Personal Meaning of Religion and Religious Activities in the Home

While it would be safe to say that people who actively participate in religious services are displaying religious behavior (even while acknowledging that some people attend religious services for social or other nonreligious reasons), it would be inacccurate to assume that people who do not attend religious services are not engaging in religious behavior. Some people may hold religious values and beliefs even though they may not translate them into participation in established religions. At least one study found that older people are more likely than younger people to hold traditional religious beliefs and are more certain of the existence of a supreme being (Gray and Moberg, 1962). Another survey found that 71 percent of the people age 65 and over said that religion was very important in their lives, whereas only 49 percent of those between the ages of 18 and 64 said that it was very important (National Council on the Aging, 1975). In addition, a study that found that fewer than half of the older respondents attended religious services regularly also found that more than three-fourths were religiously active in some way. Nearly 60 percent of those who seldom or never attended religious services reported that they regularly listened to religious services on the radio or television, prayed at home, or expressed some other type of nonorganizational religiosity (Mindel and Vaughan, 1978).

Religion and the Meaning of Life and Death

The role of religion in achieving a sense of spiritual well-being was among the topics discussed at the 1971 White House Conference on Aging (Moberg, 1971). It was concluded that the youth orientation found in American society can produce a certain "spiritual fatigue": "A sense of uselessness and rejection, inner emptiness and boredom, loneliness and fear emerges." Religious organizations and institutions can provide comfort and spiritual support to older people who are beset with the anxiety and fears that accompany the losses experienced with advancing age. For some people, religious ideas can serve as a means of dealing with existential problems, such as the meaning of life and death, as they arise in the latter part of life.

The significance of religion to the aging process is something that changes over time. It seems that the importance of religion and the amount of religious behavior varies from one historical period to another and from one generation to another. Some analysts have argued that the United States has experienced a gradual movement away from religion in the last few decades. If this were true, we would expect to find older people more involved with religious ideas and behavior; however, this would be a generational effect and not an aging effect. Other researchers have maintained that the importance of religion in a society waxes and wanes in a more or less cyclical pattern. One study (Wingrove and Alston, 1974) attempted to clarify some of these issues by conducting a cohort analysis of church attendance over a thirty-year period (from 1939 to 1969). The researchers defined a cohort as all the people who had been born within a ten-year period (e.g., between the years 1925 and 1934). They then analyzed the church attendance of each cohort for the years 1939, 1950, 1955, 1960, 1965, and 1969. The results showed that each cohort was somewhat different in its patterns of religious attendance, although there was a general tendency for most of the cohorts to have shown their highest levels of attendance between the years 1950 and 1960; all cohorts showed declines in attendance after 1965. The research indicates that any age-related pattern of religious involvement must be considered in the context of the general social mood, because religious interests in a society may rise and fall over time.

Death and Dying

In American society few, if any, topics are more taboo than death—even sex is more widely discussed than death. The reasons for the reluctance of Americans to discuss death are not entirely clear. Parsons and Lidz (1967) have speculated that the peculiar American attitude toward death is the result of a rejection of the idea that death is inevitable and therefore something to be accepted fatalistically. Americans have come to regard death as something that should be avoided and that can and should be prevented. In essence, they have come to believe that death is something that has been brought under human control; if it occurs, it should occur only among the very old. It should be remembered that according to the disengagement theory the old are supposed to withdraw from social entanglements partly because they are preparing for death in a manner that will cause little social disruption. In this view death as a physical and social fact is not an entirely taboo topic. Rather, it has been compartmentalized. It is a specialized task assigned to the old the way other tasks are assigned: through division of labor. In the case of death, the old have been assigned the duties of death work, leaving younger people more or less free from any concern or responsibility for the processes of death and dying.

Some people will not be convinced by the argument that Americans hold a functional view of death in view of the fact that many researchers have concentrated on the apparent denial of death found among many different people in many different places. Still, there is some evidence that people trust their own ability to deal with the possibility of death more than they trust others' ability to do so. For example, a group of cancer and noncancer patients were asked whether they wanted to be told that they had cancer if it was discovered during a medical examination. While over 90 percent of the respondents said that they wanted to be told, only 73 percent said that they thought everyone who had cancer should be told (Kelly and Friesen, 1977).

The Stages of Dying

Humans are like all other animals in that their death is inevitable, but they are very different in that they are the only ones who are confronted with the fact of their own death. The ability to anticipate death has allowed us to develop particular attitudes toward it, to assign social meaning to the process of dying, and to construct various rituals and ceremonies that surround the event of death.

There have been several attempts to define the process of dying; of these, probably the best known is the work of Elisabeth Kubler-Ross (1969). She maintains that dying persons pass through the following stages:

1. denial and isolation
2. anger
3. bargaining
4. depression
5. acceptance

She says that in the first stage many people refuse to believe that they are really going to die, even though they may have been told so by a physician. This disbelief leads some people to seek the opinions of other doctors or even to seek out alternative sources of information, such as faith healers.

After a time, Kubler-Ross says, the stage of denial is succeeded by the stage of anger. In many instances medical personnel are the objects of the anger of a dying patient. The anger expressed by the patient toward nurses and physicians can cause them to resent the patient, and this can lead to even greater anger and frustration on the part of the patient.

In the third stage the dying person assumes a compromising or bargaining position. Kubler-Ross likens the bargaining patient to a child who has initially reacted to a parental decision with anger but then has decided to try to alter the decision by exhibiting exemplary behavior. By switching to "good behavior," the dying person is trying to negotiate an extension of life or at least a few days free from pain and suffering.

The fourth stage finds the dying person returning to a state somewhat akin to anger, that is, depression. The depression may be due partly to the realization that bargaining through good behavior did not achieve the desired goal; but depression is also often associated with further problems or complications brought on by the patient's illness. Some people have had to undergo disfiguring treatments, or the cost of the medical care has caused them to sell items (such as a home) to which they were emotionally attached.

The fifth and final stage is the stage of acceptance. Acceptance does not mean that the dying person is embracing death or welcoming it as a friend; rather, it refers to a dying person's acquiescence in his or her fate. "Acceptance should not be mistaken for a happy stage. It is almost void of feelings. It is as if the pain had gone, the struggle is over, and there comes a time for 'the final rest before the long journey,' as one patient phrased it" (Kubler-Ross, 1969, p. 100).

The work of Kubler-Ross has been widely publicized in the popular media and is probably accepted as valid by large numbers of people; however, some researchers are cautiously skeptical about the applicability of her scheme. Kalish (1976, p. 494), for example, has concluded that the stages described by Kubler-Ross are useful as hypotheses, but in his experience

> any of these kinds of behavior may occur at any time during the dying process: The terminally ill do not move through any regular progression, but they move back and forth, sometimes rapidly and sometimes displaying denial and repression or bargaining and acceptance in consecutive moments or even simultaneously, perhaps at different levels of awareness.

Likewise, Edwin Shneidman (1976, p. 446) has stated that "while I have seen in dying persons isolation, envy, bargaining, depression, and acceptance, I do not believe that these are necessarily 'stages' of the dying process, and I am not at all convinced that they are lived through in that order, or, for that matter, in any universal order."

Glaser and Strauss (1968) have analyzed the dying process from the point of view of observers or participants in the process. They note that in addition to the physical process of dying there is a social process, the patient's "dying trajectory." There is a certain uniformity about the dying process, which in each case has seven critical junctures:

(1) The patient is defined as dying. (2) Staff and family then make preparations for his death, as he may do himself if he knows he is dying. (3) At some point, there seems to be "nothing more to do" to prevent death. (4) The final descent may take weeks, or days, or merely hours, ending in (5) the "last hours," (6) the death watch, and (7) the death itself. (Glaser and Strauss, 1968:7)

The people who are involved with the dying person attempt to organize themselves around the schedule for dying; that is, they try to determine how long it will take the person to move through these steps to arrive at number 7, the death itself. The definition that emerges regarding the movement of the dying person toward death is the dying trajectory.

Fear and Denial

While the stages of dying are not fully accepted by all researchers and await more complete empirical testing, there is a fair amount of agreement that certain elements are very often present in the dying process. The two that are mentioned most often are fear and denial. Becker (1973) maintains that there are two explanations for the human fear of death. One says that fear of death is learned and can be unlearned, the other that fear of death is a natural part of the human condition and cannot be changed. Becker has been influenced by Freudian ideas and the Frankfurt school of sociology, and these have led him to conclude that "the fear of life and the fear of death are the mainsprings of human activity" (Keen, 1974). The fear of death is so important to most of human existence, according to Becker, that humans have created a large number of rituals and beliefs in order to cope with this fear.

A number of surveys have failed to support the idea of death as a primary motive force. They have found relatively low levels of concern about death. The actual percentages vary slightly from one survey to another, partly because the questions are phrased differently and are asked in different settings, but usually less than one-fourth of those asked report fear of death (Kimsey, Roberts, and Logan, 1972; Kalish and Reynolds, 1976). It is possible, of course, that fear of death is present even in those who are not aware of it; the fact that most people do not acknowledge this fear may be a testament to the success of the rituals and beliefs that have been created to alleviate it. In this regard it has been discovered that more religious people have less anxiety about death than those who are less religious (Kalish, 1976).

If it were true that most people are afraid of death, it would seem that people who have a higher chance of dying would be more fearful than those who have little chance of dying. Thus, it would be expected that older people would be more fearful than younger people. The research evidence on the relationship between age and fear of death indicates an inverse relationship; that is, younger people are usually more fearful than older people (Kalish and Reynolds, 1976; Bengtson, Cuellar, and Rogan, 1977). Older people, however, may show less fear of death because they have already experienced a death crisis, probably at some time in middle age, and since that time have resolved their attitude toward death in a manner that has left them less fearful (Bengtson, Cuellar, and Rogan, 1977). Others have suggested (Kalish, 1976) that older people have less fear of death because, like other people, they place less value on the lives of older people. It is argued that because older people have already lived their allotted time under a normal life expectancy and thus do not feel cheated of any time, and because old age is so closely associated with death that older people have actually been socialized into accepting their own dying and death, they are more accepting of their own death. By way of contrast, younger people fear death because they value their lives highly, feel they have not yet lived their allotted time, and have not experienced any anticipatory socialization for death.

The Legitimation of Impending Death

Marshall (1975) has discovered that older persons in a retirement community are able to adjust to the presence of death in the community and even to accept with equanimity the idea of their own impending death. He argues, however, that the social legitimation of death may not occur in every setting. It is probably not enough for death to be an ever-present phenomenon within a community; it must be something that is actively dealt with, at least in a verbal sense, by the community's members. "One is also better able to face his impending death if he can observe, in a kind of role-modeling process, that the deaths of his fellows occur within a taken-for-granted framework where they are considered appropriate. The rendering of death as appropriate must be a community event in which the individual can himself participate" (Marshall, 1975, p. 1141).

The Hospice

Most people in the United States die in a health care institution. This institution is usually a hospital, but in a significant number of cases it is an extended-care facility. The majority, however, would prefer to die at home (Kalish and Reynolds, 1976). Recently there has been renewed interest in the hospice, perhaps a compromise between the home and the hospital. There are at least 40 hospices in England. In the United States, the best-known hospice is the Hospice of New Haven, in Branford, Connecticut. The New Haven hospice is modeled after St. Christopher's Hospice in London.

The ideal of the hospice is to provide a decent life for the terminally ill, a goal that is pursued in a variety of ways. First, the hospice is a cheerful, lively, colorful place that gives special consideration to the needs of the terminally ill. Its residents need special attention but do not need the specialized technical and medical equipment of the hospital. Second, the hospice extends itself into the community, attempting to serve people who are terminally ill but can continue to reside in their homes with the help of the hospice. The main task of the hospice is to provide medical and emotional support to its clients; the goal is to provide each client with a drug program to prevent pain and to help the client engage in normal activities to the extent possible, including eating regular meals. The hospice also strives to provide emotional support for the terminally ill person during the dying process as well as for the survivors during the grieving process. Hospices prefer to be regarded as places to live rather than places to die, and very often a hospice has a child care center on the premises to underscore the liveliness of the place. The cost of residence in a hospice is greater than that of residence in a typical nursing home but less than that of a hospital stay (Stoddard, 1978; Knoble, 1978).

The hospice is a compromise between the personal death that can occur when the dying person remains in familiar surroundings in the midst of the family and the impersonal death that can occur in an institution such as a hospital or nursing home; it is also a compromise between the absence of specialized medical facilities in the home and the availability of modern medical technology in the hospital. In this way the hospice provides an alternative to the increasing bureaucratization of death and dying in modern societies. Blauner (1966, p. 386) has maintained that "the dying patient in the hospital is subject to the kinds of alienation experienced by persons in other situations in bureaucratic organizations." And because the dying person becomes a depersonalized object within the bureaucratic medical setting "he is powerless in that the medical staff and the hospital organization tend to program his death in keeping with their organizational and professional needs; control over one's death seems to be even more difficult to achieve than control over one's life in our society."

Institutions that have large numbers of older people and in which death is a normal feature of the setting may still attempt to disguise or hide the existence of a dead person and suppress the news of death. Gubrium (1975) concludes that the administrators of a nursing home tried to keep the news of a death from spreading throughout the institution because they felt that such news was frightening to the patients and residents, but he did not find that the clientele were at all frightened by the news of someone dying, although most were quite curious and anxious to know about any deaths that occurred: "When someone dies at the manor, there is no general gloom among other patients and residents. As many suggest, death is a very reasonable thing to expect 'in a place like this.' When anyone hears of the death of someone he did not know well, he may be curious and politely sympathetic, but he is not especially mournful or depressed" (Gubrium, 1975:204).

Funerals

Some attention has been focused on the funeral practices of Americans in the last few years, and much of it has been very uncomplimentary to the funeral industry. Part of the public protest against the funeral industry, no doubt, revolves around the different perceptions of the role of the mortician. While morticians may regard themselves as businesspeople attempting to sell goods and services in a competitive industry, the general public expects them to serve as public officials to whom profit is a secondary concern. Thus, practices that would be accepted as standard operating procedures in any other business are regarded as deceptive and manipulative when engaged in by morticians. In her popular book *The American Way of Death* (1963), Jessica Mitford relates that morticians are instructed in how to arrange the caskets in the selection room so as to maximize profit. Any other business would be expected to try to maximize profits through an advantageous floor arrangement of its products, but morticians are condemned for applying rational thought to their business. Consumers may feel that they are at a disadvantage because they are expected to purchase funeral services while in a highly emotional state whereas the mortician can use rational thought. Whether this state of affairs is to be blamed on morticians or, instead, attributed to the attitudes toward death that cause this peculiar consumer behavior is still an open question.

Mitford (1963) has concluded that the American consumer is vulnerable to exploitation when purchasing the services of a mortician for several reasons. First, the person who is responsible for arranging a funeral is guided by the desire to do the "right thing," that is, to meet other people's expectations regarding a decent burial. People usually rely on their personal tastes, preferences, and judgments when making a purchase, but when arranging a funeral they are motivated by a desire to gain social approval. The smart mortician can presumably play on this desire and thereby bolster sales.

Second, few people are aware of burial prices; most people are loath to do comparative shopping among morticians, and even if they did they would not have enough knowledge to make an informed judgment about the quality of one casket versus another. Most people arrange very few funerals in their lifetime, and often many years go by between those funerals. It is becoming more common for people to arrange their own funerals in advance of their deaths, and this could help them become informed about prices and variations in such things as quality of service, quality and preferred style of casket, and so on; however, this trend will probably not affect the majority of people in the near future.

Third, funeral arrangements must be completed within a relatively short time, and one cannot change one's mind and return for a refund or exchange. When making most major purchases a consumer can adopt a strategy of waiting, hoping that the seller will reduce the price. But when one is purchasing funeral arrangements this strategy is not available; in fact, time constraints operate against the consumer.

On another level there is the question of why funerals should exist at all. Fulton (1976) has noted that several social theorists believe funerals serve the functions of separation and integration. A funeral marks the separation of the dead person from the ongoing life of the community, but it also serves as a rite that reinforces and reaffirms the ties among the survivors. In this sense the funeral is as much for the survivors as it is for the dead person. Fulton has concluded, moreover, that funerals actually ease the adjustment of the survivors to a life without the person who has died. He discovered in a survey of widows and widowers that those who had participated in a traditional funeral for a deceased marital partner experienced fewer adjustment problems than those who had arranged for immediate disposition of the body.

Grief and Widowhood

There has been some attempt to study the process of grieving in American society. Parkes (1970), for example, has identified four phases of grief:

1. Numbness, an initial reaction to the loss of a loved one in which the grief-stricken person is not fully cognizant of the loss that has occurred.
2. Yearning, a second phase in which the loss is recognized and the grief-stricken person begins searching to regain the lost person.
3. Disorganization and despair, in which the grieving person ceases the searching behavior of the second phase and accepts the permanence of the loss.
4. Reorganization, in which a person establishes a new orientation to life.

One study of widows in Boston found that almost all of them altered their style of dress (i.e., wore somber clothing) and practiced some degree of social withdrawal for a period following the husband's death. They began to return to more normal practices after a short time, usually reentering social life at a gradually accelerated pace. In most cases, by about two months after the husband's death the widows were "themselves" again which meant that they had accepted the death of their husbands, had redefined themselves as widows, and were ready to live their lives with an orientation to the future (Glick, Weiss, and Parkes, 1974).

The fact that American women usually survive their husbands was noted in Chapter 2. Because women have a longer life expectancy than men and usually marry men somewhat older than themselves, there are many more widows than widowers. Also, the remarriage rate for widows over age 55 in the United States is very low. Only about 5 percent of widows over 55 will remarry, and after age 65 less than 1 percent will remarry (Cleveland and Gianturco, 1976).

There does not appear to be any generally agreed-upon waiting period after the death of a spouse before dating or remarrying. Kalish (1976) reports that 23 percent of people over age 60 thought it was not necessary to wait after a death before going out with other men or women, and 20 percent felt it was unimportant to wait before remarrying. The largest number of people thought that a widow or widower should wait at least six months before dating, and at least a year before remarrying. But 29 percent felt that the surviving spouse should wait five years before dating, and 34 percent felt that there should be a five-year waiting period before remarriage.

Compared to widows in many other societies, widows in the United States have a wide variety of choices available to them with regard to the roles they may fulfill and the kinds of life style they may pursue (Lopata, 1973). This does not mean that American widows are not constrained in their choices by circumstances of wealth, family, health, and so on, but only that they are able to take a wide variety of orientations without social disapproval. A widow can remarry, continue or resume a career, concentrate on being a mother or a grandmother, or develop strong friendships and participate in the activities of voluntary associations. This relative freedom can be contrasted to the much more formalized and prescribed role of widowhood in other societies.

While the American widow has a relatively wide selection of lifestyle options available to her, it is nevertheless difficult for her to reorganize her life after the death of her husband. Just the availability of so many options makes the readjustment process a difficult one, since a number of decisions must be made. At the center of the readjustment problems lies the fact that the American family system stresses the centrality of the nuclear family and the conjugal relationship. Yet the widow is forced to restructure her life without assuming that she will have a husband, and if she is older and her children are adults she may not have a nuclear family.

It seems that widows and widowers are more likely to live alone today than in the past. Table 12.1 shows that in 1940 slightly less than 20 percent of the widowed persons in the United States lived alone, but that by 1970 this figure had grown to about 50 percent. The table also shows that there are very small differences between males and females in this regard; both are showing an increasing tendency to live alone.

Lopata (1973) has concluded that the greatest short-range needs of widows are (1) to express emotions and come to terms with widowhood through "grief work" with the help of family, friends, and counselors; (2) companionship, especially if the widow is living alone for the first time in her life; (3) to be

Table 12.1 PERCENTAGE OF THE WIDOWED LIVING ALONE, UNITED STATES, 1940–1970

	Male (%)	Female (%)	Total (%)
1940	21.2	19.0	19.6
1950	27.9	26.8	27.1
1960	38.2	35.7	36.2
1970	47.0	50.4	49.8

Source: Based on data from U.S. Bureau of the Census, in Albert Chevan and J. Henry Korson, "The Widowed Who Live Alone: An Examination of Social and Demographic Factors," *Social Forces* 51 (1972): 45–54.

protected from the hordes of people who want to give her advice—"Everyone around her is full of advice, and the bits she receives are often contradictory and irrelevant or unbeneficial from her point of view" (p. 273); (4) assistance in building self-confidence and competencies, assistance that can consist of not giving too much advice and avoiding actions that might encourage dependency; (5) help in reengaging, that is, becoming involved in social activities that will be stimulating and meaningful.

Summary

While it is often assumed that religious involvement increases with age, there are some ambiguous research findings in this regard. Higher proportions of older people have been found to express a belief in traditional religious concepts, although it has also been found that middle-aged people are somewhat more likely to attend church services. However, large proportions of older people who do not attend church services were found to be religiously active. Religious interest is probably as much a function of a person's generation as it is of his or her age, and it is quite possible that future generations of older people will be less interested in religious activity than some younger cohorts.

Older people are usually thought to be more interested in spiritual and religious matters because of the increasing proximity of death. There are, however, nonreligious ways of confronting the inevitability of death, including the life review process and the social legitimation of death noted by some gerontologists. In any case older people do not seem to be any more fearful of death than younger people, and are probably much less fearful.

SELECTED REFERENCES

Barney G. Glaser and Anselm L. Strauss, *Time for Dying* (Chicago: Aldine 1968).
Jaber F. Gubrium, *Living and Dying at Murray Manor* (New York: St. Martin's, 1975).

Richard A. Kalish, "Death and Dying in a Social Context," in *Handbook of Aging and the Social Sciences,* eds. Robert H. Binstock and Ethel Shanas (New York: Van Nostrand Reinhold, 1976), pp. 483–507.

Victor W. Marshall, "Socialization for Impending Death in a Retirement Village," *American Journal of Sociology* 80 (1975): 1124–1144.

Charles H. Mindel and C. Edwin Vaughan, "A Multidimensional Approach to Religiosity and Disengagement," *Journal of Gerontology* 33 (1978): 103–108.

Edwin S. Shneidman, ed., *Death: Current Perspectives* (Palo Alto, Calif.: Mayfield, 1976).

C. Ray Wingrove and Jon P. Alston, "Cohort Analysis of Church Attendance, 1939–1969," *Social Forces* 53 (1974): 324–331.

CHAPTER **13**

Aging and the Future

Overview. As has been pointed out throughout the book, aging is a very new field of academic study, and research, and applied practice. Most of the major developments of the aging revolution, both in the United States and in the world, will occur in the future. Because of this, social gerontology is a very future-oriented area of study, and gerontologists tend to think of aging in the past, the present, and the future as three quite distinct phenomena.

Despite the traditional view that aging signifies the approach of death, what becomes most obvious when one is studying aging is that in many ways it is very new in terms of both the experience of the individual and the development of aging generations or cohorts. At the societal level, aging societies are just emerging in world history. The inescapable conclusion that the study of social gerontology impresses on us is that aging is really a phenomenon of the future. In essentially every way, the modern meaning of aging has barely begun to develop; it is just starting to mature, and the course of its development is not much better known than the dimensions of interstellar space. Much of the excitement of the fields of gerontology and social gerontology derives from the fact that we know so very little and therefore have so much to learn. As with other research areas that are on the frontiers of knowledge, fields like extraterrestrial travel, the development of new energy sources, or the creation of new sexual roles, the challenges are exciting.

Aging in a Postindustrial Society

The future of aging holds the possibility of a large number of changes. Many of the changes that have already occurred were tied to the movement of societies from a preindustrial form to an industrial one. It was noted in Chapter 2 that the development of industrialized societies resulted in a demographic structure characterized by relatively low birthrates and low death rates. Demographic changes were also indicated by large increases in population, increases in the median ages of societies, and large increases in the number and proportion of older people in many societies. Industrialization was closely related to the emergence of older people as a large group in these societies, but the significance of aging and the development of the modern meaning of aging may be more closely related to the advent of an even newer form of society that is often referred to as postindustrial society.

Characteristics of Industrial Societies

Most people are probably familiar with the general characteristics of an industrial society, although perhaps not with its specific characteristics. Lakoff (1976) has summarized these characteristics in his "paradigm of industrial society," which includes the following elements:

1. The development of mechanical systems powered by fossil fuels and hydro-electricity.
2. Large increases in agricultural production, which allowed more resources and more workers to be utilized in primary and secondary segments of industrial production.
3. The movement of large segments of the population from the rural settings of agricultural production to the urban settings of industrial production.
4. Recognition of the differences between nonindustrialized and industrialized societies.
5. The establishment of a belief and value system based more on materialism and the secular world than on traditional values and religious beliefs.

Characteristics of Postindustrial Societies

Many of the social changes that have occurred in the last couple of decades, especially the kinds of changes that are associated with aging, have been caused by the movement of many formerly industrial societies to the status of postindustrial societies. Lakoff (1976) describes the postindustrial society as having the following characteristics:

1. New forms of energy, especially energy forms that have been developed through scientific discoveries, such as nuclear energy.
2. A labor force composed increasingly of service workers, including larger numbers of government workers, with a relative decrease in industrial workers.
3. An increased demand for higher education to meet the increased demand for highly trained technical personnel.
4. The diffusion of urban centers into metropolitan areas composed of an urban center with a larger number of suburbs.
5. The erosion of values centered on the work ethic and the emergence of a new ethic vaguely oriented toward an improvement in the quality of life.

The Role of Older People in a Postindustrial Society

Aging as a modern phenomenon emerged in the United States at about the same time that the nation was showing signs of moving into the postindustrial phase. For example, the increase in the functions of government and the accompanying increase in government and service workers coincided with the passage of the Social Security Act of 1935. Just as important, the Social Security Act and similar forms of government involvement became a reality at the very point at which the industrial society broke down: during the Great Depression of the 1930s. The establishment of government programs such as the social security system marked the acceptance of a new ideology that justified government intervention in order to secure the common good, but it also marked the beginning of a postindustrial society in which the government began consciously to compensate for the obvious instability of an industrial system based on the liberal ideology of the free market.

It is significant that the New Deal programs were established at the time of the Depression, when it was obvious to everyone that the free-exchange system did not always operate efficiently. The new government programs were attempting to avoid further problems and overcome those that already existed. Thus, the programs were trying to counteract the most serious defects of the industrial business cycle, and only secondarily (if at all) attempting to lay the foundations of a postindustrial society. It is probably for this reason that the postindustrial society retains two of the elements of the capitalist industrial society: private property and the profit motive.

Thoenes (1966) maintains that the movement toward a postindustrial society was a result of an error in the economic thinking of the industrial society, namely, that industrial organizers assumed that the capacity for economic production would always be somewhat less than the demand for the produced goods. The depression of the 1930s demonstrated, however, that expanding production did no good if there was not enough demand for the products. The postindustrial society emerged when it became necessary for the national government to enter into the economic process to ensure the adequate disposal and consumption of goods within the society. Although the American domestic economy had always been thought to operate more or less automatically, stimulated only through such means as advertising, fashion, some planned obsolescence, and the availability of consumer credit or installment buying, it now became necessary for the government to engage in some coordination of economic production and consumption. Whereas the ideal of the industrial society had been a continual increase in the gross national product, the goal of the postindustrial society was to balance the amount of goods produced with the ability of the society to consume them (Thoenes, 1966).

The depression of the 1930s showed what could happen if an industrial society overexpanded its productive apparatus. When producers accumulated a sufficient inventory of goods, but consumption of those goods was not keeping pace with production, the businesses would simply cease production and workers would be laid off. But even though layoffs and the cessation of production by individual businesses solved the immediate problem of overproduction, they caused the economy to stagnate even more, since the laid-off employees would themselves be unable to consume goods at a normal rate; thus, the society experienced an accelerated reduction in the aggregate economic demand.

The solution to the problems of the industrial society was to assign to the federal government the responsibility for coordinating economic production and consumption and thus to assure the welfare of all members of the society. This included not only responsibility for the welfare of the workers but also a responsibility to the owners of the businesses; that is, it became the goal of postindustrial society to assure the relative economic stability of workers throughout their lifespan and to assure a reasonable profit to the owners.

Even though this is a very limited perspective on the development of postindustrial society, it shows the relationship between the production and consumption functions of the industrial economy, which is crucial for understanding the economic importance of the older population in the postindustrial society. The older population can be retired from the labor force, an act that simultaneously serves to decrease the productive potential of the economy and increases the number of employment opportunities available to younger workers. Simply retiring older workers without providing them with any retirement income accomplishes very little, however. The key to the economic role of the older population in a postindustrial society is to direct a certain proportion of the national production to this group so that they can serve as consumers. In other words, if the older population is provided with a retirement income in the form of social security, older people become steady users of consumer goods and thus continually stimulate the economy.

In a postindustrial society the older population serves an entirely new economic function. Even though the retired segment of the population is no longer actively engaged in economic production, it is a fourth-level economic participant because it fills the essential role of consumer in the balancing of the production and consumption aspects of the economy. Older people become the most likely candidates for this role because they may engage in leisure and voluntary activities that would be more problematic for younger age groups. Also, since the economic status of the older population is relatively low and retirement benefits are very modest, the money received by older people is more likely to be spent on essential items such as food, housing, and clothing.

If the present social situation of older people is in many ways a product of the transition from an industrial society to a postindustrial society, then significant changes may be expected to result from any further changes in the social structure. While social science is not yet, and may never be, in a position to predict the future accurately, what follows is a discussion of possible changes that could occur in the future, based on what is known now.

The Demography of Aging

The population of the world will continue to grow older in the immediate future. The median age of the earth's population will increase during most of the twenty-first century. It must be assumed that disease control will be improved, especially in those countries which currently have relatively high rates of infant and childhood mortality. It also seems likely that there will be increased use of contraceptive techniques, which will tend to moderate the worldwide birthrate. Each of these factors will have the effect of increasing the median age of the world population and producing increasing proportions of older people in many societies.

There is every reason to believe that life expectancy at birth and at older ages will increase throughout the world. While life expectancy at birth will probably show fairly large increases in those countries which achieve a significant decrease in their rates of infant and early-childhood mortality, increases in life expectancy after age 65 will probably be much smaller. There will undoubtedly be some advances in the prevention and control of some forms of cancer, and probably some improved methods of controlling some of the chronic diseases. There is nevertheless no reason to expect large increases in life expectancy at the later stages of the life cycle.

There is also no reason to conclude that life expectancy or the population structures of any society of the world will be drastically altered or severely affected by the application or misapplication of modern forms of technology. But neither can such possibilities be entirely ruled out. The intentional use of nuclear weapons or the unintentional release of radiation as a result of a nuclear accident could have effects that would render present projections meaningless.

In the decades to come we can expect that some retirees will choose to move from cold-weather states to warm-weather states. The movement from the Northeast and the Midwest to the West and the South will probably involve a relatively small percentage of the older population, however, since most people prefer to live fairly close to their preretirement home. There is not likely to be much more age-segregated housing in the United States than currently exists. Nevertheless, with the large increases in the number of older people that can be expected between now and the middle of the twenty-first century, it is very likely that retirement communities in the warm-weather states, especially Florida, Arizona, and California, will experience continued growth in both number and size.

The educational level of the older population will increase in each succeeding generation for the next several decades. It is quite likely that the older population will also become more cognizant of its position in society and more critical of the social structure as it relates to aging.

In general, the American population should continue to mature into the middle of the twenty-first century. After that, its age structure will probably stabilize. It must be remembered, however, that any significant change in the birthrate will alter the population composition.

The Biology of Aging

Our faith in the ability of science to achieve consistent progress leads us to anticipate that the next few decades will produce some significant increases in our understanding of the biology of aging. While this is a relatively new and undeveloped area of study, a number of theories and approaches are being pursued. From these theories will eventually come some means of slowing the aging process. But even the ability to slow the aging process may not produce wide acceptance of efforts to do so. If, for example, slowing the aging process involves an elaborate, expensive, unconventional, or discomforting experience, its applicability will be limited. If the way to increase longevity proves to be a diet limited to alfalfa sprouts and goat's milk, there is no reason to believe that most people would be willing to exchange their current eating habits for increased longevity. In this connection, Comfort (1978) notes that many people are unwilling to give up cigarette smoking even if abstinence can be shown to increase longevity. If the procedure for increasing longevity is expensive, then people will be limited by their resources; if the program is government sponsored, the rich nations will be better able to carry it out than the poor nations.

Although older people have been largely ignored in nutritional studies, much more emphasis will be placed on the nutritional intake of older people in the future. It seems likely that those diseases which are related to malnutrition can be curtailed and that a nutritionally adequate and inexpensive food can be developed from vegetables fortified with the nutrients found in animal proteins. Alfin-Slater and Friedman (1978, p. 74) even predict a significant increase in life expectancy as a result of nutritional improvements: "It is estimated that adherence to these new, nutritionally optimal, prescribed diets may extend healthy longevity by 30 years; and healthy, productive centenarians should not be uncommon 25 years in the future."

Aging Around the World

While I have already stated that the world population is expected to grow older during the next few decades, we can anticipate other age-related changes to occur on a worldwide scale. The expected increase in longevity should bring about a relative increase in the female population and a corresponding decrease in the male population. In other words, the increasing maturation of the world population will probably alter the sex ratio in favor of females. This shift will occur primarily in the last third of the life cycle, which means that the number of widows will increase.

As the number and proportion of older people increases throughout the world, it should be expected that old age will become an increasingly recognized social status. Societies that have already experienced a large increase in their older population will serve as models for those that have not yet done so. The mistakes made by the former will provide a lesson to the latter, although it is nearly as certain that some societies will choose to avoid those mistakes while others will choose to repeat them. A sense of shared identity may develop among older people around the world, although this possibility seems remote given traditional national loyalties. A more universal definition of the role of the old may develop, however, and this definition may cross-cut many nationalities.

It is unclear what the future holds with regard to the power of older people. On the one hand, traditional wisdom says that older people in societies that are undergoing industrialization will experience a decline in status and power; on the other hand, it may well be that older people will increase their power as they consolidate their position in postindustrial societies. If the older cohorts in such societies are successful in increasing their power and influence, this could also serve to increase the awareness and participation of older people in the developing nations.

It is certain that different societies will maintain certain differences in the position and participation of older people; distinct cultural traditions, differences in social structure, and unique historical developments will ensure that aging will not become a similar experience in all societies. At the same time, if the process of industrialization is a synthesizing phenomenon, then the process of aging may become much more homogeneous in the future than it has been in previous periods of human history.

The Psychology of Aging

The next few decades will undoubtedly see many changes in the psychology of aging, both in the performance levels of older people and in social attitudes about the mental capacities of older people. Even the limited amount of current research, much of it based on inadequate cross-sectional research designs, has shown that the mental capacities of most older people are much greater than was previously supposed. The newer cohorts of older people are going to be increasingly well educated, and many more of them will have worked all of their adult lives in nonmanual occupations that have utilized their mental capacities throughout their adult lives. It is also quite likely that many more adults will be involved in higher education throughout their lives and that some will even undertake new fields of study after retirement from other occupational areas. All of these factors will contribute to the intellectual advancement of the older population and will demonstrate both to themselves and to other people that mental rigor and aging are congenial phenomena. In the past some older people have made significant intellectual contributions, but these were thought to be unusual or extraordinary cases. The future will show that the typical person can maintain a high level of mental acuteness throughout his or her life.

As older people demonstrate the capacities they retain in their later years, the social stereotypes of old age will change accordingly. Many of the negative ideas that people currently associate with growing older are based on inaccurate information or none at all, and when the older population demonstrates that these ideas are invalid the social attitudes will change.

We currently know so little about the ways personalities change over the life cycle and the personality types that are found in old age that the future will surely show major advances in this area. It will probably take much longer for social psychologists to determine the effect of generation on personality development, even though this effect may be quite significant.

Work, Retirement, and Leisure

Max Weber, the German sociologist who greatly influenced the development of contemporary sociology, made famous the idea that industrial society was permeated by a religious source of moral support, namely, the protestant ethic and the spirit of capitalism. This development of a "work ethic" was the dynamic component of the capitalist industrial society, especially in the early industrial societies that were heavily dependent on the labor power of large numbers of workers. In a postindustrial society, however, the increasing automation of many jobs has reduced the need for labor power, and the work ethic has been joined by a developing "leisure ethic." At one time people saw leisure as something that would help them work better, whereas today there are many leisure-oriented people who work in order to better enjoy their leisure time.

Older people have generally benefited from the emergence of the leisure ethic, at least in the sense that the leisure orientation provides an outlet for many people who have lived most of their lives in a society dominated by the work ethic. People who strongly support the work ethic sometimes are disturbed by mandatory retirement. For some, retirement presents a very difficult problem of adjustment. But retirement should be much less of an adjustment problem for leisure-oriented people. In retirement, they are free to pursue their major interests. In terms of people's attitudes toward retirement, the future will probably see more workers embracing retirement and fewer workers fearing it.

The major hitch in retirement in the future is very likely to be the same as that experienced by many people today: money. A leisure-oriented retirement requires more than a subsistence level of income, and if it is not available the retirement of the future may be as frustrating as it has been in the past. It is fairly certain that social security benefits will not rise to the level that would be needed for a leisure-oriented retirement, at least not before the latter half of the twenty-first century. More people will be eligible for a private pension, and increasing numbers of retired couples will have been dual-career couples throughout their working lives. Both of these factors will operate to increase the income of the average person or couple in retirement. It is hoped that more people will begin to plan early for retirement, and this could cause people to devote more of their earnings to providing for economic security and an adequate level of income in their retirement years.

Another development that may be on the horizon is the possibility that retirement may become more difficult to achieve. In recent years the issue of mandatory retirement was an emotional one for supporters of the work ethic, but in the future the problem may be reversed. Because of the declining birthrate in the United States and other mature societies, certain organizations and businesses may be very reluctant to lose their most valuable employees to retirement. In such a situation social pressures may develop for people to continue working past the age at which they are eligible for retirement, perhaps even beyond the point at which there is any economic advantage for them in doing so.

It does not seem likely that any society will raise the age at which workers become eligible for retirement, at least not in the next few decades, but it would be precipitous to rule out this possibility for the long term. If there were a movement to raise the retirement age, it would probably begin with the private pension plans, and thus the social security systems might not need to raise their age standards. It seems likely, in any event, that retirement will become increasingly popular in the years ahead, especially if retirees can be assured of an adequate income that will allow them to pursue an alternative life style of their own choosing.

The Political Economy of Aging

Older people in many societies will become a much more significant political force, but there probably are limits to the amount of power they will be able to exercise. The greater number of older people, combined with their increased education and increased ability to participate in political affairs, will surely provide the foundation for an age-related political force. The older population is a heterogeneous group, however, with significantly different goals, and it is most likely that the older population will be even more heterogeneous in the future. Some political issues will be related to the age structure of the society, but most will be only marginally related to age per se. Most political issues of the future, therefore, will probably divide age groups rather than unite them.

Some contemporary political issues are age-related; for example, older people have demonstrated a tendency to recognize specific issues that affect them, such as health care, and a large majority often have similar opinions on these issues. Age based organizations such as the American Association of Retired Persons and the Gray Panthers, as well as the mass media, are creating a belief in age identification, especially among older persons. In addition, at least in the recent past, older people in the United States have been essentially unopposed by other organized interest groups, and have been able to form coalitions with other political groups such as the Democratic party, the labor unions, and some professional and social-service groups.

The potential increase in the political power of the older population of the United States is indicated in Table 13.1, which shows actual and projected changes in the voting-age population from 1900 to 2030. The over-65 population was only 6.8 percent of the over-18 population of the United States in 1900, only 9.8 percent in 1940, and 14.9 percent in 1970; it is projected to be 24.2 percent of the over-18 population in 2030. As a segment of the voting-age population, the over-65 group will account for nearly one-fourth of those who are eligible to vote by 2030. The middle-aged group, those between the ages of 45 and 64, will remain nearly unchanged between 1970 and 2030, whereas the youngest segment of the voting-age population, those between the ages of 18 and 44, will decrease from 54.1 percent to 46.3 percent of the voting-age population.

Future research will be able to shed a great deal more light on the effects of generation. It will be possible, for example, to study the effects of maturation on a particular generation. The youth of the 1960s were known, for example, for their acceptance of relatively radical political ideals (i.e., they were relatively radical compared to the generations immediately preceding them). Will this cohort remain relatively radical throughout life? Will it still be a relatively radical generation when it's become older? My guess is that there will be some continuity of political ideals in particular cohorts, which would mean that the

Table 13.1 VOTING POPULATION OF THE UNITED STATES, 1900–2030, BY AGE GROUP

	1900	1940	1970	2030 (Projection)
18–44	70.1%	61.6%	54.1%	46.3%
45–64	23.1%	28.6%	31.1%	29.5%
65 +	6.8%	9.8%	14.9%	24.2%
Total	100%	100%	100%	100%

Sources: U.S. Bureau of the Census, *Historical Statistics of the United States, Colonial Times to 1970*, bicentennial edition (Washington, D.C.: U.S. Government Printing Office, 1975), and "Projections of the Population of the United States: 1977 to 2050," *Current Population Reports*, Series P–25, no. 704 (Washington, D.C.: U.S. Government Printing Office, 1977).

generation of the 1960s will be relatively active politically for the rest of its life.

The economic status of the older populations of many societies, including the United States, will probably improve in the next few decades and in the next century. Larger groups of workers will become eligible for private pensions that will supplement their social security benefits, but it is unlikely that older people will benefit from large increases in social security payments. To the extent that the economies of the industrialized societies expand, older people should be able to claim a share of the increased wealth, but the relative economic position of the older population will probably remain at current levels.

Many industrialized societies have developed a framework for the provision of social services to the older population, with the result that many American communities offer some limited services through senior centers. The level of service will probably increase, although at an uncertain pace, and the quality of the services will improve as more people are trained to provide such services.

Aging and the Family

One of the effects of greater longevity on the family is the potential for a much larger family system. Instead of a family that extends over three or maybe four generations, there will be many more families with members from five or even six generations. However, the nuclear family has become firmly established as the core of the American family system, and it appears that intense family relationships are unlikely to extend much beyond a single generation in either direction. Most of the research on grandparents shows that relationships between them and their grandchildren are relatively weak, at least compared with relationships between parents and their children. It thus seems unlikely that great-grandparents will have significant relationships with their great-grandchildren. Even if the family of the future is extended over more generations, this does not necessarily imply that strong family relationships will be extended over more generations.

The development of a leisure ethic may operate against the development of stronger extended-family systems in the sense that leisure-oriented older people will be more active and involved in activities that might cause them to go outside the family setting more often. On the other hand, the leisure orientation may provide the basis for more intensive interaction between parents and children throughout the adult years. A couple who have raised their children may find that they share with their own parents an interest in boating or camping or any number of other leisure pursuits. Companionship of this sort between adult children and their parents could extend, on the average, over a longer period than the relationship between parents and young children. But even if more adult children and their parents develop companionship relations based on leisure pursuits, both generations will probably remain independent; that is, each generation will retain its own home and independent life style.

The conjugal relationship of married couples over the life cycle is already undergoing significant change, especially in terms of sexual equality. This trend will surely become more established in the years to come. Since the childbearing and child rearing years have become a much smaller component of the conjugal life cycle, the affectionate, companionate, and sexual elements of the relationship have taken on greater meaning and significance. In this sense couples of the future are probably going to define a "good marriage" much more strictly, and this will probably be reflected in a higher divorce rate at all stages of the life cycle.

Sexual activity among older people will probably increase in the future, both because of the greater sexual capacities of a healthier older population and as a result of increased social acceptance of the value of sexual activity for people of all ages.

Social Problems

One of the most significant changes that we can anticipate in the future is an end to the perception of aging as a deviant status. As they increase in numbers, older people will no longer be thought of as unusual or as synonymous with frailty or disease or death. The later stages of the life cycle will become accepted as a normal status, indicating general social acceptance of the inevitability of aging.

The normal status of the process of growing older will also modify the image of older people as an easily duped or victimized group, a change that should discourage some offenders from concentrating on older people. This change should eventually have the effect of reducing older people's fear of being victimized, and decreasing their feelings of vulnerability. This, in turn, will encourage them to live their lives in a less inhibited, less fearful way.

It would be heartening to be able to predict that nursing homes and extended-care facilities will show remarkable improvements in the next few decades, but there is no reason to believe they will do so. There will probably be a core of high-quality institutions, staffed by well-trained, conscientious people, that provide excellent care; but these institutions will undoubtedly be expensive to operate and thus will probably be exceptional rather than typical. The average institution might show some improvement in its programs as more people are trained to work as professionals in geriatric settings, but it will have to be willing to pay appropriate salaries. The economics of the extended-care facility will remain a long-term problem that will not be solved by exposés or even by well-intentioned administrators and staff members. It seems most likely that below-average and inadequate institutions will be around for the foreseeable future. There will be increasing demand for the geriatric extended-care facility, and there will be proprietors who will meet this need by warehousing older people, turning a profit by providing inadequate services and utilizing incompetent administrators and untrained staff who are paid minimum wages. Laws governing the operation and administration of extended-care facilities will help, but it is currently impossible for government inspectors to monitor the daily activities of every institution; moreover, only those institutions which are grossly abusive toward their patients or are in open violation of the laws are subject to prosecution. As the number of institutions increase along with the number of patients in such institutions, the situation could very likely grow worse.

Death and Dying

One of the by-products of the social legitimation of aging may be the development of a more pragmatic approach to death and dying. There is already a movement to legitimize the concept of death with dignity, an idea that seems destined to gain greater acceptance among older people. The development of hospices around the country could aid significantly in the adoption of new social attitudes toward death and dying as well as ease the pain and trauma of dying. The funeral industry will probably change to accommodate changing attitudes toward death, although it seems that formal funerals probably serve an essential function for many of the relatives and friends of the dead person, and thus are likely to remain a feature of death in the United States.

Summary

In a social sense aging is closely related to the structure of society. Most social gerontologists view the experience of aging as shaped by a number of forces that have existed in the last few centuries; in the years to come, however, the aging population will begin to exert an independent influence on the rest of the social structure. It is, of course, impossible to know what form the aging experience will take in the future, although it is possible to make some reasonable predictions. In general, a more positive view of the aging process will probably be widely accepted, a change in social attitudes that will be brought on partly by the increase in the number of older people and partly by the achievements of this age group. The older people of the next few decades will have considerable influence on the meaning of aging in many societies.

SELECTED REFERENCES

Robert J. Havighurst, "The Future Aged: The Use of Time and Money," *Gerontologist* 15 (1975): 10–15.

Lissy F. Jarvik, *Aging into the 21st Century: Middle-Agers Today* (New York: Gardner Press, 1978).

Sanford A. Lakoff, "The Future of Social Intervention," in *Handbook of Aging and the Social Sciences,* eds. Robert H. Binstock and Ethel Shanas (New York: Van Nostrand Reinhold, 1976), pp. 643–663.

Bibliography

Achenbaum, W. Andrew. "The Obsolescence of Old Age in America, 1865–1914." *Journal of Social History,* 8 (1974):48–62.

Adams, David. "Correlates of Satisfaction Among the Elderly." *Gerontologist,* 11 (1971):64–68.

Aldous, Joan. "Intergenerational Visiting Patterns: Variation in Boundary Maintenance as an Explanation." *Family Process,* 6 (1967):235–251.

Alvirez, David, and Frank D. Bean. "The Mexican American Family." *Ethnic Families in America: Patterns and Variations,* eds. Charles H. Mindel and Robert W. Habenstein. New York: Elsevier, 1976, pp. 271–292.

Antunes, George E., et al. "Patterns of Personal Crime Against the Elderly: Findings from a National Survey." *Gerontologist,* 17 (1977):321–327.

Arieti, Silvano, ed. *American Handbook of Psychiatry,* 2nd ed. New York: Basic Books, 1974, vol. 1.

Atchley, Robert C. "Disengagement Among Professors." *Journal of Gerontology,* 26 (1971):476–480.

———."Orientation Toward the Job and Retirement Adjustment Among Women." In *Time, Roles, and Self in Old Age,* ed. Jaber F. Gubrium. New York: Human Sciences, 1976.

Auerbach, Doris N., and Richard L. Levenson. "Second Impressions: Attitude Change in College Students Toward the Elderly." *Gerontologist,* 17 (1977):362–366.

Bahrick, H. P., P. O. Bahrick, and R. P. Wittlinger. "Fifty Years of Memory for Names and Faces: A Cross-sectional Approach." *Journal of Experimental Psychology,* 104 (1975):54–75.

Baizerman, Michael, and David L. Ellison. "A Social Role Analysis of Senility." *Gerontologist,* 11 (1971):163–170.

Bakerman, Seymour. *Aging Life Processes.* Springfield, Ill.: Charles C Thomas, 1969.

Baltes, Paul B., and K. Warner Schaie. "Aging and IQ—The Myth of the Twilight Years." *Psychology Today,* 7, no. 10 (1974):35–38, 40.

———, eds. *Life-Span Developmental Psychology: Personality and Socialization.* New York: Academic, 1973.

Barfield, Richard E., and James N. Morgan. *Early Retirement: The Decision and the Experience.* Ann Arbor: University of Michigan, Institute for Social Research, 1969.

Barrows, Charles H., and Lois M. Roeder. "Nutrition," In *Handbook of the Biology of Aging,* eds. Caleb E. Finch and Leonard Hayflick. New York: Van Nostrand Reinhold, 1977, pp. 561–581.

Bean, P. In *The Social Control of Drugs.* New York: Wiley, 1974.

Becker, Ernest. *The Denial of Death.* New York: Free Press, 1973.

Beeson, Diane. "Women in Studies of Aging: A Critique and Suggestion." *Social Problems,* 23 (1975): 52–59.

Bendix, Reinhard, and Seymour Martin Lipset, eds. *Class, Status, and Power,* 2nd ed. New York: Free Press, 1966.

Benet, Sula. *Abkhasia: The Long-Living People of the Caucasus.* New York: Holt, Rinehart and Winston, 1974.

Bengtson, Vern L., Jose B. Cuellar, and Pauline K. Ragan. "Stratum Contrasts and Similarities in Attitudes Toward Death." *Journal of Gerontology,* 32 (1977): 76–88.

Bengtson, Vern L., and Neal E. Cutler. "Generations and Intergenerational Relations: Perspectives on Age Groups and Social Change. In *Handbook of Aging and the Social Sciences,* eds. Robert H. Binstock and Ethel Shanas. New York: Van Nostrand Reinhold, 1976.

Bengtson, Vern L., James J. Dowd, David H. Smith, and Alex Inkeles. "Modernization, Modernity, and Perceptions of Aging: A Cross-cultural Study." *Journal of Gerontology,* 30 (1975):688–695.

Berkowitz, B. "Changes in Intellect with Age." *Journal of Genetic Psychology,* 107 (1965):3–14.

Bhanthumnavin, Kowit, and Marvin M. Schuster. "Aging and Gastrointestinal Function." *Handbook of the Biology of Aging,* eds. Caleb E. Finch and Leonard Hayflick. New York: Van Nostrand Reinhold, 1977, pp. 709–723.

Binstock, Robert H. "Interest Group Liberalism and the Politics of Aging." *Gerontologist,* 12 (1972):265–280.

Binstock, Robert H., and Ethel Shanas, eds. *Handbook of Aging and the Social Sciences,* New York: Van Nostrand Reinhold, 1976.

Birren, James E., ed. *Handbook of Aging and the Individual.* Chicago: University of Chicago Press, 1959.

———. *The Psychology of Aging.* Englewood Cliffs, N.J.: Prentice-Hall, 1964.

Birren, James E., and Vivian Clayton. "History of Gerontology." *Scientific Perspectives and Social Issues,* eds. Diane S. Woodruff and James E. Birren. New York: Van Nostrand Reinhold, 1975, pp. 15–27.

Birren, James E., and K. Warner Schaie, eds. *Handbook of the Psychology of Aging,* New York: Von Nostrand Reinhold, 1977.

Bjorksten, Johan. "The Crosslinkage Theory of Aging." *Journal of the American Geriatrics Society,* April 1968.

Blauner, Robert. "Death and Social Structure." *Psychiatry,* 29 (1966):378–394.

———. "Work Satisfaction and Industrial Trends in Modern Society." In *Class, Status, and Power,* 2nd ed., eds. Reinhard Bendix and Seymour Martin Lipset. New York: Fress Press, 1966, pp. 473–487.

Blenkner, Margaret. "Social Work and Family Relationships in Later Life with Some Thoughts on Filial Maturity." *Social Structure and the Family: Generational Relations,* eds. Ethel Shanas and Gordon F. Streib. Englewood Cliffs, N.J.: Prentice-Hall, 1965, pp. 46–59.

Blood, Robert O., and Donald M. Wolfe. *Husbands and Wives: The Dynamics of Married Living.* New York: Free Press, 1960.

Bock, E. Wilbur. "Aging and Suicide: The Significance of Marital, Kinship, and Alternative Relations." *Family Coordinator,* 21 (1972):71–79.

Botwinick, Jack. *Aging and Behavior.* New York: Springer, 1973.

Brittain, John A. *The Payroll Tax for Social Security.* Washington, D.C.: Brookings Institution, 1972.

Brody, Harold, and N. Vijayashanka. "Anatomical Changes in the Nervous System." In *Handbook of the Biology of Aging,* eds. Caleb E. Finch and Leonard Hayflick. New York: Van Nostrand Reinhold, 1977, pp. 241–261.

Brown, Mollie, ed. *Readings in Gerontology.* St. Louis: C. V. Mosby, 1978.

Burgess, Ernest W. ed. *Aging in Western Societies.* Chicago: University of Chicago Press, 1960.

Busse, Ewald W., and Eric Pfeiffer, eds. *Behavior and Adaptation in Later Life,* 2nd ed. Boston: Little, Brown, 1977.

Butler, Robert N. "The Life Review: An Interpretation of Reminiscence in the Aged." ed. Bernice L. Neugarten *Middle Age and Aging: A Reader In Social Psychology.* Chicago: University of Chicago Press, 1968, pp. 486–496.

Butler, Robert, and Myrna I. Lewis. *Aging and Mental Health,* 2nd ed. St. Louis: C. V. Mosby, 1977.

Cain, Leonard D. "Aging and the Law." In *Handbook of Aging and the Social Sciences,* eds. Robert H. Binstock and Ethel Shanas. New York: Van Nostrand Reinhold, 1976, pp. 342–368.

California Department of Justice. *Understanding the New California Nursing Home Law.* Sacramento, Calif.: Office of the Attorney General, 1976.

Canestrari, Robert E. "Paced and Self-paced Learning in Young and Elderly Adults." *Journal of Gerontology,* 18 (1963):165–168.

Capel, W. C., B. M. Goldsmith, and K. J. Waddell. "The Aging Narcotic Addict: An

Increasing Problem for the Next Decades." *Journal of Gerontology,* 27 (1972): 102–106.

Carp, Frances M. "Housing and Living Environments of Older People." *Handbook of Aging and the Social Sciences,* eds. Robert H. Binstock and Ethel Shanas. New York: Van Nostrand Reinhold, 1976, pp. 244–271.

Chatfield, Walter F. "Economic and Sociological Factors Influencing Life Satisfaction of the Aged." *Journal of Gerontology,* 32 (1977):593–599.

Citibank of New York. "Afraid You Won't Find a New Job? Wait 10 Years and It May be a Workers' Market." *Los Angeles Times,* August 20, 1978, pt. 7, p. 12.

Cleveland, William P., and Daniel T. Gianturco. "Remarriage Probability After Widowhood: A Retrospective Method." *Journal of Gerontology,* 31 (1976):99–103.

Cohn, Richard M. "Age and the Satisfactions from Work." *Journal of Gerontology,* 34 (1979):264–272.

Comalli, Peter M., Jr. "Cognitive Functioning in a Group of 80–90-year-old Men." *Journal of Gerontology,* 20 (1965):14–17.

———. "Life Span Changes in Visual Perception." In *Life Span Developmental Psychology,* eds. L. R. Goulet and P. B. Baltes. New York: Academic, 1970.

Cooper, R. M., et al. "The Effect of Age on Taste Sensitivity." *Journal of Gerontology,* 14 (1959):56–58.

Cowgill, Donald O., and Lowell D. Holmes, eds. *Aging and Modernization.* New York: Appleton-Century-Crofts, 1972.

Crouch, Ben M. "Age and Institutional Support: Perceptions of Older Mexican Americans." *Journal of Gerontology,* 27 (1972):524–529.

Cumming, Elaine, and William E. Henry. *Growing Old.* New York: Basic Books, 1961.

Davies, David. *The Centenarians of the Andes.* Garden City, N.Y.: Anchor Books/ Doubleday, 1975.

Decker, David L. "Sociological Theory and the Social Position of the Aged." *International Journal of Contemporary Sociology,* 15 (1978):303–317.

Decker, T. Newell. "A Survey of Hearing Loss in an Older Age Population." *Gerontologist,* 14 (1974):402–403.

Demming, J. A., and S. L. Pressey. "Tests 'indigenous' to the Adult and Older Years." *Journal of Counseling Psychology,* 4 (1957):144–148.

Demos, John. *A Little Commonwealth: Family Life in Plymouth Colony.* New York: Oxford University Press, 1970.

———. "Old Age in Early New England." In *The American Family in Social-historical Perspective,* 2nd ed., ed. Michael Gordon. New York: St. Martin's, 1978, pp. 220–256.

Denckla, W. Donner. "A Time to Die." *Life Sciences,* 16 (1975):31– .

———. "Pituitary–Thyroid Aris and Aging." *Hypothalamus, Pituitary, and Aging,* eds. Arthur V. Everitt and John A. Burgess. Springfield, Ill.: Charles C Thomas, 1976, pp. 703–705.

———. "Role of the Pituitary and Thyroid Glands in the Decline of Minimal O_2 Consumption with Age." *Journal of Clinical Investigation,* 53 (1974):572–581.

Deutscher, Irwin. "The Quality of Postparental Life." In *Middle Age and Aging,* ed. Bernice L. Neugarten. Chicago: University of Chicago Press, 1968, pp. 263–268.

Donahue, Wilma. "Aging: A Historical Perspective." In *Research Utilization in Aging,* Publication no. 1211. Bethesda, Md.: Public Health Service, 1964, pp. 7–15.

Dowd, James J., and Vern L. Bengtson. "Aging in Minority Populations: An Examination of the Double Jeopardy Hypothesis." *Journal of Gerontology,* 33 (1978): 427–436.

Drevenstedt, Jean. "Perceptions of Onsets of Young Adulthood, Middle-age, and Old Age." *Journal of Gerontology,* 31, no. 1 (1976):53–57.

Duffy, John. *The Healers: The Rise of the Medical Establishment.* New York: McGraw-Hill, 1976.

Duvall, Evelyn M. *Family Development.* Philadelphia: Lippincott, 1971.

Edwards, John N. and David L. Klemmark. "Correlates of Life Satisfaction: A Reexamination." *Journal of Gerontology,* 28 (1973):497–502.

Eisele, F. "Age and Political Change: A Cohort Analysis of Voting Among Careerists in the U.S. Senate, 1947–1970." Unpublished doctoral dissertation, New York University.

Engen, Trygg. "Taste and Smell." In *Handbook of the Psychology of Aging,* eds. James E. Birren and K. Warner Schaie. New York: Van Nostrand Reinhold, 1977, pp. 554–561.

Erber, Joan T. "Age Differences in Recognition Memory." *Journal of Gerontology,* 29 (1974):177–181.

Everitt, Arthur V. "Conclusion: Aging and Its Hypothalamic–Pituitary Control." In *Hypothalamus, Pituitary, and Aging,* eds. Arthur V. Everitt and John A. Burgess. Springfield, Charles C Thomas, 1976, pp. 676–701.

Everitt, Arthur V., and John A. Burgess, eds. *Hypothalamus, Pituitary, and Aging.* Springfield, Ill.: Charles C Thomas, 1976.

Feifer, H., and A. B. Branscomb. "Who's Afraid of Death?" *Journal of Abnormal Psychology,* 81 (1973):282–288.

Feldman, Harold, and Margaret Feldman. "The Family Life Cycle: Some Suggestions for Recycling." *Journal of Marriage and the Family,* 37 (1975):277–284.

Fengler, A., and Vivian Wood. "The Generation Gap: An Analysis of Attitudes on Contemporary Issues." *Gerontologist,* 12 (1972):124–128.

Finch, Caleb E., and Leonard Hayflick, eds. *Handbook of the Biology of Aging.* New York: Van Nostrand Reinhold, 1977.

Fischer, David Hackett. *Growing Old in America,* exp. ed. New York: Oxford University Press, 1978.

Fishel, J. "Party Ideology and the Congressional Challenger." *American Political Science Review,* 63 (1969):1213–1232.

Fox, Judith Huff. "Effects of Retirement and Former Work Life on Women's Adaptation in Old Age." *Journal of Gerontology,* 32 (1977):196–202.

Fozard, James L., et al. "Visual Perception and Communication." In *Handbook of the Psychology of Aging,* eds. James E. Birren and K. Warner Schaie. New York: Van Nostrand Reinhold, 1977, pp. 497–534.

Freedman, Richard. "Sufficiently Decayed: Gerontophobia in English Literature." In *Aging and the Elderly,* eds. Stuart F. Spicker, Kathleen M. Woodward, and David D. Van Tassel. Atlantic Highlands, N.J.: Humanities, 1978, pp. 49–61.

Fried, Edrita G., and Karl Stern. "The Situation of the Aged Within the Family." *American Journal of Orthopsychiatry,* 18 (1948):31–54.

Friedmann, Eugene A., and Harold L. Orbach. "Adjustment to Retirement." In *American Handbook of Psychiatry,* 2nd. ed., ed. Silvano Arieti. New York: Basic Books, 1974, 1, 609–645.

Fulton, Robert. "The Traditional Funeral and Contemporary Society." In *Acute Grief and the Funeral,* eds. Vanderlyn R. Pine, Austin H. Kutscher, David Peretz, Robert C. Slater, Robert DeBellis, Robert J. Volk, and Daniel J. Cherico. Springfield, Ill.: Charles C Thomas, 1976, pp. 23–40.

Gilbert, Jeanne G., and Raymond F. Lever. "Patterns of Declining Memory." *Journal of Gerontology,* 26 (1971):70–75.

Glamser, Francis D. "The Importance of Age to Conservative Opinions: A Multivariate Analysis." *Journal of Gerontology,* 29 (1974):549–554.

Glaser, Barney G., and Anselm L. Strauss. *Awareness of Dying.* Chicago: Aldine, 1966.
———. *Time for Dying.* Chicago: Aldine, 1968.

Glenn, Norval D. "Aging and Conservatism." *Annals of the American Academy of Political and Social Science,* 415 (1974):176–186.
———. "Aging, Disengagement, and Opinionation." *Public Opinion Quarterly,* 33 (1969):17–33.

Glenn, Norval, and M. Grimes. "Aging, Voting and Political Interest." *American Sociological Review,* 33 (1968):563–575.

Glenn, Norval D., and Richard E. Zody. "Cohort Analysis with National Survey Data." *Gerontologist,* 10 (1970):233–240.

Glick, Ira O., Robert S. Weiss, and C. Murray Parkes. *The First Year of Bereavement.* New York: Wiler, 1974.

Goldfarb, Alvin I., Neil J. Hochstadt, Julius H. Jacobson, and Edwin A. Weinstein. "Hyperbaric Oxygen Treatment of Organic Mental Syndrome in Aged Persons." *Journal of Gerontology,* 27 (1972):212–217.

Gordon, Chad, Charles M. Gaitz, and Judith Scott. "Leisure and Lives: Personal Expression Across the Life Span." In *Handbook of Aging and the Social Sciences,* eds. Robert H. Binstock and Ethel Shanas. New York: Van Nostrand Reinhold, 1976, pp. 310–341.

Gordon, Michael, ed. *The American Family in Socio-Historical Perspective,* 2nd ed. New York: St. Martin's, 1978.

Goulet, L. R., and P. B. Baltes, eds. *Life-span Developmental Psychology.* New York: Academic, 1970.

Gray, Robert M., and David O. Moberg. *The Church and the Older Person.* Grand Rapids, Mich.: Wm. B. Eerdmans, 1962.

Grebler, Leo, Joan W. Moore, and R. C. Guzman. *The Mexican American People.* New York: Free Press, 1970.

Greenfield, Sidney M. "Love and Marriage in Modern America: A Functional Analysis." *Sociological Quarterly,* 6 (1965):361–377.

Greven, Philip J., Jr. "Family Structure in Seventeenth-century Andover, Massachusetts." In *The American Family in Social-Historical Perspective,* 2nd ed., New York: St. Martin's, 1978, pp. 20–37.

Gross, Ronald, Beatrice Gross, and Sylvia Seidman, eds. *The New Old: Struggling for Decent Aging.* Garden City, N.Y.: Anchor Books/Doubleday, 1978.

Gruman, G. J. *A History of Ideas About the Prolongation of Life: The Evolution of Prolongevity Hypothesis to 1800.* Philadelphia: American Philosophical Society, 1966.

Gubrium, Jaber F. *Living and Dying at Murray Manor.* New York: St. Martins, 1976.

———. ed. *Time, Roles, and Self in Old Age.* New York: Human Sciences, 1976.

Gutmann, E. "Muscle." In *Handbook of the Biology of Aging.* New York: Van Nostrand Reinhold, 1977, pp. 445–469.

Haan, Norma, and David Day. "A Longitudinal Study of Change and Sameness in Personality Development: Adolescence to Later Adulthood." *International Journal of Aging and Human Development,* 5 (1974):11–39.

Haanes-Olsen, Leif. "Earnings-replacement Rate of Old-age Benefits, 1965–75, Selected Countries." *Social Security Bulletin,* 41 (1978):3–14.

Harman, D. "The Free Radical Theory of Aging: The Effect of Age on Serum Mercaptan Levels." *Journal of Gerontology,* 15 (1960):38–40.

———. "Free Radical Theory of Aging." *Journal of Gerontology,* 23 (1968):476–482.

———. "Prolongation of the Normal Lifespan and Inhibition of Spontaneous Cancer by Antioxidants." *Journal of Gerontology,* 16 (1961):247–254.

Havighurst, Robert J. "The Future Aged: The Use of Time and Money." *Gerontologist,* 15 (1975):10–15.

———. "Personality and Patterns of Aging." *Gerontologist,* 8 (1968):20–23.

Hayflick, Leonard. "The Limited in Vitro Lifetime of Human Diploid Cell Strains." *Experimental Cell Research,* 37 (1965):614–636.

———. "Cytogerontology." In *Theoretical Aspects of Aging,* ed. Morris Rockstein. New York: Academic, 1974, pp. 83–103.

———. "The Cellular Basis for Biological Aging." In *Handbook of the Biology of Aging,* eds. Caleb E. Finch and Leonard Hayflick. New York: Van Nostrand Reinhold, 1977, pp. 159–186.

Hayflick, Leonard, and Paul Moorhead. "The Serial Cultivation of Human Diploid Cell Strains." *Experimental Cell Research,* 25 (1961):585–621.

Haynes, Suzanne G., Anthony J. McMichael, and Herman A. Tyroler. "Survival After Early and Normal Retirement." *Journal of Gerontology,* 33 (1978):269–278.

Heenan, Edward F. "Sociology of Religion and the Aged: The Empirical Lacunae." *Journal for the Scientific Study of Religion,* 11 (1972):171–176.

Hendricks, Jon, and C. Davis Hendricks. *Aging in Mass Society.* Cambridge, Mass.: Winthrop, 1977.

Henle, P. "Recent Trends in Retirement Benefits Related to Earnings." *Monthly Labor Review,* 95 (1972):12–20.

Herman, Eufemiusz. "Senile Hypophyseal Syndromes." In *Hypothalamus, Pituitary, and Aging,* eds. Arthur V. Everitt and John A. Burgess. Springfield, Ill.: Charles C Thomas, 1976, pp. 157–170.

Heyman, Dorothy K., and Frances C. Jeffers. "Wives and Retirement: A Pilot Study." *Journal of Gerontology,* 23 (1968):488–496.

Hickey, Tom. "Association for Gerontology in Higher Education—A Brief History."

In *Gerontology in Higher Education: Perspectives and Issues,* eds. Mildred M. Seltzer, Harvey Sterns and Tom Hickey. Belmont, Calif.: Wadsworth, 1978, pp. 2–11.

Hill, Reuben. *Family Development in Three Generations.* Cambridge, Mass.: Schenkman, 1970.

Hobman, David, ed. *The Social Challenge of Aging.* New York: St. Martin's, 1978.

Hochschild, Arlie Russell. "Disengagement Theory: A Critique and Proposal." *American Sociological Review,* 40 (1975):553–569.

Holtzman, Abraham. *The Townsend Movement.* New York: Bookman Associates, 1963.

Hudson, Robert B., and Robert H. Binstock. "Political Systems and Aging." *Handbook of Aging and the Social Sciences,* eds. Robert H. Binstock and Ethel Shanas. New York: Van Nostrand Reinhold, 1976, pp. 369–400.

Hulicka, Irene M., and Joel L. Grossman. "Age-group Comparisons for the Rise of Mediators in Paired-associate Learning." *Journal of Gerontology,* 220 (1967): 46–51.

Hunt, C. "Private Integrated Housing in a Medium Size Northern City." *Social Problems,* 7 (1960):196–209.

Jackson, Jacquelyne J. "Aged Negroes: Their Cultural Departures from Statistical Stereotypes and Rural–Urban Differences." *Gerontologist,* 10 (1970):140–145.

Jackson, Jacquelyne J., and Bertram E. Walls. "Myths and Realities About Aged Blacks." In *Readings in Gerontology,* ed. Mollie Brown. St. Louis: C. V. Mosby, 1978, pp. 95–113.

Jacobs, Eleanor A., Peter M. Winter, Harry J. Alvis, and S. Mouchly Small. "Hyperoxygenation Effect on Cognitive Functioning of the Aged." *New England Journal of Medicine,* 281 (1969):753–757.

Jacobs, Jerry. *Older Persons and Retirement Communities: Case Studies in Social Gerontology.* Springfield, Ill.: Charles C Thomas, 1975.

Jarvik, Lissy F. *Aging into the 21st Century: Middle-agers Today.* New York: Gardner, 1978.

Jarvik, L. F., and J. E. Blum. "Cognitive Declines as Predictors of Morality in Twin Pairs." In *Prediction of Life Span,* eds. E. Palmore and F. C. Jeffers. Lexington, Mass.: D. C. Heath, 1971, pp. 199–211.

Jarvik, L. F., and A. Falek. "Intellectual Stability and Survival in the Aged." *Journal of Gerontology,* 18 (1963):173–176.

Jaslow, Philip. "Employment, Retirement, and Morale Among Older Women." *Journal of Gerontology,* 31 (1976):212–218.

Kalish, Richard A. "Death and Dying in a Social Context." In *Handbook of Aging and the Social Sciences,* eds. Robert H. Binstock and Ethel Shanas. New York: Van Nostrand Reinhold, 1976, pp. 483–507.

Kalish, Richard A., and D. K. Reynolds. *Death and Ethnicity: A Psychocultural Study.* Los Angeles: University of Southern California Press, 1976.

Kamerman, Sheila B., and Alfred J. Kahn. "Community Services for the Aged." In *Social Services in the United States.* Philadelphia: Temple University Press, 1976.

Kaplan, Howard B., and Alex D. Pokorny. "Aging and Self-attitude: A Conditional Relationship." *Aging and Human Development,* 1 (1970):241–250.

Karcher, Charles J., and Leonard L. Linden. "Family Rejection of the Aged and Nursing Home Utilization." *International Journal of Aging and Human Development,* 5 (1974):231–244.

Kart, Cary S., Eileen S. Metress, and James F. Metress. *Aging and Health: Biologic and Social Perspectives.* Menlo Park, Calif.: Addison-Wesley, 1978.

Kasschau, Patricia L. "Age and Race Discrimination Reported by Middle-aged and Older Persons." *Social Forces,* 55 (1977):728–742.

Kastenbaum, Robert, and Sandra E. Candy. "The 4% Fallacy: A Methodological and Empirical Critique of Extended Care Facility Population Statistics." *Aging and Human Development,* 4 (1973):15–21.

Keen, Sam. "The Heroics of Everyday Life: A Theorist of Death Confronts His Own End." *Psychology Today,* 7 (1974): 70–72.

Kelly, William D., and Stanley R. Friesen. "Do Cancer Patients Want to Be Told?" *Ethical Issues in Death and Dying,* ed. Robert F. Weir. New York: Columbia University Press, 1977, pp. 3–8.

Kerckhoff, Alan C. "Family Patterns and Morale in Retirement." In *Social Aspects of Aging,* eds. Ida H. Simpson and John C. McKinney. Durham, N.C.: Duke University Press, 1966, pp. 173–194.

Keys, A. "Nutrition for the Later Years of Life." *Public Health Reports,* 67 (1952): 484–489.

Keyssar, A. "Widowhood in Eighteenth-century Massachusetts: A Problem in the History of the Family." *Perspectives on American History,* 8 (1974):83–119.

Kimsey, L. R., J. L. Roberts, and D. L. Logan. "Death, Dying and Denial in the Aged." *American Journal of Psychiatry,* 129 (1972):161–166.

Kinsey, A. C., W. B. Pomeroy, and C. R. Martin. *Sexual Behavior in the Human Male.* Philadelphia: W. B. Saunders, 1948.

Kleemeier, R. W. "Intellectual Change in the Senium." *Proceedings of the Social Statistics Section of the American Statistical Association,* 1962, pp. 290–295.

Knoble, John. "Living to the End: The Hospice Experiment." In *The New Old,* eds. Ronald Gross, Beatrice Gross, and Sylvia Seidman. Garden City, N.Y.: Anchor Books/Doubleday, 1978, pp. 396–399.

Knox, David H., Jr. "Conceptions of Love at Three Developmental Levels." *The Family Coordinator,* 19 (1970):151–157.

Kogan, Nathan, and Florence C. Shelton. "Beliefs About 'Old People': A Comparative Study of Older and Younger Samples." *Journal of Genetic Psychology,* 100 (1962):93–111.

Kohn, Robert R. "Heart and Cardiovascular System." In *Handbook of the Biology of Aging,* eds. Caleb E. Finch and Leonard Hayflick. New York: Van Nostrand Reinhold, 1977, pp. 281–317.

Kubler-Ross, Elisabeth. *On Death and Dying.* New York: Macmillan, 1969.

Kurtzman, Joel, and Phillip Gordon. *No More Dying: The Conquest of Aging and the Extension of Human Life.* Los Angeles: J. P. Tarcher, 1976.

Lakoff, Sanford A. "The Future of Social Intervention." In *Handbook of Aging and the Social Sciences,* eds. Robert H. Binstock and Ethel Shanas. New York: Van Nostrand Reinhold, 1976, pp. 643–663.

Larson, Reed. "Thirty Years of Research on the Subjective Well-being of Older Americans." *Journal of Gerontology,* 33 (1978):109–125.

Laslett, Peter. "Societal Development and Aging." *Handbook of Aging and the Social Sciences,* eds. Robert H. Binstock and Ethel Shanas. New York: Van Nostrand Reinhold, 1976, pp. 87–116.

Lasswell, Harold, and D. Lerner, eds. *World Revolutionary Elites: Studies in Coercive Ideological Movements.* Cambridge, Mass.: M.I.T. Press, 1966.

Lazarsfeld, Paul F., William H. Sewell, and Harold Wilensky, eds. *The Uses of Sociology.* New York: Basic Books, 1967.

Leaf, Alexander. *Youth in Old Age.* New York: McGraw-Hill, 1975.

Lebowitz, Barry D. "Age and Fearfulness: Personal and Situational Factors." *Journal of Gerontology,* 30 (1975):696–700.

Lemon, Bruce W., Vern L. Bengtson, and James A. Peterson. "An Exploration of the Activity Theory of Aging: Activity Types and Life Satisfaction Among In-movers to a Retirement Community." *Journal of Gerontology,* 27 (1972):511–523.

Lopata, Helena Znaniecki. *Occupation: Housewife.* New York: Oxford University Press, 1971.

———. *Widowhood in an American City.* Cambridge, Mass.: Schenkman, 1973.

Maddox, George L. "Selected Methodological Issues." *Normal Aging: Reports from the Duke Longitudinal Study, 1955–1969,* ed. Erdman Palmore. Durham, N.C.: Duke University Press, 1970, pp. 18–27.

Maeda, Daisaku. "Aging in Eastern Society." In *The Social Challenge of Aging,* ed. David Hobman. New York: St. Martin's, 1978, pp. 45–72.

Main, Jeremy. "A Word to the Wise About Old Age Groups." *Money,* March 1975, pp. 44–48.

Makinodan, Takashi. "Immunity and Aging." In *Handbook of the Biology of Aging,* eds. Caleb E. Finch and Leonard Hayflick. New York: Van Nostrand Reinhold, 1977, pp. 379–408.

Mannheim, Karl. *Essays on the Sociology of Knowledge.* New York: Oxford University Press, 1952.

Marascuilo, L. and K. Penfield. "A Northern Urban Community's Attitudes Toward Racial Imbalances in Schools and Classrooms." *School Review,* 74 (1966):359–378.

Marshall, Victor W. "Socialization for Impending Death in a Retirement Village." *American Journal of Sociology,* 80 (1975):1124–1144.

Martel, Martin U. "Age–Sex Roles in American Magazine Fiction (1890–1955)." In *Middle Age and Aging,* ed. Bernice L. Neugarten. Chicago: University of Chicago Press, 1968, pp. 47–57.

Masters, W. H., and V. E. Johnson. *Human Sexual Response.* Boston: Little, Brown, 1966.

———. *Human Sexual Inadequacy.* Boston: Little, Brown, 1970.

Mazess, Richard B., and Sylvia H. Forman. "Longevity and Age Exaggeration in Vilcabamba, Ecuador." *Journal of Gerontology,* 34 (1979):94–98.

McGill, Dan M. *Fundamentals of Private Pensions,* 3rd ed. Homewood, Ill.: Richard D. Irwin, 1975.

John C. McKinney. "Typifications, Typologies, and Sociological Theory." *Social Forces,* 48 (1969):1–12.

Medvedev, Zhores A. "Caucasus and Altay Longevity: A Biological or Social Problem?" *Gerontologist,* 14 (1974):381–387.

Miller, Michael B., Herbert Bernstein, and Harold Sharkey. "Family Extrusion of the Aged Patient: Family Homeostasis and Sexual Conflict." *Gerontologist,* 15 (1975):291–296.

Miller, Stephen J. "The Social Dilemma of the Aging Leisure Participant." In *Older People and Their Social Worlds,* eds. Arnold M. Rose and Warren A. Peterson. Philadelphia: F. A. Davis, 1965, pp. 77–92.

Mindel, Charles H., and Robert W. Habenstein, eds. *Ethnic Families in America.* New York: Elsevier, 1976.

Mindel, Charles H., and C. Edwin Vaughan. "A Multidimensional Approach to Religiosity and Disengagement." *Journal of Gerontology,* 33 (1978):103–108.

Mitford, Jessica. *The American Way of Death.* New York: Simon and Schuster, 1963.

Moberg, David O. "Religiosity in Old Age." *Gerontologist,* 5 (1965):78–87.

———. *Spiritual Well-being: Background and Issues.* Washington, D.C.: White House Conference on Aging, 1971.

Moenster, Phyllis A. "Learning and Memory in Relation to Age." *Journal of Gerontology,* 27 (1972):361–363.

Munnell, Alicia H. *The Future of Social Security.* Washington, D.C.: Brookings Institution, 1977.

Murdock, George P. *Social Structure.* New York: Macmillan, 1949.

National Center for Health Statistics. *Health in the Later Years of Life.* Washington, D.C.: U.S. Government Printing Office, 1971.

National Council on the Aging. *The Myth and Reality of Aging in America.* Washington, D.C., 1975.

National Institute of Senior Centers. *Senior Centers: Report of Senior Group Programs in America.* Washington, D.C.: National Council on the Aging, 1975.

Neugarten, Bernice L., ed. *Middle Age and Aging.* Chicago: University of Chicago Press, 1968.

Neugarten, Bernice L. "Personality and Aging." In *Handbook of the Psychology of Aging,* eds. James E. Birren and K. Warner Schaie. New York: Van Nostrand Reinhold, 1977, pp. 626–649.

———. "The Future and the Young-old." *Gerontologist,* 15 (1975):4–9.

Neugarten, Bernice L., and Nancy Datan. "Sociological Perspectives on the Life Cycle." *Life-span Developmental Psychology: Personality and Socialization,* ed. Paul B. Baltes and K. Warner Schaie. New York: Academic, 1973, pp. 53–69.

Neugarten, Bernice L., Robert J. Havighurst, and Sheldon S. Tobin. "Personality and Patterns of Aging." *Middle Age and Aging,* ed. Bernice L. Neugarten. Chicago: University of Chicago Press, 1968, pp. 173–177.

Neugarten, Bernice L., and Karol K. Weinstein. "The Changing American Grandparent." In *Middle Age and Aging: A Reader in Social Psychology,* ed. Bernice L. Neugarten. Chicago: University of Chicago Press, 1968, pp. 280–285.

Newman, G., and C. R. Nichols. "Sexual Activities and Attitudes in Older Persons." *Journal of the American Medical Association,* 173 (1960):33–35.

Northcott, Herbert C. "Too Young, Too Old—Age in the World of Television." *Gerontologist,* 15 (1975):184–186.

Nye, F. Ivan, and Felix M. Berardo. *The Family: Its Structure and Interaction.* New York: Macmillan, 1973.

O'Brien, Beatrice, ed. *Aging: Today's Research and You.* Los Angeles: University of Southern California Press, 1978.

Orgel, L. E. "The Maintenance of the Accuracy of Protein Synthesis and Its Relevance to Aging." *Proceedings of the National Academy of Science,* 49 (1963):517–521.

———. "The Maintenance of the Accuracy of Protein Synthesis and Its Relevance to Aging: A Correction." *Proceedings of the National Academy of Science,* 67 (1970):1476.

Ostfeld, Adrian M. "The Aging Brain: Alzheimer's Disease and Senile Dementia— Discussant's Perspective." In *Epidemiology of Aging,* eds. Adrian M. Ostfeld and Dan C. Gibson. Washington, D.C.: U.S. Government Printing Office, 1975, pp. 129–135.

Ostfeld, Adrian M., and Dan C. Gibson, eds. *Epidemiology of Aging.* Washington, D.C.: U.S. Government Printing Office, 1975.

Palmer, Gladys L. "Factors in the Variability of Response in Enumerative Studies." *Journal of the American Statistical Association,* 38 (1943):143–152.

Palmore, Erdman. "Attitudes Toward Aging as Shown by Humor." *Gerontologist,* 11 (1971): 181–186.

———. "The Effects of Aging on Activities and Attitudes." *Gerontologist,* 8 (1968): 259–263.

———. *The Honorable Elders.* Durham, N.C.: Duke University Press, 1975.

———. *Normal Aging: Reports from the Duke Longitudinal Study, 1955–1969.* Durham, N.C.: Duke University Press, 1970.

Palmore, Erdman. "Total Change of Institutionalization Among the Aged." *Gerontologist,* 16 (1976):504–507.

Palmore, Erdman, and W. Cleveland. "Aging, Terminal Decline, and Terminal Drop." *Journal of Gerontology,* 31 (1976):76–81.

Palmore, Erdman, and F. C. Jeffers, eds. *Prediction of Life Span.* Lexington, Mass.: D. C. Heath, 1971.

Palmore, Erdman B., and Kenneth Manton. "Modernization and Status of the Aged: International Correlations." *Journal of Gerontology,* 29 (1974):205–210.

Parkes, C. Murray. " 'Seeking' and 'Finding' a Lost Object." *Social Science and Medicine,* 4 (1970):187–201.

Parsons, Talcott. "Aging in American Society." *Law and Contemporary Problems,* 27 (1962):22–35.

———. "Toward a Healthy Maturity." *Journal of Health and Human Behavior,* 2 (1960):163–173.

Parsons, Talcott, and Victor Lidz. "Death in American Society." In *Essays in Self- destruction,* ed. Edwin S. Shneidman. New York: Science House, 1967, pp. 133–140.

Pascarelli, E. F. "Drug Dependence: An Age-old Problem Compounded by Old Age." *Geriatrics,* 29 (1974):109–115.

Pascarelli, E. F. and W. Fischer. "Drug Dependence in the Elderly." *International Journal of Aging and Human Development,* 5 (1974):347–356.

Penalosa, Fernando. "The Changing Mexican American in Southern California." *Sociology and Social Research,* 51 (1967):404–417.

Perkins, Frances. *The Roosevelt I Knew.* New York: Viking, 1946.

Peters, George R. "Self-conceptions of the Aged, Age Identification, and Aging." *Gerontologist,* 11 (1971):69–73.

Peterson, David. "An Overview of Gerontology Education." In *Gerontology in Higher Education: Perspectives and Issues,* eds. Mildred M. Seltzer, Harvey Sterns, and Tom Hickey. Belmont, Calif.: Wadsworth, 1978, pp. 14–26.

Peterson, David M., and Charles W. Thomas. "Acute Drug Reactions Among the Elderly." *Journal of Gerontology,* 30, no. 5 (1975):552–556.

Peterson, William. *Population,* 3rd ed. New York: Macmillan, 1975.

Pfeiffer, Eric. "Sexuality in the Aging Individual." *Journal of the American Geriatric Society,* 20 (1974):481–

——. "Sexual Behavior in Old Age." In *Behavior and Adaptation in Late Life,* 2nd ed., eds. Ewald W. Busse and Eric Pfeiffer. Boston: Little, Brown, 1977, pp. 130–141.

Pfeiffer, Eric, Adriaan Verwoerdt, and Hsioh-Shan Wang. "Sexual Behavior in Aged Men and Women: Observations on 254 Community Volunteers." *Archives of General Psychiatry,* 19 (1968):753–758.

Philibert, Michel A. *An Essay on the Development of Social Gerontology.* University of Michigan, Division of Gerontology, 1964, mimeo.

——. "The Emergence of Social Gerontology." *Journal of Social Issues,* 2 (1965): 4–12.

Pine, Vanderlyn R., Austin H. Kutscher, David Peretz, Robert C. Slater, Robert DeBellis, Robert J. Volk, and Daniel J. Cherico, eds. *Acute Grief and the Funeral.* Springfield, Ill.: Charles C Thomas, 1976.

Plath, David W. "Japan: The After Years." In *Aging and Modernization,* eds. Donald O. Cowgill and Lowell D. Holmes. New York: Appleton-Century-Crofts, 1972.

Pollman, A. William. "Early Retirement: A Comparison of Poor Health to Other Retirement Factors." *Journal of Gerontology,* 26 (1971):41–45.

Posner, Judith. "Notes on the Negative Implications of Being Competent in a Home for the Aged." *International Journal of Aging and Human Development,* 5, no. 4 (1974):357–364.

Pratt, Henry J. *The Gray Lobby.* Chicago: University of Chicago Press, 1976.

Putnam, Jackson K. *Old Age Politics in California.* Stanford, Calif.: Stanford University Press, 1970.

Raskind, M., and C. Eisdorfer. "Psychopharmacology of the Aged." In *Drug Treatment of Mental Disorders,* ed. L. L. Simpson. New York: Raven, 1976, pp. 237–266.

Reichard, Suzanne, Florine Livson, and Paul G. Peterson. *Aging and Personality.* New York: Wiley, 1962.

Resnik, H. L. P. and Joel M. Cantor. "Suicide and Aging." *Journal of the American Geriatrics Society,* 18 (1970):152–158.

Richman, Joseph. "The Foolishness and Wisdom of Age: Attitudes Toward the Elderly as Reflected in Jokes." *Gerontologist,* 17 (1977):210–219.

Riegel, K. F., and R. M. Riegel. "Development, Drop and Death." *Developmental Psychology,* 6 (1972):306–319.

Riley, Matilda White, and Anne Foner. *Aging and Society,* vol. 1, *An Inventory of Research Findings.* New York: Russell Sage Foundation, 1968.

Riley, M. W., M. E. Johnson, and A. Foner, eds. *Aging and Society,* vol. 3, *A Sociology of Age Stratification.* New York: Russell Sage Foundation, 1971.

Robertson, A. Haeworth. "Financial Status of Social Security Programs After the Social Security Amendments of 1977." *Social Security Bulletin,* 41 (1978): 21–30.

Robertson, Joan F. "Grandmotherhood: A Study of Role Conceptions." *Journal of Marriage and the Family,* 39 (1977):165–174.

Rockstein, Morris, ed. *Theoretical Aspects of Aging.* New York: Academic, 1974.

Rockstein, Morris, and Marvin Sussman. *Biology of Aging.* Belmont, Calif.: Wadsworth, 1979.

Rollins, Boyd C., and Kenneth L. Cannon. "Marital Satisfaction over the Family Life Cycle: A Reevaluation." *Journal of Marriage and the Family,* 36 (1974):271–282.

Rollins, Boyd C., and Harold Feldman. "Marital Satisfaction over the Family Life Cycle." *Journal of Marriage and the Family,* 32 (1970):20–28.

Roosevelt, Franklin D. *The Public Papers and Addresses of Franklin D. Roosevelt,* ed. Samuel I. Rosenmen. New York: Random House, 1938, 5 vols.

Rose, Arnold M. *The Power Structure.* New York: Oxford University Press, 1967.

———. "The Subculture of the Aging: A Framework for Research in Social Gerontology." In *Older People and Their Social World,* eds. A. M. Rose and W. A. Peterson. Philadelphia: F. A. Davis, 1965, pp. 3–16.

Rose, Arnold M., and Warren A. Peterson, eds. *Older People and Their Social World.* Philadelphia: F. A. Davis, 1965.

Rosenfeld, Albert. *Prolongevity.* New York: Knopf, 1976.

Rosenweig, Mark R., and Lyman W. Porter, eds. *Annual Review of Psychology,* 26 (1975).

Rossman, Isadore. "Anatomic and Body Composition Changes with Aging." *Handbook of the Biology of Aging,* eds. Caleb E. Finch and Leonard Hayflick. New York: Van Nostrand Reinhold, 1977, pp. 181–221.

Rowe, Alan R. "Scientists in Retirement." *Journal of Gerontology,* 28 (1973):345–350.

———. "The Retired Scientist: The Myth of the Aging Individual." *Time, Roles, and Self in Old Age,* ed. Jaber F. Gubrium. New York: Human Sciences, 1976, pp. 209–219.

Rowe, Alan R., and Charles R. Tittle. "Life Cycle Changes and Criminal Propensity." *Sociological Quarterly,* 18 (1977):223–236.

Rubin, Isadore. *Sexual Life After Sixty.* New York: Basic Books, 1965.

Ruzicka, L. T. "Suicide, 1950–1971." *World Health Statistics Report,* 29 (1976):396–412.

Sachuk, Nina N. "Population Longevity Study: Sources and Indices." *Journal of Gerontology,* 25 (1970):262–264.

Sauvageot, J. Paul. "Gerontology and Geriatrics in Professional Curricula of Medical Schools." In *Gerontology in Higher Education: Perspectives and Issues,* eds. Mildred M. Seltzer, Harvey Sterns, and Tom Hickey. Belmont, Calif.: Wadsworth, 1978, pp. 228–231.

Schaie, K. Warner, and Kathy Gubbin. "Adult Development and Aging." *Annual Review of Psychology,* eds. Mark R. Rosenweig and Lyman W. Porter. Vol. 26 (1975):65–96.

Schaie, K. Warner, and Iris A. Parham. "Stability of Adult Personality Traits: Fact or Fable?" *Journal of Personality and Social Psychology,* 34 (1976):146–158.

Schaie, K. Warner, and Charles R. Strother. "A Cross-sequential Study of Age Changes in Cognitive Behavior." *Psychological Bulletin,* 70 (1968):671–680.

Schlesinger, J. A. *Ambition and Politics: Political Careers in the United States.* Chicago: Rand McNally, 1966.

Schluderman, E., and J. P. Zubek. "Effect of Age on Pain Sensitivity." *Perceptual and Motor Skills,* 14 (1962):295–301.

Schonfield, D. "Theoretical Nuances and Practical Old Questions: The Psychology of Aging." *Canadian Psychologist,* 13 (1972):252–266.

Schorr, Alvin. *Filial Responsibility in the Modern American Family.* Washington, D.C.: U.S. Government Printing Office, 1960.

Schreiber, E. M., and L. R. Marsden. "Age and Opinions on a Government Program of Medical Aid." *Journal of Gerontology,* 27 (1972):95–101.

Schuckit, Marc A. "Geriatric Alcoholism and Drug Abuse." *Gerontologist,* 17 (1977): 168–174.

Schuckit, Marc A., and P. L. Miller. "Alcoholism in Elderly Men: A Survey of a General Medical Ward." *Annals of New York Academy of Sciences,* 273 (1975): 558–571.

Schulz, James H. *The Economics of Aging.* Belmont, Calif.: Wadsworth, 1976.

Seelbach, Wayne C. "Gender Differences in Expectations for Filial Responsibility." *Gerontologist,* 17 (1977):421–425.

Selmanowitz, Victor J., Ronald L. Rizer, and Norman Orentreich. "Aging of the Skin and Its Appendages." In *Handbook of the Biology of Aging,* eds. Caleb E. Finch and Leonard Hayflick. New York: Van Nostrand Reinhold, 1977, pp. 496–509.

Seltzer, Margaret M., and Robert C. Atchley. "The Concept of Old: Changing Attitudes and Stereotypes." *Gerontologist,* 11 (1971):226–230.

Seltzer, Mildred M., Harvey Sterns, and Tom Hickey, eds. *Gerontology in Higher Education: Perspectives and Issues.* Belmont, Calif.: Wadsworth, 1978.

Shanas, Ethel, and Gordon F. Streib, eds. *Social Structure and the Family: Generational Relations.* Englewood Cliffs, N.J.: Prentice-Hall, 1965.

Shanas, Ethel, Peter Townsend, Dorothy Wedderburn, Henning Friis, Paul Milhoj, and Jan Stehower. *Old People in Three Industrial Societies.* New York: Atherton, 1968.

Shelanski, Michael L. "The Aging Brain: Alzheimer's Disease and Senile Dementia." *Epidemiology of Aging*, eds. Adrian M. Ostfeld and Don C. Gibson. Washington, D.C.: U.S. Government Printing Office, 1975, pp. 113–127.

Sherwood, Sylvia. "Malnutrition: A Social Problem." *International Journal of Aging and Human Development*, (1970):70–78.

Shichor, David, and Solomon Kobrin. "Note: Criminal Behavior Among the Elderly." *Gerontologist*, 18 (1978):213–218.

Shneidman, Edwin S., ed. *Death: Current Perspectives*. Palo Alto, Calif.: Mayfield, 1976.

Shneidman, Edwin S. "Death Work and Stages of Dying." In *Death: Current Perspectives*, ed. Edwin S. Shneidman. Palo Alto, Calif.: Mayfield, 1976, pp. 443–451.

Shneidman, Edwin S., ed. *Essays in Self-destruction*. New York: Science House, 1967.

Shulman, Norman. "Life-cycle Variations in Patterns of Close Relationships." *Journal of Marriage and the Family*, 37 (1975):813–821.

Siegel, Barry. "Children: A Dark Cloud over Sun City." *Los Angeles Times*, May 22, 1977, pt. 5, pp. 1, 16, 17.

Siegler, Ilene C., and Jack Botwinick. "A Long-term Longitudinal Study of Intellectual Ability of Older Adults: The Matter of Selective Subject Attention." *Journal of Gerontology*, 34 (1979):242–245.

Simmons, Leo W. *The Role of the Aged in Primitive Society*. New Haven, Conn.: Yale University Press, 1945.

Simpson, L. L., ed. *Drug Treatment of Mental Disorders*. New York: Raven, 1976.

Simpson, Ida H., and John C. McKinney, eds. *Social Aspects of Aging*. Durham, N.C.: Duke University Press, 1966.

Skogan, Wesley G. "The Validity of Official Crime Statistics: An Empirical Investigation." *Social Science Quarterly*, 55 (1974):25–38.

Snee, John, and Mary Ross. "Social Security Amendments of 1977: Legislative History and Summary of Provisions." *Social Security Bulletin*, 41 (1978):3–20.

Spanier, Graham B., Robert A. Lewis, and Charles L. Cole. "Marital Adjustment over the Family Life Cycle: The Issue of Curvilinearity." *Journal of Marriage and the Family*, 37 (1975):263–275.

Spengler, Joseph J. *Population and America's Future*. San Francisco: W. H. Freeman, 1975.

Spicker, Stuart F., Kathleen M. Woodward, and David D. Van Tassel, eds. *Aging and the Elderly: Humanistic Perspectives in Gerontology*. Atlantic Highlands, N.J.: Humanities, 1978.

Spreitzer, Elmer, and Eldon E. Snyder. "Correlates of Life Satisfaction Among the Aged." *Journal of Gerontology*, 29 (1974):454–458.

Stahmer, Harold M. "The Aged in Two Ancient Oral Cultures: The Ancient Hebrews and Homeric Greece." In *Aging and the Elderly*, eds. Stuart F. Spicker, Kathleen M. Woodward and David D. Van Tassel. Atlantic Highlands, N.J.: Humanities, 1978, pp. 23–36.

Stannard, Charles T. "Old Folks and Dirty Work: The Social Conditions for Patient Abuse in a Nursing Home." *Social Problems*, 20 (1973):329–342.

Stehouwer, Jan. "Relations Between Generations and the Three Generation Household in Denmark." In *Social Structure and the Family: Generational Relations*, eds. Ethel Shanas and Gordon F. Streib. Englewood Cliffs, N.J.: Prentice-Hall, 1965, pp. 142–162.

Sterne, Richard S., James E. Phillips, and Alvin Rabushka. *The Urban Elderly Poor*. Lexington, Mass.: Lexington Books, 1974.

Stinnett, Nick, Linda Mittelstet Carter, and James E. Montgomery. "Older Persons' Perceptions of Their Marriages." *Journal of Marriage and the Family*, 34 (1972): 665–670.

Stix, Harriet. "Retiring the Age Limit at Hastings Law." *Los Angeles Times*, May 15, 1977, pt. 4, pp. 20–22.

Stoddard, Sandol. *The Hospice Movement*. New York: Vintage Books, 1978.

Streib, Gordon F. "Intergenerational Relations: Perspectives of the Two Generations on the Older Person." *Journal of Marriage and the Family*, 27 (1965):469–474.

———. "Social Stratification and Aging." In *Handbook of Aging and the Social Sciences*, eds. Robert H. Binstock and Ethel Shanas. New York: Van Nostrand Reinhold, 1976, pp. 160–185.

Streib, Gordon F. and Harold L. Orbach. "The Development of Social Gerontology and the Sociology of Aging." In *The Uses of Sociology*, eds. Paul F. Lazarsfeld, William H. Sewell and Harold Wilensky. New York: Basic Books, 1967, pp. 612–640.

Streib, Gordon F., and Clement J. Schneider. *Retirement in American Society*. Ithaca, N.Y.: Cornell University Press, 1971.

Streib, Gordon F., and Wayne E. Thompson. "The Older Person in a Family Context." In *Handbook of Social Gerontology*, ed. Clark Tilbitts. Chicago: University of Chicago Press, 1960, pp. 447–488.

Sudnow, David. *Passing On*. Englewood Cliffs, N.J.: Prentice-Hall, 1967.

Sundeen, Richard A. "The Fear of Criminal Victimization and Attitudes Toward Criminal Justice Agencies and Practices: A Comparative Study Among Elderly." Paper presented at the annual meeting of the American Society of Criminology, Tucson, Arizona, 1976.

Sundeen, Richard A., and James T. Mathieu. "The Fear of Crime and Its Consequences Among Elderly in Three Urban Communities." *Gerontologist*, 16 (1976):211–219.

Tamke, Susan S. "Human Values and Aging: The Perspective of the Victorian Nursery." In *Aging and the Elderly*, eds. Stuart F. Spicker, Kathleen M. Woodward and David D. Van Tassel. Atlantic Highlands, N.J.: Humanities, 1978, pp. 63–81.

Tappel, A. L. "Will Antioxidant Nutrients Slow Aging Processes?" *Geriatrics*, 23 (1968):97–105.

Tibbitts, Clark, ed. *Handbook of Social Gerontology*. Chicago: University of Chicago Press, 1960.

Tissue, Thomas. "Old Age and the Perception of Poverty." *Sociology and Social Research*, 56 (1972):331–344.

Tonna, Edgar A. "Aging of Skeletal–Dental Systems and Supporting Tissues." In *Handbook of the Biology of Aging,* eds. Caleb E. Finch and Leonard Hayflick. New York: Van Nostrand Reinhold, 1977, pp. 470–495.

Treas, Judith. "Aging and the Family." In *Aging: Scientific Perspectives and Social Issues,* eds. Diana S. Woodruff and James E. Birren. New York: Van Nostrand Reinhold, 1975, pp. 92–108.

Troll, Lillian, Sheila J. Miller, and Robert C. Atchley. *Families in Later Life.* Belmont, Calif.: Wadsworth, 1979.

Turnbull, Colin M. "The Mountain People." *Readings in Aging and Death: Contemporary Perspectives,* ed. Steven H. Zarit. New York: Harper & Row, 1977.

U.S., Bureau of the Census. *Census of Population: 1970,* Final Report. Washington, D.C.: U.S. Government Printing Office, 1973.

———. "Demographic Aspects of Aging and the Older Population in the United States." *Current Population Reports,* Special Studies, Series P-23, no. 59. Washington, D.C., May 1976.

———. "Historical Statistics of the United States, Colonial Times to 1970." Bicentennial Ed. Washington, D.C., 1975.

———. "Projections of the Population of the United States: 1977 to 2050." *Current Population Reports,* Series P-25, no. 704. Washington, D.C., 1977.

U.S., Department of Health, Education and Welfare, Administration on Aging. *Older Americans Act of 1965, as Amended.* Washington, D.C.: U.S. Government Printing Office, 1976.

———. Social Security Administration. *Social Security Programs in the United States.* Washington, D.C.: U.S. Government Printing Office, 1973.

U.S., Department of Justice. *Criminal Victimization in The United States, 1973.* Washington, D.C.: U.S. Government Printing Office, 1976.

———. *Uniform Crime Reports for The United States.* Washington, D.C.: U.S. Government Printing Office, 1975.

U.S., House of Representatives, Select Committee on Aging. *Federal Responsibility to the Elderly: Executive Programs and Legislative Jurisdiction.* Washington, D.C.: U.S. Government Printing Office, 1976.

U.S., Senate, Special Committee on Aging. *Fraud and Abuse Among Practitioners Participating in the Medicaid Program.* Washington, D.C.: U.S. Government Printing Office, 1976.

———. *Women and Social Security: Adapting to a New Era,* 94th Cong., 1st sess. Washington, D.C.: U.S. Government Printing Office, 1975.

Upton, Arthur C. "Pathobiology." In *Handbook of the Biology of Aging,* eds. Caleb E. Finch and Leonard Hayflick. New York: Van Nostrand Reinhold, 1977, pp. 513–535.

Vazquez, Jacinto, and Takashi Makinodan. "Aging and the Immune System: A Brief Summary of Current Knowledge." *Epidemiology of Aging,* eds. Adrian M. Ostfeld and Don C. Gibson. Washington, D.C.: U.S. Government Printing Office, pp. 161–173.

Vogel, F. Steven. "The Brain and Time." In *Behavior and Adaptation in Late Life,* 2nd ed., eds. Ewald W. Busse and Eric Pfeiffer. Boston: Little, Brown, 1977, pp. 228–239.

Wake, Sandra Byford, and Michael J. Sporakowski. "An Intergenerational Comparison of Attitudes Towards Supporting Aged Parents." *Journal of Marriage and the Family,* 34 (1972):42–48.

Walford, Roy L. *The Immunologic Theory of Aging.* Baltimore: Williams & Wilkins, 1969.

Wang, H. S. "Organic Brain Syndromes: Conceptual and Practical Issues." *Behavior and Adaptation in Late Life,* 2nd ed., eds. Ewald W. Busse and Eric Pfeiffer. Boston: Little, Brown, 1977, pp. 240–263.

Watson, Wilbur H., and Robert J. Maxwell. *Human Aging and Dying: A Study in Sociocultural Gerontology.* New York: St. Martin's, 1977.

Weaver, Jerry L. "The Elderly as a Political Community: The Case of National Health Policy." *Western Political Quarterly,* 29 (1976):610–619.

Webber, Irving L., David W. Coombs, and J. Selwyn Hollingsworth. "Variations in Value Orientations by Age in a Developing Society." *Journal of Gerontology,* 29 (1974):676–683.

Weg, Ruth B. "Changing Physiology of Aging: Normal and Pathological." *Aging: Scientific Perspectives and Social Issues,* eds. Diana S. Woodruff and James E. Birren. New York: Van Nostrand Reinhold, 1975, pp. 229–256.

———. *Nutrition and the Later Years.* Los Angeles: University of Southern California Press, 1978.

Weir, Robert F., ed. *Ethical Issues in Death and Dying.* New York: Columbia University Press, 1977.

Weiss, A. D. "Sensory Functions." In *Handbook of Aging and the Individual,* ed. James E. Birren. Chicago: University of Chicago Press, 1959, pp. 503–542.

Wingrove, C. Ray, and Jon P. Alston. "Cohort Analysis of Church Attendance, 1939–1969." *Social Forces,* 53 (1974):324–331.

Wiseman, Robert F. *Spatial Aspects of Aging.* Washington, D.C.: Association of American Geographers, 1978.

Wiseman, Robert F., and Mark A. Virden. "Spatial and Social Dimensions of Intraurban Elderly Migration." *Economic Geography,* 53 (1977):1–13.

Wiswell, Robert. "Vigor Maintained." In *Aging: Today's Research and You,* ed. Beatrice O'Brien. Los Angeles: University of Southern California Press, 1978, pp. 70–82.

Wood, Vivian, and Joan F. Robertson. "The Significance of Grandparenthood." In *Time, Roles, and Self in Old Age,* ed. Jaber F. Gubrium. New York: Human Sciences, 1976, pp. 278–355.

Woodruff, Diana S., and James E. Birren. "Age Changes and Cohort Differences in Personality." *Developmental Psychology,* 6 (1972):252–259.

———. eds. *Aging: Scientific Perspectives and Social Issues.* New York: Van Nostrand, 1975.

Zarit, Steven H., ed. *Readings in Aging and Death: Contemporary Perspectives.* New York: Harper & Row, 1977.

Zimberg, Sheldon. "The Elderly Alcoholic." *Gerontologist,* 14 (1974):221–224.

Index

Social theories (*cont'd*)
  phenomenological, 146–147
  uses of, 140–143
Special Committee on Aging (U.S. Senate), 191–192, 239, 240
Status, experience of aging and, 75–76
Strokes, 57, 59
Suicide, 236
  by country, 233–234
  older population, 231–234
  social environment and, 233
Supplemental Security Income (SSI), 177, 183–184
Survivor's insurance, 181–182
Synagogue attendance, 250

Taste, sense of, 99
Teeth, loss of, 56
Telephone Reassurance program, 196
Tender Loving Greed (Mendelson), 243
Terminal drop, 103
Townsend, Francis E., 154
Townsend Movement, 154–158, 160
  popularity of, 155
  Social Security Act and, 156–158
Tranquilizers, 236
Transportation services program, 196

Undernutrition, 65–66
Uniform Crime Reports, 234–235
Union party, 155
United Fund, 195
United Nations, 28
U.S. Bureau of the Census, 31, 84, 211, 217
U.S. Department of Agriculture, 176–177
U.S. Department of Health, Education and Welfare, 176–177
U.S. Department of Justice, 237
U.S. Department of Labor, 177
U.S. Housing and Urban Development, 177
U.S. Public Health Service, 5
U.S. Supreme Court, 165
Universals of aging, 71–74
Universities, gerontology curricula of, 7–8

University of Chicago, 5
University of Southern California, 159
Urban areas, aging experience and, 88–89
Urban-rural residence (people 65 years of age and older), 41
Urine retention, 58

Valium, 236
Veterans Administration, 176–177
Victimization of the old, 237–239
Victorian period, 3–4
Vietnam War, 144–145
Vilcabamba people, 66, 76, 77–78
Vision, 98–99
Visiting nurse program, 196
Vital rates, 26
Vitamin B_{12}, 57
Vitamin E, 3, 51
Voter participation (election of 1972), 164
Voting behavior, 161–164

Weber, Max, 270
Wechsler Adult Intelligence Scale (WAIS), 100, 101
White House Conference on Aging (1971), 84, 251
Widowhood, 258–260
  in colonial society, 204–205
Women
  and retirement from work, 122, 126–127
  and social security, 191–192
"Women and Social Security: Adapting to a New Era" (Special Committee on Aging), 191–192
Work
  age discrimination in, 127–128
  future and, 270–271
  meaning of, 120–121
  See also Retirement
Wrinkles, 56

Zero order resources, 153
  See also Political economy